R.L.GALLUN

D1482271

Cereal diseases
their pathology and control

D. Gareth Jones and Brian C. Clifford

Cereal diseases

their pathology and control

First published 1978
© Copyright D. Gareth Jones and Brian C. Clifford, 1978

Published by BASF United Kingdom Limited, Agrochemical Division,
Lady Lane, Hadleigh, Ipswich, Suffolk IP7 6BQ

Printed in England by Perivan Press Limited

ISBN 0 950 2752 1 2

Acknowledgements

We would like to record our thanks to BASF United Kingdom Limited for their generous sponsorship of this book and for the use of many of their excellent colour photographs of cereal diseases. The help of Gordon Angell, Ken Mason, Gavin Hardy, Judith Moate, Huw Phillips and Alan Frost is particularly acknowledged in this respect. We also are indebted to many other colleagues, in the U.K. and abroad, for their help in collecting together the large number of photographs which, we hope, will be a most important feature of the book. Although specific acknowledgement is given where appropriate we should like to record thanks to Prof. John F. Schafer, Prof. Ralph J. Green Jr., Prof. A. J. Ullstrup, Dr. R. F. Line, Dr. J. K. Doodson, Dr. M. J. Richardson, Prof. J. Colhoun and Dr. C. V. Cutting.

Many other agrochemical companies also readily contributed detailed information on the nature and use of the many fungicidal and bactericidal products now in current use. The writing of this book could not have been achieved without constant recourse to the published results of the research of many hundreds of plant pathologists, past and present. We acknowledge our debt to these publications here and explain that references to original papers or to text-books are only included either as a supplement to our text or to provide details of critical experimental techniques referred to in the text.

The compendium of cereal diseases owes much to the Descriptions of Pathogenic Fungi and Bacteria and to the Descriptions of Plant Viruses, both published by the Commonwealth Mycological Institute and in the case of the latter, in conjunction with the Association of Applied Biologists. We are most grateful to these organizations for permission to use this published material. On an individual basis, we are most grateful to Dr. Ellis Griffiths, Dr. G. M. Evans, Dr. R. N. Jones, Dr. P. D. Hewett, Dr. D. B. Slope, Dr. J. E. King, Dr. Huw Thomas, Dr. R. M. Habgood and we are pleased to recognize the help and encouragement given by Prof. Hugh Rees of the Department of Agricultural Botany and Prof. J. P. Cooper, Director of the Welsh Plant Breeding Station and our friends and colleagues in the University College of Wales, Aberystwyth.

DGJ
BCC
August 1978

Dedication

To Dorothy, Steven and Laura (BCC)
Anita, Huw, Phillip and Justin (DGJ)

Contents

Preface   ix

Chapter 1   **General introduction**   *page* **1**
Introduction, the cereal crops, cultivation and
management, the disease problem.

Chapter 2   **Nature of pathogenicity**   *page* **16**
Concept of pathogenicity, host range of pathogens,
variability in pathogens, the infection process.

Chapter 3   **Nature of resistance**   *page* **36**
Disease escape, tolerance, genuine disease
resistance, resistance mechanisms, genetics of
resistance.

Chapter 4   **Pathological techniques**   *page* **52**
Disease diagnosis, isolation of fungal and bacterial
pathogens, culture and inoculum production,
preservation and storage, inoculation and infection,
incubation and sympton expression, observing
host:parasite relations, disease assessment, monitoring
pathogen populations, maintenance of physiologic races
in isolation, experimental design.

Chapter 5   **Resistance breeding techniques**   *page* **95**
Why breed for resistance? Sources of resistance,
characterization of resistance, utilization of resistance,
breeding methods, strategies, the identification and
prediction of stability, assessment of the value of
resistance, conclusions.

Chapter 6   **Control of plant diseases**   *page* **128**
              Objectives, regulatory methods, cultural methods,
              biological methods, physical methods, chemical methods,
              major groups of non-systemic agricultural fungicides,
              systemic fungicides, fungicide insensitivity, seed
              treatments, disease forecasting, integrated control.

              List of plates   *page* **161**

              Compendium of cereal diseases   *page* **167**

              Glossary   *page* **259**

              Index   *page* **264**

              Index to compendium   *page* **278**

Preface

It is the hope of the authors that this book will help towards the objective of increased cereal crop yields by providing the basis for a better understanding of the many problems associated with cereal diseases and their control. An attempt has been made to bring together an outline of the theory and practice of cereal pathology. At first the reader is introduced to the cereal crops, their distribution and importance to man. The next two chapters deal with the principles of cereal pathology and are designed to provide an understanding of the nature of pathogenicity and host resistance. The remaining three chapters are intended to act as a guide – a 'workshop manual' – for pathologists and breeders and consist of a chapter on pathological techniques, one on breeding for resistance and finally, a synthesis of the various control measures and their integrated application. The compendium of diseases, illustrated by many colour plates, includes diseases of wheat, barley, oats, rye and maize and is intended as a source of reference to the biology and natural history of the pathogens of these crops. Included also are notes on handling the pathogens, their culture and storage. Specific methods, where they apply, are presented in the description of the disease but, where more general methods apply, the reader is referred to chapters 4, 5 and 6. Only limited references are given for further general reading or where specific techniques, keys or procedures are not fully described or illustrated in the text.

The book, which has been contributed to equally by the two authors, does not claim to be an exhaustive treatise but hopefully includes methods and information of value to the student and practitioner of cereal crop protection. It is hoped that students will be provided with an understanding of cereal pathological problems and their solution and new workers in the field with a basis from which to initiate research and development programmes. In chapters 4 and 5, particular consideration has been given to describing simple techniques which can be used where resources are limited, especially in developing countries. This latter need has become apparent to us from our involvement with training programmes for overseas students, in particular the M.Sc. course in plant breeding at the University College of Wales and the Welsh Plant Breeding Station at Aberystwyth. A glossary of terms is also included and the key words for this are indicated by bold face type in the text.

DGJ

BCC

Chapter 1 **General Introduction**

It is not overstating the case to say that cereal cultivation is the linch-pin of civilization as we know it. The dramatic events in our primaeval past which resulted in the decline of man the nomadic hunter and the ascent of man the cultivator and husbander, completely changed the course of human history. These changes were brought about by man's realization that the seeds of certain grasses could be harvested, stored and sown again the following season to produce more grain for himself, his animals and to sow yet again.

Nowhere else in agriculture have the skills of the breeder, the pathologist, the chemist and farmer been better expressed than in those crops which belong to the family *Gramineae*. The evolution of this most important family of agricultural plants enabled man to develop a more settled existence. Today's needs for a plentiful supply of cheap energy to fuel industrial civilization are parallel to primitive man's perhaps less perceived needs for such a fuel to drive his muscle-powered evolution. This need was met by the cereal grain which embodied energy from the sun, concentrated and stored ready for use. A cereal field became the launch-pad for the ascent of man. Man, a compassionate animal, could now support those less fitted to survive in a harsh primitive world – the old, the young and the infirm. With the cultivation of cereals and the domestication of animals more people were released from the primary task of survival to become priests, poets, artists, doctors and philosophers thus transforming the quality of man's existence.

Traditionally, wheat, barley, oats and rye have been considered as crops adapted to temperate regions. Maize, whilst accompanying rice, sorghum and millet as crops of warm temperate and tropical regions, is now expanding rapidly into temperate regions due to the development of new varieties. Such diversity implies differences in cultivation and husbandry. A great number of problems might also be expected. Not the least of these problems are those associated with the loss of yield due to pests and diseases. Such invaders of our basic food supplies represent a threat to our continued existence. Populations are expanding so fast that we are no longer able, as were the ancient Egyptians, to store sufficient grain to tide us over years of low production and, consequently, stability of grain yield has become of paramount importance.

Modern high yielding varieties of cereals can support larger human populations than ever before and it is essential that this support be maintained or the magnitude of suffering would surpass all that has gone before. One of the key ways in which yields can be stabilized is through the control of plant disease. Much of today's disease problem has been brought about by modern man. One of the common features of all cereal crops has been their cultivation on an ever increasing scale, often providing an agronomically uniform and genetically identical target for plant pathogens. In such an environment, a suitable parasite is able to develop in epidemic proportions. The example of the Southern corn leaf blight epidemics in the early 1970s in the U.S.A. is a case in point. From the beginning, disease has taken its share of the harvest to the point where it is now estimated that, on average, one-ninth of the cereal crop is lost to disease each year. This, despite our entry into the space and atomic era. Clearly, there are many lessons to be learned.

Since the beginning of the 20th century there has been a tremendous research input to attempt to combat plant diseases by the use of resistance in the host plant. Although plant species, including cereals, are resistant to the majority of pathogenic organisms, some organisms have evolved special relationships with their hosts. It is these special relationships that are of importance to the crop protectionist. A clue to the magnitude of the problem of disease control comes from an appreciation of the fact that host and parasite have co-evolved over thousands of years, the outcome in wild populations being a dynamic balance. In agriculture, we are concerned with shifting this balance in favour of the host plant with the object of maximizing crop yields. This shift is being brought about principally through the incorporation of genetic resistance into desirable varieties by breeding. In a few instances, this approach has met with considerable success but, in others, resistance has been ephemeral due to changes in the pathogen's virulence which have resulted in the host's resistance becoming ineffective. In response to the appearance of new pathogen races, the plant breeder hastily searched for other sources of resistance to incorporate into yet more varieties. More often than not this, in its turn, has resulted in the 'break-down' of resistance by yet more new pathogenic races appearing producing a 'boom and bust' cycle of new varieties which is wasteful of resources and falls far short of the objective of stable yields.

It is perhaps not the type of resistance that has been used that has led to these problems but rather the way in which it has been used. In most regions of the world only a few varieties are grown as farmers seek to benefit from the new high yielding varieties, the results of much modern research and development. The cereal acreage in the United Kingdom has almost doubled since the mid 1950s and, during this intensification, the number of varieties has dropped dramatically. In 1970, for example, two varieties accounted for two-thirds of the winter wheat acreage and two varieties for half the barley acreage. Such intensification has often been accompanied by increases in damage due to disease. These large areas of homogeneous germplasm provide an ideal substrate for the appropriate pathogens especially if the plants had been hitherto protected by a highly specific resistance.

Similarly, although a new era in cereal crop protection has dawned with the development of highly specific and effective 'systemic' fungicides, their widespread use may result in the emergence of strains of pathogens that are insensitive to normal concentrations of the chemicals. Such potential vulnerability of the host plant is of major concern. Current thinking inclines to the view that a more stable solution to cereal disease problems is likely to come through better management in conjunction with a more efficient use of genetic host resistance and chemical fungicides. An integrated approach is thought likely to be the best way of stabilizing cereal yields, each constituent control measure increasing the efficiency of the others and, at the same time, acting as insurance policies against the failure of a single measure.

The cereal crops

The first cereals were probably cultivated about 9,000 years ago by neolithic man. He had recognized that the seeds of certain grasses, when separated from the chaff, were a rich source of food. He also realized that if he stored some of these seeds he would be able to sow them the following season and thus replenish his supply of food. A close look at history indicates that each major civilization was dependent on one or more grain crops; the Greeks, Romans and Western civilizations were dependent upon wheat and barley although oats and rye were grown to a limited extent, the Chinese civilization relied upon rice and the Aztec Indians based their nutrition on maize.

All true cereals are from the family *Gramineae*. The most important are wheat, rice, maize, barley, oats, rye, sorghum and millets. This book, however, considers only wheat, oats, barley, rye and maize, these being the most important in the temperate and cool temperate regions of the world. Cereals are the main source of food for mankind, either as a food source rich in energy producing carbohydrate or as food for our animals from which we derive much of our protein. In the poorer areas of the world, cereals also provide a large fraction of the protein intake for millions of people. This can lead to serious deficiency diseases, such as kwashiorkor, because the cereals arc both low in protein and in essential amino acids such as lysine. At a low level of subsistence, many more people can exist on a given amount of cereal grain than if it was fed to animals and they and their products fed to the population. This results in differences in the cereals grown in a country depending on how they will be

3

used. In countries with an almost vegetarian diet the emphasis is on wheat, rice and rye but as standards of living improve more and more maize, barley and oats are grown to feed the animals required to cater for change to a more proteinaceous diet. In most countries, however, there is an additional requirement for cereals to provide the carbohydrate raw materials for brewing and distilling.

Wheat

Wheat is believed to have originated in the Middle East and is thought to be the result of an accidental hybridization between the diploid einkorn *Triticum* species with a wild grass-like *Aegilops* species. Some of the progeny must have been tetraploid, the emmer wheats, and these again hybridized with another diploid *Aegilops* species. From this cross the hexaploid wheats including the bread wheats, *Triticum aestivum*, were derived. The polyploid species contain genomes which have been derived from *Aegilops* and *Triticum* and are a classic example of evolution through **amphidiploidy**. They behave like typical genomic **allopolyploids** in that their chromosomes pair in a diploid-like fashion and the mode of inheritance is disomic. The *Triticum* species form a polyploid series based on $x = 7$ and consist of three different ploidy levels: diploids ($2n = 2x = 14$), tetraploids ($2n = 4x = 28$) and hexaploids ($2n = 6x = 42$).

It is thought that wheat was first cultivated domestically about 7500 BC and grains have been found in prehistoric Turkish settlements as well as in the 'fertile crescent' which ran through Mesopotamia, now Iraq and Syria. Wheat became a cultivated crop in the United Kingdom about 2000 BC but it wasn't until modern times, in fact in the 15th century, that the crop was first recorded in North America. There has been a considerable change during the evolution of the cultivated wheat from the wild wheat. Its self-pollinating habit has helped to fix desirable mutants and characteristics such as a brittle rachis, which aids seed dissemination have been lost. Similarly, the wild type, with its closed glumes and 'hulled' seed, has been replaced by today's types with easily threshed naked grain.

Both the diploid 'einkorn' and the tetraploid 'emmer' wheats were cultivated in the fertile crescent and later in other countries around the Mediterranean but it was emmer that was the most important cereal until 1000 BC when another tetraploid wheat, *T. turgidum* var *durum*, largely replaced it. The *durum* wheats were a more advanced form and incorporated the free-threshing character. The hexaploid *T. aestivum* probably came into cultivation a little later than the diploid and tetraploid forms, probably about 7000 BC. They were more suited to continental type climates than the Mediterranean type tetraploids adapted to mild winters and dry summers. This was due to the additional genome which was of Asiatic origin and its presence allowed the hexaploid wheats to penetrate into Asia, Europe and eventually to encompass the world.

As more and more wheat came into cultivation there was continuous adaptation and sometimes conscious selection for specific environments and requirements. By breeding and selection, the yields have been increased, the grain is larger and more uniform and flour quality has been improved. Today, the plant breeder has achieved tremendous yields. This has been achieved both by increasing the size and number of grains per head and by incorporating such characteristics as resistance to plant pathogens and pests. Many of the new varieties have a dwarfed growth to reduce the amount of lodging under high rates of fertilizer application. These dwarf varieties, incorporating the genes for this character from the Japanese variety Norin 10, were introduced into Mexican spring wheat by Nobel Prize Winner N. E. Borlaug and became the basis of the so-called 'green revolution', altering the agriculture of such countries as India and Pakistan so that they became self-supporting for this cereal.

There is much still to do in the improvement of wheat. One of the approaches to obtaining increased yields is to exploit heterosis. This involves the production of F_1 hybrid wheat, a method that has been common in maize breeding for several decades. Breeders have already obtained male sterile lines and fertility restoring genes are also available. Such developments may yet see even greater advances in this crop whilst the breeder and the pathologist combine their efforts to reduce the vast losses which regularly occur as a result of disease.

Oats

The history of oats does not date as far back as wheat or barley, in fact the first oats seem to have been grown in Europe and then not until about 1000 BC. The centre of origin is probably the Mediterranean basin where oats probably evolved first as a weed in the wheat and barley crops and later as a selection from these weed oats. The crop did not reach America until AD 1602.

Avena species occur at three ploidy levels, diploids ($2n = 2x = 14$), tetraploids ($2n = 4x = 28$) and hexaploids ($2n = 6x = 42$). As in wheat, there is some evidence indicating evolution from the diploid types through to the hexaploids. There is cytological evidence, for example, which indicates that the diploid A. *strigosa* donated one genome to the hexaploids and there is further evidence of a link between the tetraploid A. *barbata* group which is essentially autopolyploid in origin and is derived directly from the *A. strigosa* diploids. However, the exact pathway of evolution of the hexaploid oats based on *A. sterilis* is not clear and the *barbata* group does not appear to have contributed to the hexaploid types.

The cultivated species today include the diploid *A. strigosa* and *A. brevis*, the tetraploid *A. abyssinica* and the hexaploids *A. sativa*, *A. byzantina* and *A. nuda*. The two major cultivated species, *sativa* and *byzantina* differ in the position at which the rachilla fractures at threshing, the free-threshing *nuda* forms having apparently evolved from *sativa* or *byzantina*. The two hexaploid wild oat species *A. sterilis* and *A. fatua* are the most likely progenitors of our cultivated hexaploids although the consensus of opinion seems to favour evolution through *sterilis* with its wider distribution and aggressiveness.

Climatic factors are mainly responsible for the geographic distribution of oats. Mostly they are grown above 30°N. and below 30°S. latitude. The oat crop is mainly used as livestock feed and is particularly suitable for horses. It is unsuitable for pigs unless it is crushed. The oat grains are normally husked with the lemmas and paleas tightly enclosing the grain. The grain itself is rich in protein (about 16%) and fat (about 8%) but its total nutrient value is much less than barley. This is mainly due to the high husk content (about 20–25%) and it is mainly the lower nutritive value that has contributed to its decline in recent years in terms of the area sown, being mostly replaced by barley. Oats are also a popular human food being used as oatmeal in baking or as rolled oats for porridge.

It seems unlikely that the oat crop will increase in popularity unless free-threshing types with the *sativa* background are produced. Yields have been improved consistently over the past fifty years and much of the breeders' attention has been given to incorporate resistance to disease into his selections.

Barley

Barley (*Hordeum vulgare*) is a most important cereal, the origin of which remains largely unresolved. It has been dated as far back as 8000 BC. It is a self-pollinating diploid ($2n = 2x = 14$) which probably originated from the two-rowed wild type *H. spontaneum*. All the earliest barley finds in archeological excavations were two-rowed in which the grain was tightly held in the husk. The six-rowed, naked grain types appeared by about 6000 BC and, it is believed, originated from *H. agriocrithon* which is found wild in Tibet. In the two-rowed types, there are three spikelets at each node of the rachis but only the central one produces a grain, the two lateral spikelets being female-sterile whereas in the six-rowed types, all spikelets produce grains.

The barley grain is very nutritious, having on average more protein than maize and considerably less oil. It was the standard food of many populations in the Middle and Near East and there are many early writings describing its food value. Some of the ancient gladiators built up their strength on barley and athletes of that era were often rewarded with prizes of barley. It has a high fibre content due to the husks' close proximity to the grain and this reduces its digestibility in comparison with maize. However, protein as high as 18% of which the lysine content makes up about one-fifth, has recently been reported in some Ethiopian barleys. The crop is used for animal feed, the production of malts for brewing and, directly as human food. Over half the world's production of barley goes in the production of feeding stuffs for animals and poultry. For brewing, a high quality grain is required. It should be fully mature, plump and have a nitrogen content between 1·35 and 1·75%. The starch content should be high and there should be enough enzymes available to carry out the fermentation of starch into sugars. Both two-rowed and six-rowed varieties can have these characteristics although European maltsters appear to prefer the two-rowed types whilst in the United States it is the six-rowed varieties that find favour. The present trends are for varieties that can withstand high levels of nitrogen fertilizer and that have either a better feed or malting quality. Attempts are also being made to exploit heterosis and there are many hybrid barley programmes in being in con-sequence. Losses due to disease also pose problems and there has been much emphasis placed on the incorporation of genetic resistance.

Rye

Rye (*Secale cereale*) is the most winter hardy of the cereals hence it is found predominantly in the colder northern and eastern parts of Europe and the U.S.S.R. It is also tolerant of drought, acid soils and low fertility. It is closely related to wheat but has much narrower glumes and paleae. All *Secale* species are diploid ($2n = 2x = 14$) except for a few tetraploid species which have been artificially produced. It is a secondary crop whose antiquity only dates back as far as 1000 BC. It probably arose as a weed of wheat and barley crops and the wild rye can still be found in some areas of Turkey, Morocco, Iran and Afghanistan. The genus *Secale* is very small but two distinct groups of wild species can be separated, both of which appear to have contributed to the evolution of the cultivated *S. cereale*. The annual weed rye species, such as *S. ancestrale, S. segetale* and *S. afghanicum* are very similar cytologically to the cultivated rye. The perennial rye species such as *S. ciliatoglume* and *S. dalmaticum* belong to the *S. montanum* group which differs from

S. cereale in having two major interchanges involving three pairs of chromosomes. During the course of its evolution, *S. cereale*, by natural or imposed selection, has changed from the successful coloniser, with a capacity for growth even in areas where barley and wheat would fail, into the more upright plant with the non-shattering head that is known today.

Unlike the other temperate cereals, rye is self-sterile and an outbreeder, being pollinated by wind action. This characteristic has imposed different breeding techniques upon the crop. This has usually involved the isolation of selected inbred lines which are then crossed in all combinations to determine their combining ability. The best parents are then used as the basis of a new variety. The rye grain is very similar to wheat in its composition and is naked. Glutenin, very important if bread is to be made, is absent from the protein fraction and thus its uses are somewhat restricted. It is the source of flour for the 'black bread' which was eaten extensively by the peasant population in Europe and Russia during the 18th and 19th century. The grain is also malted for the production of beer, whisky and gin. In many areas, rye is used as an early spring forage crop, it being mainly autumn sown and will usually have made considerable growth by the spring. It is normally harvested in June and July. There are prospects for exploiting heterotic effects and male sterile cytoplasmic factors and restorer genes are available. Synthetic autopolyploids ($2n = 4x = 28$) have been produced on a small scale and this is an area which may see further developments.

Maize
The centre of origin of maize (*Zea mays*) is in America with the first evidence of its cultivation dating back to about 5000 BC in Mexico. Its botanical origin is a little uncertain but it is thought that its close relative teosinte (*Euchlaena mexicana*) has contributed to its genotype although there is no archeological evidence to support this view. Teosinte and maize are both diploid ($2n = 2x = 20$) and there are certain close similarities both in chromosome and certain external morphological characteristics. Teosinte also crosses readily with maize and the progeny is fertile.

Most of the world production of maize is concentrated in North America and southern Europe, the Corn Belt region of the north central states of the U.S.A. producing about half of the world's total. Other areas of intensive cultivation include some African countries, Argentina, Mexico and Brazil with the U.S.S.R., Rumania, Italy, Hungary, Yugoslavia and France representing the main European countries.

Several quite distinct types of maize are recognized and are regarded as sub-species of *Zea mays*. The *dent* type owes it name to the depression which develops in the kernel when the soft starch within dries. The *flint* type does not become indented and has a lower soft starch content. The *flour* type contains a very high proportion of soft starch. The *sweet corn* type is sweet because the sugars within the kernel are not converted to starch during ripening. The *pop corn* type has small hard kernels, with very little soft starch, which burst on heating. Maize is a high carbohydrate crop but it is normally deficient in the amino acids lysine and tryptophan which are essential in a balanced feed for non-ruminants and man, and also in nicotinic acid. However, the *opaque*-2 mutant recently discovered confers upon its carrier the ability to synthesize both lysine and tryptophan and this is most important from the standpoint of human and animal nutrition. Because of the nutrient deficiencies of maize, the greater part of the crop is channelled into livestock feed. It does form the staple diet in many African and Latin American countries where it is ground up to produce a flour that is often eaten as a gruel. There is also a growing market for the sweet corn types especially since the recent expansion of domestic deep-freezers for storage.

With the introduction of new and improved varieties of maize, especially those which are more nutritionally acceptable, there is likely to be an increase both in the yield and the area sown to this crop. There has already been an expansion into N.W. Europe although, in the United Kingdom, much of this has been associated with ensilage of the green crop. There is much interest in breeding methods and the production of F_1 hybrid corn has been the basis for recent developments in the breeding of other cereals. Much is now known of yield components, standability and resistance to disease. Much has been learned about the problems of genetic vulnerability from the Southern corn leaf blight epidemics in the U.S.A. in 1970, where, by introducing the 'Texas' male sterile cytoplasm into many varieties, susceptibility to this disease was also introduced. The current techniques of inter-crossing selected and tested inbred plants to more rapidly produce hybrids, offer the breeder a better chance both to quickly improve the agronomic characters of his varieties and to introduce resistance to pests and diseases. Coupled with improved techniques of screening, especially in the laboratory plus the advent of tissue culturing, the plant breeder has many and useful advantages on his side.

Cultivation and management

Before embarking on any farming system that includes cereals a thorough knowledge should be obtained of the requirements of the particular crop in terms of land preparation, technology of sowing, fertilizer rates and management during the growing season. The preparation of the seed bed is all important in most crops and, for all cereals, it is essential that the land should have been worked over in plenty of time before sowing to produce a good even tilth of adequate moisture level and which is normally rolled to give a firm seed bed. Although in some systems 'direct drilling' is now the normal practice, conventional land preparation by ploughing, probably to a depth of about 20 cm followed by a harrowing or even a passage with a rotary cultivator, is still the more widely used method. It is important not only to break up the larger soil aggregates but also to incorporate decaying crop residues and any weeds. However, it should be emphasized that too much soil disturbance can result in a loss of soil moisture and this would be detrimental to the germination of the sown seed, especially maize.

Except in the case of the small peasant farmer who sows his seed either broadcast or by hand placement in the case of maize, most cereals are normally drilled into a shallow row which is shaped by some form of coulter. The coulters precede the drill spout down which the seed is either delivered by gravity or by some mechanism which feeds the drill tube. A recent innovation has been the practice of drilling the seed directly into soil with no prior cultivation. It is usual to kill off any vegetation or the remains of a previous cereal crop and to 'direct drill' through the dead vegetation. This practice is certainly cheaper and quicker than the traditional methods of cultivation but there is a higher requirement for nitrogen due to the reduced level of mineralization of soil nitrogen in the absence of the incorporation of organic matter into the soil during normal cultivation techniques. In most cases, cereal seed will be treated with a fungicide to control seed-borne pathogens. This treatment has, more often than not, involved the use of organo-mercurial compounds. However, in many countries the use of mercury compounds has been banned and in many others there had been a change over to a mixture of one of the systemic fungicide compounds, for example carboxin, and a contact fungicide such as thiram.

The requirement for fertilizers will be determined both by the fertility status of the soil, the cereal to be grown and the time of sowing. It is normal to apply both potash and phosphate prior to seed drilling and this may be accompanied by an application of nitrogen. The nitrogen requirement is mostly met by splitting the application with the second, heavier application, being given in the spring in the case of autumn sown crops and perhaps as late as May or June, during the stem extension phase, in the spring sown crops where it can be directed towards the process of grain filling rather than tillering and straw production. The timing of application of nitrogen to wheat is most important. Applications in the vegetative stages prior to heading result in increased grain yield, applications after heading results in additional protein in the seed, improving both the nutritive value and the baking quality. With barley grown for malting, a low nitrogen content is required and this limits the use of nitrogenous fertilizers.

In the spring, the application of a post-emergence chemical spray to control weeds is now almost a routine practice. The timing of such sprays, normally hormonal weedkillers to control broad-leaves weeds, is critical. The optimum time is when the plants are fully tillered but not after the start of 'jointing' or 'shooting'. Graminaceous weed species such as wild oats (*Avena fatua* and *A. sterilis*), blackgrass (*Alopecurus myosuroides*) and couchgrass (*Agropyron repens*) are more difficult to control although there are chemical herbicides which are recommended for their control, for example, a formulation of a dalapon sodium salt is in use for the control of couch and other perennial grasses but here, the chemical is applied after harvesting the cereal crop. Similarly, wild oats and blackgrass can be checked in a wheat crop by an application of a formulation of barban (12·5% w/v). It must be applied when the wild oats are in the 1–2½ leaf stage or the blackgrass at the 2 leaf stage. Another formulation of barban (23·5% w/v) can be used for the control of wild oats in spring barley crops but must not be used in wheat or other crops.

Other management practices during the growing season include the application of foliar sprays of growth regulating chemicals such as chlormequat which has the effect of reducing straw length. The dwarfed crop is less prone to lodging and there is also some evidence that the effects of eyespot disease (*Pseudocercosporella herpotrichoides*) are also reduced. Fungicides for the control of diseases caused by airborne pathogens may also be applied during the growing season. Their time of application will depend upon the nature of the disease but, in general, they would be applied during the stem extension phase and are rarely applied after heading, although a pre-harvest spray has been shown to be beneficial in barley by reducing the contamination of the grain by seed-borne pathogens.

The application of a second nitrogen dressing and the use of fungicides, especially systemics, in the maturing crop has led to the adoption of a 'tramline' system of drilling the small seeded cereals in which drills are left blank for tractor wheelings

(Fig. 1.1). The progress of tractor and accompanying machinery through a cereal field inevitably causes physical damage to the crop and, before the introduction of more persistent and effective systemics, the loss of yield that would occur after several applications of a conventional protectant fungicide made this form of treatment uneconomical.

Wheel damage to the crop up to GS5–6 (first node detectable) (Growth stages, see Fig. 4.3) is unlikely to affect yield as compensation occurs but after this stage yield loss increases up to about 190 kg/ha (1½ cwt/acre) in a 4·40 tonne/ha (35 cwt/acre)

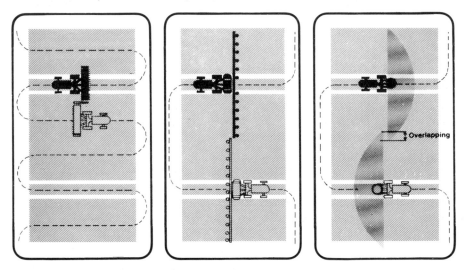

Fig. 1.1 *The preparation of 'tramlines' for foliar spray application.*

crop, at GS 10·5 (full ear emergence). This estimate is based on the use of a spray boom about 9 m (30 ft) wide. Now, with the higher value of the cereal crop and the introduction of 'tramline' farming, spraying has become a common practice even up to the heading stage. The use of tramlines is a well-established procedure in Western Europe, and the system has several advantages over standard systems of field marking used for crop spraying.

1 Well-defined wheelways help to ensure accurate spraying of crop chemicals.
2 One set of wheelings in the crop reduces crop damage and secondary growth which might occur as a result of repeated applications.

3 Late application of fertilizers and fungicides is made easier and these can help to increase yields and control damaging pests and diseases.

The most reliable method is to close the two drill coulters which match the wheel spacing of the equipment to be used for subsequent field work. Alternatively, a single coulter can be blocked and the second lane of the wheelway formed when the drill travels back across the field in the opposite direction. The technique is gaining popularity in the United Kingdom and is most suited to the winter crop but, with an increased awareness of the advantages and greater standardization of equipment, it will become part of normal routine for the cereal farmer.

The disease problem

Cereals are subject to attack by many groups of fungi, bacteria, viruses, insects and nematodes. The damage they produce may cause considerable reductions in grain yield and quality. The extent of the problem varies with the nature of the pathogen and the severity of the attack but it has been estimated that there is an annual reduction in yield of about 12% on a world basis. There can be no doubt that modern agricultural systems have largely contributed to this problem of pests and disease. The adoption of the extensive method of monoculturing cereals coupled with a desire for a uniform crop have been the two features which have dramatically accentuated the disease problem. In addition, the liberal use of nitrogen fertilizers has produced yet more problems such as lodging and an increase in the severity of certain diseases. It is now known, for example, that nitrogen not only produces the lush succulent growth that in itself is highly susceptible to certain plant pathogens but also that it increases the sporulation capacity of the diseased tissue in powdery mildew-infected cereals and thus feeds the epidemic.

The discovery of genes in the host plant controlling resistance led to the initiation of many plant breeding programmes designed to incorporate these genes into varieties of cereals which also had desirable agronomic qualities. This approach seemed quite sound and the feeling was that, given enough plant breeders, the disease problem would disappear. However, the reality was quite different. In most cases, the incorporation of genetic resistance into new varieties led to the 'boom and bust' cycle where, due to the high degree of selection pressure placed on the pathogen population, mutant races capable of overcoming the resistance increased in the population at the expense of the previous pathogen races which could not infect the new host plants. Thus, in breeding for resistance, an element of genetic vulnerability was also introduced which commonly led to the withdrawal of the new variety. Crop vulnerability to disease may be artificially induced, as in the case of breeding for resistance, or it may be natural where the host and the parasite, having evolved separately, are eventually brought together. When a host plant is moved into an area in which it has previously not been grown it might well encounter indigenous parasites against which it has no resistance. The converse is also true and is exemplified by the introduction of *Puccinia polysora*, the causal organism of Southern corn rust, into Africa in the 1940s. It is believed that the pathogen was imported on green cobs and it quickly spread. The local varieties, although very heterogeneous, were highly susceptible and many infected individuals were killed outright. The fact that the surviving plants, under strong selection pressure for resistance, formed the basis of the current varieties with a better background of resistance is a salutary lesson both to plant breeders and pathologists. Genetic vulnerability was added to by the popularity which the new varieties attracted. In place of the traditional system of a great diversity of varieties, presumably incorporating many forms and levels of resistance, the new varieties were very uniform and were grown widely providing new virulent races with a large target population. The ensuing epidemics reduced the profitable life of the host varieties, and in many commercial wheats, this has resulted in a change of variety about every four years. There is a difference in the magnitude of the problems associated with foliar diseases of cereals as compared with root diseases. Unfortunately, the foliar diseases, with rusts and powdery mildew heading the attack, have rather dominated the scene and many root diseases have been neglected by researchers on a priority basis.

Many cereal pathogens are seed-borne and this important epidemiological fact has resulted in a variety of control measures aimed at the elimination of the pathogen at this source. Such control measures as protectant chemicals, hot water treatment and, lately, systemic fungicides have been very successful and diseases such as the smuts (*Ustilago spp.*) and bunts (*Tilletia spp.*) and certain *Helminthosporium* species have been reduced to almost negligible proportion in many countries. Root diseases pose many problems not the least being that they may pass more or less unnoticed. It must be emphasized that subclinical attacks by root pathogens can still cause reductions in yield. Their control is usually very difficult as it is not yet economical or, in many cases practical, to chemically sterilize large tracts of soil. The approach to the foliar diseases of cereals has been much more energetic. The pathologist and the breeder had the results of his efforts to control these diseases displayed for all to see and, all too often, the picture was none too pleasant. The breakdown of resistance based on single genes has led to pathologists placing a greater emphasis on the more stable polygenically controlled resistance and there have also been developments to make better use of varieties incorporating monogenic resistance. In this respect, the use of multilines and composite mixtures is in its infancy as a science but coupled with advances in the technology of cereal cultivation and in the more efficient use of fungicides there would seem to be a good chance of improving on present day yields through a reduction in disease losses. The decisive factor will probably emerge as a result of detailed epidemiological studies leading to accurate forecasting systems. The aim of this book is to provide information on all aspects of the pathology of cereal diseases in an attempt to achieve some of the objectives discussed above.

Further reading

Evolution of Crop Plants *Editor N. W. Simmonds, Longman, London, 1976*
Technology of Cereals, with special reference to wheat *by N. L. Kent, 2nd edition, Oxford, Pergamon, 1975*
The Principles of Plant Pathology *by S. A. J. Tarr, Macmillan, 1972*
Plant Pathology *by J. H. Walker, McGraw-Hill, 1969*
Plant Pathology; An Advanced Treatise *Editors J. G. Horsfall and A. E. Dimond, Academic Press, New York and London, 1959*
Diseases of Crop Plants *Editor J. H. Western, Macmillan, 1971*
Plant Virology, The Principles *by A. Gibbs and B. D. Harrison, Edward Arnold, 1976*

Chapter 2 **Nature of pathogenicity**

Concept of pathogenicity

A simple definition of the term **pathogenicity** is 'the ability of a genus or species to cause disease'. **Virulence** is the ability of an individual entity within a group of strains, *formae speciales* or isolates to cause disease under defined conditions. The term **aggressiveness** is applied to physiologic races of a pathogen that differ in the severity of their pathological effects but which do not interact differentially with host varieties.

A distinction should now be made between a parasite and a pathogen. The term **pathogen** applies only to biotic agents of disease, nematodes, fungi, bacteria and viruses in the case of cereal diseases, although two new types of pathogens of other crop species have been described in recent years. The first is a wall-less, membrane-bound, mycoplasma-like organism and the second, minute RNA molecules with no protein coat which have been given the name **viroids**. When an organism lives on or in some other organism, obtaining its nutrient supply from the latter and conferring no benefit in return, then it can be defined as a **parasite**. Parasitism can therefore be seen to be closely associated with pathogenicity, for the withdrawal of nutrients from a host plant inevitably leads to a reduction in some growth process and might even result in the plant's death. To this extent, pathogenicity may be considered as the interference of some essential functions in the plant by the parasite and this is a description commonly used to define a diseased plant.

Plant parasites can be conveniently divided into two groups depending upon whether or not they can live in the absence of the living plant. Those viruses, nematodes, powdery mildew and rust fungi which normally grow and reproduce only on living hosts have, traditionally, been classified as **obligate parasites**. The remainder of the fungi and all the bacteria should therefore be classified as non-obligate parasites, having the ability to live on both living and dead host tissues. Within this category there is a wide variation of types. Those with a strongly developed parasitic habit have been termed **facultative saprophytes** whilst those which are only weakly parasitic have been termed **facultative parasites**. The confusion that may be generated when using these terms is both apparent and unnecessary and the fact that some fungi once classified as obligate parasites can now be grown on artificial media also makes this category somewhat redundant.

A change in terminology was obviously required and the organisms which coexist with the host tissue for an extended period and do not kill the host rapidly, formerly the obligate parasites, are better described as **biotrophs**. Typical of this category of cereal pathogens are the rusts, smuts and powdery mildews and they are classified as such, regardless of whether or not they can be cultured artificially, if they obtain their nutrients normally from living host tissue. An organism that derives the greater part of its nutrient supply from dead host tissue causing a rapid death of part or all of its host was formerly known as a facultative saprophyte or parasite, and is now called a **necrotroph**. This latter category contains a very diverse collection of organisms, varying from the leaf-spotting fungi which attack living tissue in the same manner as biotrophs but continue to develop and sporulate after the tissue is dead, to those organisms that kill the host tissues in advance of their penetration, death being achieved by toxins or enzymes.

To the plant pathologist, these two categories of plant pathogens have important implications. The requirement of biotrophs for living host tissue means that it is difficult, in many cases impossible, to culture the organism artificially in the laboratory. The study of plant viruses and many important cereal pathogens is hampered in this way although some fungi which were once thought to be nutritionally demanding can now be cultured on relatively simple media. Some species of cereal rust fungi, for example, can now be successfully cultured away from their hosts. Another important implication concerns the inoculum hazard presenting itself annually by the necrotrophic fungi which can survive the inter-crop period on crop debris.

The concept of pathogenicity has not always been an accepted fact. Its early opponents favoured the theory of 'spontaneous generation' believing that the observed signs of the pathogen on diseased plants arose as a result of some malfunctioning in the host which was attributable to biological agencies. This is not to say that disease conditions were not recognized as being important or that control measures were not attempted. The early Greeks and Romans had recorded the incidence of blights, blasts, mildews and rusts as being of considerable social and economic importance. Their attempts at control were purely arbitrary, the usual maxim being that if a chemical was particularly pungent then it ought to be toxic to any malady of their plants.

It took scientists until the mid-nineteenth century to disprove the hypothesis of spontaneous generation and much of the credit has been given to Tyndall and Pasteur although Prévost had earlier demonstrated that bunt of wheat (*Tilletia caries*) was caused by a fungus whose spores were carried on the outside of the cereal grain. Here then was the explanation of why this disease could be prevented by soaking the seed in a copper sulphate solution. The cereal rusts had been known for centuries although there was no information about the causal organism. In 1805, Banks suggested that both the uredospore and teleutospore stages found on the wheat plant belonged to the same fungus. He also put forward the view that there might also be an association between the common barberry and the wheat black stem rust pathogen (*Puccinia graminis tritici*). However it took another sixty years before de Bary finally published the complete life-cycle of this pathogen and confirmed its **heteroecious** nature.

The involvement of bacteria as plant pathogens came a little later with the work of Burrill and Erwin Smith leading the way forward. However, it was well into the 20th century that bacterial pathogens of cereals were recognized and identified although they do not figure prominently in the list of damaging cereal pathogens.

To the ancient Romans the word **virus** meant poison. Its meaning altered during the course of time so that, at present, it is only applied to a heterogeneous group of minute, biotrophic pathogens. In the first half of the present century, all sub-microscopic plant pathogens were considered to be viruses but it is now known that many diseases previously referred to as virus diseases are caused by mycoplasma-like organisms. **Mycoplasmas** are the smallest free-living microorganisms, having ribosomes and both RNA and DNA. They possess a unit membrane but, unlike bacteria, lack a rigid cell wall and are therefore highly pleomorphic. Plant viruses, on the other hand, consist of a single or double strand of nucleic acid surrounded by a protein coat. Most plant viruses contain RNA (ribonucleic acid) but a small proportion contain DNA (deoxyribonucleic acid). Virus diseases of cereals are now recognized as being of considerable importance although it wasn't until 1952 that the first virus disease of the *Gramineae* was recorded in the United Kingdom. This was the discovery of cocksfoot streak virus by Kenneth Smith. Since then, many more diseases of cereals and grasses have been recorded throughout the world.

Host range of pathogens

Variation in plant pathogens encompasses all aspects of physiology, morphology and, just as importantly, the kinds of plants and the tissues of those plants that they can attack. At one extreme there are those pathogens which are very specific, being restricted to a single species. Less specific are those pathogens that attack within a single genus. With a wider host range still are those pathogens with the ability to attack many taxonomic groups of higher plants. There may be genetical and physiological reasons for this variation although the controlling factors are not completely understood. However, there is at least one limiting factor to universal pathogenicity by a particular pathogen and that is host plant resistance. This phenomenon is more widespread than is perhaps realized and it is as well not only to emphasize that diseased plants are the exception rather than the rule but also that individual pathogens are able to parasitize only a very small proportion of the huge spectrum of plants available to them.

The biotrophic pathogens can be represented by the cereal rusts and powdery mildews as examples of the highly specific category. It is thought that this specificity as to the kind of host they attack is the result of the close adaptation of the pathogen to its host, both 'partners' having evolved in parallel. Of world-wide importance is the black stem rust pathogen (*Puccinia graminis*) which has a restricted host range within the *Gramineae*, being particularly important on wheat. To distinguish between forms of this fungus which are adapted to the various host genera, sub-divisions have been made within the pathogen species. These *formae speciales* are given the nomenclature of the host species predominantly attacked. The form which attacks wheat is called *P. graminis tritici* whilst *P. graminis avenae* attacks oats and *P. graminis secale* attacks rye. These sub-divisions are not absolute and there is a limited amount of promiscuity over the host range.

The degree of specificity becomes even more precise with the further sub-division of each adapted form into **physiologic races**, each of which can only attack a clearly defined spectrum of host varieties. The relationship of each physiologic race to its potential hosts depends upon the compatability of the genetic systems in both host and pathogen. From an evolutionary point of view the two systems must have developed in parallel with a mutation to virulence in a pathogen population being countered by the selection, either in nature or by the plant breeder, of hosts able to resist the new pathogen race. This is the basis of the 'gene for gene' theory that will be discussed elsewhere in this book. This extreme of specificity creates many problems, not the least being that any change in the pathogenicity spectrum of the pathogen results in an alteration of the potential host range that may be attacked.

Within a given host range there is yet another form of specificity and this is concerned with the host tissue attacked. Some pathogens are specific to certain plant parts whilst others are very much more extensive in their colonization. Many root-infecting fungi never infect the foliage, a good example being the take-all pathogen (*Gaeumannomyces graminis*). The ergot pathogen (*Claviceps purpurea*) is restricted to the floral organs. Of an intermediate category are those pathogens capable of attacking all plant tissues above the ground and here *Erysiphe graminis* and *Septoria nodorum* provide excellent examples.

Variability in pathogens

One of the most significant facts in biology is that individuals produced as a result of sexual processes will be different in genotype and possibly phenotype both from each other and from their parents. This variation is the result of the recombination of chromosomal genetic factors during **meiosis**, a process which is now well understood. Variation can also result from an exchange or admixture of extra-chromosomal factors which are situated in the cytoplasm. The production of variation in a population is only one side of the coin, its establishment and maintenance in the population is the other. New variants will be exposed to all manner of competition, not the least being, in the case of new physiologic races of pathogenic fungi, the success in being deposited upon a susceptible host. The host population itself greatly influences this selection and establishment process. A widely grown resistant host variety exerts a high selection pressure on the pathogen population in terms of presenting a new compatible race with a large target area.

Changes in the pathogen may also occur as a result of non-sexual processes. Perhaps the most common of these is **mutation** but it is also known that variability can be produced through the processes known as **heterokaryosis** and the **parasexual cycle**. The variation produced may involve any characteristic whether it be morphological or physiological. It might simply produce changes in the shape and colour of the organism or it might alter its rate of growth or reproduction. These latter changes will certainly effect the competitive ability of the new organisms. Most changes will be of a relatively unimportant nature and would go unnoticed to the casual observer. A change in virulence, with its effect upon host range might very well place a hitherto resistant species or variety under attack and lead to considerable yield losses.

Variability whether it is produced by recombination, mutation or any other process, produces a re-assortment of genetic material in a completely random manner. On this basis, it might be predicted that changes which are to the pathogen's advantage will occur at about the same frequency as those which are disadvantageous. Nothing is further from the reality of the situation. To take mutations as a good example, the overwhelming majority will be deleterious and the organism is almost bound to suffer. In fact, the majority of new pathogen variants will be so inferior in some respect that they will fail to survive, their existence may never be recorded. The reason for this is that there are likely to be many attributes necessary for pathogenicity and a re-assortment process is more likely to result in a loss of one of these than in the gain of an additional attribute. There will, of course, be exceptions and such variants may be selected out by the host population as already described. With little competition and a susceptible host, the variant quickly establishes itself in the pathogen population and will remain until such time as the host is replaced by another incorporating resistance against the variant.

This sequence, often repeated, forms the background to the situation that has existed for several decades in cereal resistance breeding and has resulted in a regular turn-over of cereal varieties and a dynamic situation in the pathogen population.

Mutation

Most changes in the characteristics of pathogens are the result of recombination during sexual processes. Recombination is, of course, limited to the genetic material constituting the parental genotypes. Changes in absolute terms must involve mutation. Mutations occur spontaneously in all living organisms but only those that produce morphological changes or endow a selective advantage will ever be recognized in nature. Mutations normally occur as single random events affecting only one character, the changed character can then be inherited in the normal way. Most fungi and bacteria are haploid and the mutation will be expressed immediately. Most rust fungi, however, have two phases, a **homokaryon** made up of haploid uninucleate cells and a **dikaryon** made up of binucleate cells. As most of the life cycle of rust fungi is dikaryotic then they can be considered as functional diploids. This situation has important implications in terms of the expression of a new character produced by mutation as, in the diploid situation, a change to virulence in one allele may be masked by the dominant avirulent partner allele. In this case, the new virulence may not be expressed until sexual recombination brings together two recessive virulent alleles in the same genotype.

Mutations affecting virulence can alter the host range of a particular physiologic race of a pathogen and, it is thought, are the main reasons for the appearance of new races of cereal powdery mildews and rusts and probably many other pathogens. Furthermore, the mutant gene, as a permanent member of the genotype, will be a participant in sexual and parasexual processes and, possibly, recombinants will be produced possessing different host ranges to those of the existing pathogen population. Mutations may thus be regarded as the basis for variation in all plant pathogens.

Recombination during sexual reproduction

The majority of fungi, being haploid, have only a very brief diploid phase, the diploid nucleus resulting from fertilization very often undergoing meiosis very soon after **karyogamy**. There is now evidence from DNA measurements that some Oomycetes are predominantly diploid and we have already seen that many Basidiomycetes are functionally diploids by virtue of their extended dikaryon phase. In those fungi with a sexual stage, and there are many lacking this stage, meiosis results in a random recombination of genetic material. This happens through the processes of crossing-over between linked genes on homologous chromosomes and the independent segregation of genes in different homologous pairs. The amount of variability released by recombination is related to the breeding system of the particular fungal species. On the one extreme are the **homothallic** fungi which are essentially self-compatible and in which sexual reproduction can take place on a single thallus. In homothallic fungi the extent of outcrossing will be close to zero and there will be very little opportunity for recombination between genetically different individuals. On the other extreme, there are the **heterothallic** fungi with physiologically distinct mycelia upon which are produced compatible male and female gametes. Here, the extent of outcrossing might approach 100%. Other fungi fall between these two extremes with simple systems based on two mating types determined by alternative alleles at a single locus.

Amongst the pathogens of cereal crops, especially the rusts and smuts, it has been possible to experimentally hybridize single spore isolates and to study the morphological, physiological and pathogenic changes in the progeny. In many instances, the new variants only differered in characters of little interest but, occasionally, new physiologic races with a different host range to the parents have been produced. Genetic studies of naturally occurring fungal populations have also indicated that hybrids are present which have combined the pathogenicity spectra of both parents. A good example is the black stem rust fungus, *Puccinia graminis*. This is a heteroecious rust spending part of its life cycle on cereals and grasses and part on certain species of barberry, of which the most important is common barberry, *Berberis vulgaris*. Two asexual spore stages are found on the cereals and grasses, the uredospore and teleutospore stages. Both uredospores and teleutospores are dikaryotic but on the germination of the teleutospores, fusion of the two nuclei occur to produce a diploid. A meiotic division then occurs and the resulting haploid nuclei migrate one each to four basidiospores produced as outgrowths of the basidium. The fungus has two mating types (+) and (−) and two of each type are represented in the four basidiospores. Two sexual spore stages are produced on the barberry, the pycniospore and aecidiospore stages, the barberry being infected by the basidiospores. Each infection can give rise to a **pycnium** and its mating type and those of the pycniospores will be the same as that of the basidiospore causing the infection. For the production of aecidiospores it is necessary for the dikaryon to be reconstituted and this can be achieved if pycniospores of the (+) mating type fuse with hyphae of a pycnium of the (−) mating type. The aecidiospores will now be dikaryotic and can infect the appropriate cereal or grass host producing infections which will give rise to dikaryotic uredospores. This knowledge of the full life-cycle of this rust fungus enabled pathologists to understand the sexual mechanism and to appreciate how new pathogenic races could arise by recombination during meiosis. This understanding was further emphasized by the work of Stakman and his colleagues in the U.S.A. who found a greater diversity of physiologic races near to the alternate host, the barberry, than distant to this source of variation. The importance of the sexual stage and the barberry bushes led to the many barberry eradication schemes in the U.S.A.

Heterokaryosis
In some fungi, hyphae or parts of hyphae contain nuclei which are genetically different, generally of two different kinds. This condition, is known as **heterokaryosis** and the phenomenon is commonly brought about after **hyphal anastomosis** between mycelia of the two parental genotypes. In the Basidiomycotina, the heterokaryon can be seen in its most stable form, the dikaryon, with its regularly binucleate cells which can be considered as functionally diploid.

In the Ascomycotina and Deuteromycotina some fungi possess cells containing numerous nuclei and these may be heterokaryotic. The underlying implication of this state is that the fungus may respond to selection by varying the proportions of the dissimilar nuclei in the cells. There can be no doubt that heterokaryosis is involved in the production of fungal variation. Studies involving observations on sectoring and on variation in progeny arising from single spores have suggested heterokaryosis in *Cochliobolus sativus*, *Leptosphaeria avenaria* and *Helminthosporium gramineum*. Such variants, it can be argued, may have arisen by mutation but there is good experimental evidence to support heterokaryosis in these pathogens. In *Cochliobolus sativus*, the causal organism of root rot, spot blotch and head blight in cereals, hyphal-tip transfers from mixtures of **auxotrophic** strains produced mycelia that grew through several 'generations' on minimal medium. Both parental strains, as well as heterokaryons, were obtained from single-conidium isolations from heterokaryons. When a single heterokaryon was grown on eight separate occasions on the same medium, parental ratios varying from 1:2 to 1:19 were found. If the heterokaryon was grown on a medium selective for one parent, nearly 100% dissociation occurred. (Tinline, Can. J. Bot., **40**; 425, 1962). It is obvious that heterokaryosis does occur in *C. sativus* and that dissociation is common. However, it must be said that the extent of heterokaryosis in plant pathogens is probably not as much as was at first thought and until unequivocal and positively confirmed evidence is presented that hetero-karyosis affects pathogenicity or virulence, its role in cereal pathology must remain conjectural.

The parasexual cycle
In heterokaryotic fungal mycelium, there is always the opportunity for dissimilar nuclei to fuse and produce diploids. **Mitotic recombination** can then occur producing a random re-assortment of genetic material which is released in the progeny after haploidization. This sequence of events has been described as the parasexual cycle and was first demonstrated in the laboratory by Pontecorvo (Ann. Rev. Microbiol., **10**; 393, 1956) working with the non-pathogenic *Aspergillus nidulans.* It has since been reported in many pathogenic fungi.

Cochliobolus sativus is heterothallic with one pair of alleles controlling incom-patibility. The sexual stage has only been found in the laboratory although compatible strains can be found regularly in nature. By using several markers such as spore colour, resistance to antibiotics and nutrient requirements, it has been shown that the diploid strains produced in the laboratory gave rise to second order mitotic recom-binants providing positive confirmation of parasexuality in this pathogen. Proof of diploidy in cereal pathogens was given by experiments with the eyespot pathogen, *Pseudocercosporella herpotrichoides*, where nuclei of certain isolates were shown to have double the amount of *DNA* of the parental isolates from which they originated (Davies and Jones, Heredity, **25**; 137, 1970).

Parasexuality has also been proposed as being the mechanism of producing new physiologic races in several rusts, including *P. graminis tritici* and *P. coronata* and in some smuts, like *U. hordei* and *U. maydis*. In an experiment with *P. coronata* (Bartos, Fleischmann, Samborski and Shipton., Can. J. Bot., **47**; 267, 1969) two races were used as inocula. Of the cultures recovered from infected plants almost 30% were of one parental race and about 50% of the other. Of the remainder, nine new races were identified giving a clear indication that nuclei had been exchanged between the two parental races and that mitotic recombination of genetic material had occurred. In such rust fungi as *P. graminis tritici*, mitotic recombination may represent a most important method of generating new races, especially in countries such as Australia where the sexual stage of the fungus is rare due to the scarcity of the alternate host, the barberry. For other rust fungi with no known sexual stage, *P. striiformis* is a good example, mitotic recombination is the only means of genetic re-assortment. Parasexual recombination has also been shown to occur in the smut fungi. *U. maydis* produces galls in embryonic tissues of maize. Using auxotrophic strains differing in mating type, seedlings were inoculated from which stable **prototrophic** strains were isolated which could be demonstrated to be heterozygous diploids (Holliday, Genet Res., **2**; 231, 1961). Clearly, mitotic recombination was operating in this fungus.

In the example given above, the evidence rules out other methods of recombination leaving parasexuality as the most likely explanation. Demonstrating the parasexual cycle in nature is made difficult because of the complexity of the marker techniques but it could well be the most important evolutionary mechanism in the imperfect fungi, the Deuteromycotina. There is obviously a need for much more positive evidence, especially in terms of cytology and genetics but there can be no doubting the potential of this mechanism in producing variation in cereal pathogens.

The infection process

Pathogenesis embraces the sequence of events which begin when the pathogen contacts an infectible region of the plant. If the pathogen is deposited directly within the host tissues then immediate pathogenic reactions are likely to take place. Such is the case when the pathogen enters through a wound or natural opening as in the case of many bacterial plant diseases. Most fungal inocula, however, are deposited on the surfaces of plants, the initial site of contact being described as the **infection court** and this may be either an aerial or a subterranean surface of the plant.

The environment surrounding the leaves, the **phylloplane**, will be very different from that surrounding the roots, the **rhizoplane**. Desiccation and extreme fluctuations of temperature are the enemies of the pathogen propagule on the leaf surface in contrast to the root environment which provides a buffer against such vagaries. Soil-borne pathogens usually reach the plant surface either by growing vegetatively towards the host plant or by producing motile spores which travel in the soil moisture. The deposition of the air-borne pathogen is normally achieved fortuitously through the agencies of wind or rain-splash. Most viruses, many bacteria and some fungi are carried to plants by insects or other vectors. Having arrived at the plant surface the pathogen must now gain entry and begin the infection process.

The infection process can be divided into three phases (i) pre-penetration, (ii) penetration, (iii) post-penetration. Each phase is separate in terms of pathogen activity but, in fact, each is a continuation of the organism's preceding activity. There is a great diversity between pathogens in the manner in which every step of the infection process proceeds. Some pathogens gain easy access into the plant through natural openings or wounds, others have to contend with the complex process of penetrating the unbroken plant surface. Some pathogens, after completing the infection process, are capable of attacking any plant organ but others, the majority, show some degree of tissue specialization. The pathogen causing ergot of rye (*Claviceps purpurea*) is a good example, being confined to the floral organs. The eyespot fungus of wheat and barley (*Pseudocercosporella herpotrichoides*) is restricted to the stem and leaf sheath bases whereas the loose smut fungus (*Ustilago nuda*) starts its disease cycle as mycelium in the grain and then passes upwards within the developing plant to eventually transform the ear into a mass of black teleutospores on the rachis skeleton. The more specialized the pathogen, the obligate parasites or biotrophs are the best examples, the greater the difficulty in infecting damaged tissues, the reason being their requirement for living host cells to sustain their development.

Pre-penetration
The most important activity in this phase is the germination of the spore although it should be emphasized that infection may be carried out by completely vegetative structures such as the runner hyphae of *Gaeumannomyces graminis*. In many respects, the process of spore germination is analogous to that of seed germination in that water is absorbed, hydrolytic enzymes activated and energy derived from the breakdown of reserve food materials.

The resulting product of spore germination will depend upon the nature of the spore. Commonly, the spore will produce a hypha-like outgrowth known as a **germ-tube** (Fig. 2.1). These germ-tubes may arise from special exit points such as the germ-pores of the rust uredospores or they may emerge directly through the spore wall as in the case of the promycelium of the smut fungi. In the context of germination it is also necessary to distinguish between resting spores and propagative spores for, in the case of resting spores, there is always a period of dormancy or a delay between the time of spore production and their becoming sufficiently mature to germinate. A good example of this is the requirement for overwintering of teleutospores of certain *Puccinia* species before germination can take place. Propagative spores, on the other hand, are thin-walled and generally short-lived. They will normally germinate immediately on encountering favourable conditions. The actual time required for germination varies but most mature spores germinate within approximately one to six hours.

Fig. 2.1 *Germination of* Erysiphe graminis *conidia on the leaf surface (WPBS).*

There are many external factors which can influence the germination process and there will be many situations and periods of time when environmental conditions will be unfavourable. Moisture, temperature, light and pH constitute the main requirements but certain biological factors can also be involved.

With most fungal spores, a film of moisture on the plant's surface is normally essential for germination. There are exceptions and there is evidence that the ability to germinate in dry conditions is related to the water content of the spore. Conidia of *Erysiphe graminis* contain over 75% water in contrast to about 10% in many other fungal spores. This gives the powdery mildew fungus an almost total independence of free water for germination. In fact, germination of this fungus is inhibited by the existence of a water film on the leaf surface.

Spores can germinate over a wide range of temperatures varying from just above freezing-point to 30°C. The optimum temperature varies with the pathogen, *Erysiphe graminis* germinates best at 20°C. but the optimum varies according to the air humidity. *Ustilago zeae*, on the other hand, has a high optimum temperature of about 30°C. whilst some species of *Tilletia* germinate best at about 5°C. It should be pointed out, in this context, that these temperature optima have been calculated from laboratory experiments where temperatures can be standardized and maintained over long periods. The field situation is very much different. Here, there will always be a diurnal rhythm of temperatures and, on almost all days, temperature fluctuates considerably. An unfavourable temperature, however, although causing a delay in germination, loses its inhibitory influence once germination has commenced and the resulting final germination count may not be very different to that resulting in conducive conditions.

Light often has a most definite effect on the sporulation process in fungi. This can be seen in the photosporogenic reactions of *Septoria tritici* and *S. nodorum* to near ultra-violet or 'black light'. Light does not have such a big influence on the spore germination process unless it is sufficiently intense to cause heating. However, it has been shown that rust uredospores germinate better in red-yellow light than in light of shorter wave-lengths.

Most fungal spores can germinate over a wide range of *pH* values although it has not been established whether spore germination alone is affected or whether it affects germination and growth of the pathogen or whether it simply alters the host's susceptibility to infection by this pathogen.

Spore germination may also be influenced by biological factors which, in some cases, may be stimulatory and, in others, inhibitory. These factors may be solutes diffusing from the plant's surface, substances produced by the fungi themselves or the inhibitory effects of certain soils producing a well-known but little understood phenomenon called 'fungistasis'. An interesting effect produced by the fungi themselves is the 'density effect' noted in some rust fungi. Here, a mass of spores exhibit self-inhibition whereas germination proceeds normally if density is reduced.

Of all the factors affecting spore germination there can be no doubt that the most important are moisture and temperature and it would appear that, in most years, spore germination is not severely limited by the environment.

Penetration

Whether the pathogen propagule has completed the germination process success-fully or whether it was already at the plant surface in a form capable of causing infection, the next stage is to penetrate its host. Cereal plant viruses enter their hosts almost exclusively with the help of insect vectors. Plant pathogenic bacteria have to rely on wounds, vectors and natural openings for their point of entry. Many plant-pathogenic fungi, in contrast, are capable of penetrating directly through plant surfaces. The process of direct penetration is well worthy of description. The fungus can enter in this way either by using physical force or by chemically degrading the plant surface. It could well be that both processes are involved in all direct entry methods. However, before describing the penetration process it will be of value to comment upon the nature of the barriers the fungus has to overcome.

Much work has been carried out to elucidate the structure of the outer epidermal walls and the overall picture obtained is very complex. The outermost layer, the cuticle, is a spongy framework of cutin interspersed with wax platelets. It forms a continuous layer over the outer epidermal walls of the shoots but not the roots. To the foliar or stem pathogen of cereals, the cuticle presents the first physical obstacle in the penetration process although there may also be an added barrier in the form of epidermal hairs. The cuticle, being hydrophillic, can swell depending upon the water content of the leaf. This swelling may affect the resistance of the cuticle to penetration by fungal hyphae. The cuticle may also contain substances which may be inhibitory to certain pathogens. In the primary roots of plants, the outer cell walls may also be impregnated with lipid materials, including suberin and cutin, although it is not thought that this protective layer extends to the active apical region of the root.

Direct penetration   There are many examples of fungi that can penetrate the unbroken surface of plants although the precise mechanism for this form of attack is still not fully understood. Physical force exerted by the infection hyphae is undoubtedly involved but chemical processes must also be activated. Direct penetra-tion is normally accompanied by **appressorium** formation (Fig. 2.2). The appres-sorium is a swelling of the tip of the developing germ-tube which secretes substances which enable the appressorium to adhere to the plant surface. A small protuberance then develops from the underside, the **penetration peg**, and this is able to directly penetrate the cuticularized plant surface. The theory of the involvement of mechani-cal pressure in the penetration of the cuticle has been confirmed by many experiments using non-plant materials as media for penetration. Gold leaf and various paraffin-wax membranes can be pierced by penetration pegs and this evidence is further substantiated by the fact that fungal penetration may be impeded and even prevented in areas where the cuticle is especially thick. It is also worth emphasizing that penetration is not exclusive to penetration pegs developing from

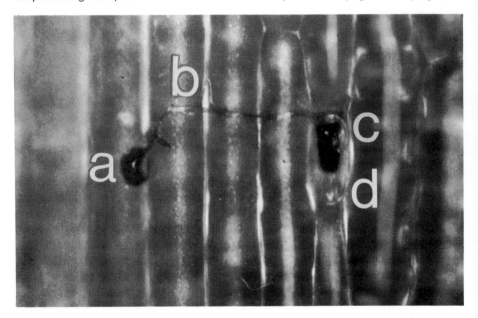

Fig. 2.2 *Germinating uredospore of* P. hordei *producing an appressorium over a host plant stomate.* a – *uredospore,* b – *germ-tube,* c – *appressorium,* d – *stomate (WPBS).*

germ-tubes. An exception is the take-all fungus (*Gaeumannomyces graminis*) which infects cereal roots by means of its runner-hyphae.

Much evidence has now been accumulated which demonstrates the production of enzymes by pathogens. Many fungi have been shown to be able to degrade cutin, cellulose and pectin during penetration. The cuticle, with its complex structure will require a number of enzymes for its degradation. Cutinases will be required for the initial breakdown of cutin into fatty and hydroxy-fatty acids. These breakdown products will, in turn, require other enzymes for their degradation and much work has been done with cereal pathogens to confirm the production of pectic and cellulolytic enzymes which could well be involved in the breakdown of the minor cuticular constituents. Some fungi readily produce cutinase and pectinase in culture but this is not sufficient evidence to positively confirm enzyme activity in the penetration process although differential staining techniques have been able to demonstrate localized dissolution of the cuticle and cell wall in close proximity to the penetration peg.

The penetration of barley leaves by *Erysiphe graminis hordei* has been extensively studied using scanning electron microscopy. When the spore and its germ-tube and penetration peg are removed, the micrographs show penetration holes with round, smooth edges. This can be taken as being evidence of the involvement of enzyme activity in the penetration process. The evidence is good but not altogether conclusive as it will also be seen that the host cuticle is displaced and pushed part-way into the penetration hole, a configuration which can only result from the application of mechanical force. In this example, and indeed with other fungal pathogens, penetration might well be the result of mechanical pressure acting at a site which was simultaneously being 'softened up' by enzymatic activity.

In many diseases caused by biotrophic parasites there is no massive penetration of host cells by hyphae. After initial penetration, such fungi produce short branches which then enter the cell where the ends develop into either simple or complex structures called **haustoria**. Haustoria are presumed to be highly absorptive and so facilitate the interchange of nutrients between host and parasite. Mostly, haustoria occur in the parenchyma cells as in the rusts (Fig. 2.3) but the powdery mildews of cereals produce their haustoria exclusively in the epidermis (Fig. 2.4). An interesting feature of the development of the haustorium in *Puccinia graminis tritici* is the fact that it does not indent the cell wall as it emerges into the cell lumen. This would suggest that the act of penetration is the result of chemicals produced by the developing haustorium rather than mere mechanical pressure.

Natural openings Many bacterial and fungal plant pathogens gain access to the plant interior through natural openings. Of the natural openings in cereal plants, the stomates provide the most common point of entry. Typical of the fungi with this mode of entry are the cereal rusts. When a uredospore of a rust fungus germinates on a cereal leaf the germ-tube grows until it approaches a stomate. There is then a migration of the protoplasm from the older parts to the distal tip The end of the germ-tube then swells to form an appressorium which lies over the stomatal aperture (Fig. 2.2). A wedge-shaped protuberance then grows out of the base of the

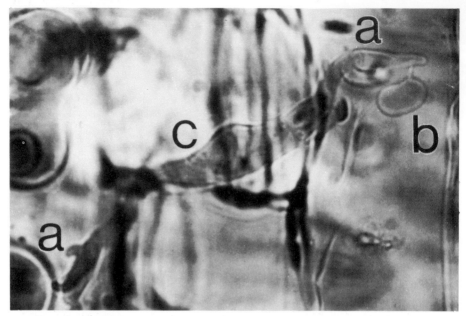

Fig. 2.3 *Development of hyphae of* P. hordei *(post-penetration) showing an haustorium in the host cell.* a – hyphae, b – haustorium, c – sub-stomatal vesicle.

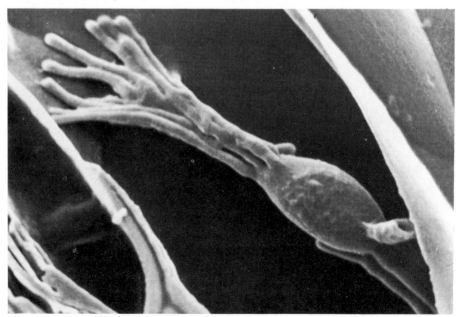

Fig. 2.4 *Scanning electron-micrograph of an haustorium of* Erysiphe graminis *(WPBS).*

appressorium and enters the stomatal cavity. The wall of a cell adjoining the stomatal cavity is then penetrated by hyphae and a haustorium is produced as already described. Stomates are also a common entry point for the eyespot fungus (*Pseudocercosporella herpotrichoides*) but, in this example, once the fungus has entered the stomatal cavity it normally forms a **stroma** before pushing its way into the adjacent mesophyll cells.

It might appear, at first sight, that stomatal penetration would provide easier access for the fungal germ-tube than direct penetration of the cuticle. However, the fungus is not in a parasitic relationship with the plant within the stomatal chamber and still has to carry out the processes involved in penetrating between or through the adjacent host cells. Stomates, however, do provide a most important entry point for many fungal pathogens and are the only pathways of entry for many parasitic bacteria. Not to be confused with natural openings is the infection of the floral organs by many cereal pathogens. *Ustilago nuda*, which causes loose smut of wheat and barley, enters its host by the penetration of either the exposed stigma surface or the pericarp wall by dikaryotic mycelium at flowering time. A similar entry point is used by the ergot fungus (*Claviceps purpurea*). In this pathogen, ascospore discharge occurs at the time of anthesis of the host so that the ascospores have the opportunity of reaching the stigma surface either through the action of rain-splash or by insect dispersal. The germinating ascospores penetrate the stigma and infect the developing ovaries. Very soon after infection, a layer of conidiophores is produced on the surface of the ovary and this produces a mass of minute conidia embedded in a sweet yellow fluid, the 'honey-dew'. These conidia can also be passively carried by insects to healthy flowers where they germinate within 24 hours and penetrate the ovary at its base. In both these examples, entry is gained from within the cereal floret but the mechanism is one of direct penetration rather than through a natural opening.

Post-penetration

Once penetration has been achieved, if the pathogen is to succeed in its parasitism of the host, colonization of the host tissues must occur. Colonization may be a very localized phenomenon in which the pathogen produces a very restricted effect. A good example of such localized effects is the leaf spot disease of barley (*Selenophoma donacis*) with its characteristic, scattered pale oval spots with a brown or purplish margin. Plants may also be systemically colonized as in the case of loose smut of wheat and barley (*Ustilago nuda*) where the mycelium within infected grain grows through the tissues of the developing plant to eventually transform the spikelets into a mass of spores.

Colonization may also be extensive and, in these cases, large scale necrosis may result. Many cereal diseases produce quite devastating effects on the plants although the extent of the colonization may differ. In the powdery mildew disease (*Erysiphe graminis*), the extent of the colonization is only into the epidermis where abundant haustoria are produced (Fig. 2.4) to sustain and support the superficial mat of mycelium which may eventually cover a very large area of the leaf surface. *Septoria nodorum*, the glume blotch pathogen, initially produces small, localized, necrotic lesions but these rapidly extend and coalesce to produce extensive leaf damage. Much of the distal parts of the leaves senesce prematurely and it is believed that this is an effect of a toxin produced by the pathogen.

The colonization of wheat leaves by the black stem rust fungus (*Puccinia graminis tritici*) illustrates how individual colonies on a leaf are very localized yet severe damage occurs when many separate colonies of the pathogen develop simultaneously on the same leaf. The fungus grows intercellularly in the leaf mesophyll, occasionally sending its haustoria into adjacent cells. A very restricted mycelial colony is produced from which a small mat of mycelium differentiates just below the host epidermis. When the fungus sporulates the uredial pustule erupts through this outer plant layer. There is no massive breakdown of infected tissue and only a slight chlorosis is normally associated with the individual pustule.

To become well established in a host, a pathogen must be able to obtain a suitable supply of nutrients. The extent of colonization will therefore vary depending upon the genotype of the pathogen and the host plant and also the environment. Successful penetration of the cuticle and/or the cell wall does not necessarily guarantee the further development of the pathogen within the plant. Many obstacles may be encountered, both physical and chemical, progress may even be completely halted by some resistance mechanism in the host. In the susceptible plant, however, the pathogen is able to continue its cycle of development.

Further reading

Plant Pathogenesis *by H. Wheeler, Advanced Series in Agricultural Sciences 2, Springer-Verlag, Berlin, Heidelberg, New York, 1975*
Genetics of Host-Parasite Interaction *by P. R. Day, W. H. Freeman and Company, 1974*
Heterokaryosis and Variability in Plant-Pathogenic Fungi *by J. R. Parmeter, Jr., W. C. Snyder and R. E. Reichle, in* Annual Review of Phytopathology, 1; *51, 1963*

Physiology of Penetration and Infection *by N. T. Flentje, in* Plant Pathology Problems and Progress 1908–1958, *Editors C. S. Holton, et. al., University of Wisconsin Press, 1959*
Physiological Plant Pathology *by R. K. S. Wood, Blackwell, Oxford, 1967*
Pathogenic Root-infecting Fungi *by S. D. Garrett, Cambridge University Press, 1970*
Recent Advances in the Genetics of Plant Pathogenic Fungi *by R. K. Webster, in* Annual Review of Phytopathology, 12; *331, 1974.*
Current Status of the Gene for Gene Hypothesis *by H. H. Flor, in* Annual Review of Phytopathology, 2; *275, 1971*
Structural Concepts of Host: Pathogen Interfaces *by C. E. Bracker and L. J. Littlefield, in* Fungal Pathogenicity and the Plant's Response, *Editors R. J. W. Byrde and C. V. Cutting, Academic Press, New York and London, 1973*

Chapter 3 **Nature of resistance**

The response to infection by a particular pathogen of a heterogeneous population of plants is usually extremely varied. Some plants may be highly susceptible and the resulting disease may ultimately cause their death. Other plants, in contrast, may be immune but there is a continuous range of response in between these two extremes. Most plants have some mechanism for either avoiding or reducing the potential impact of pathogens and it must be emphasized that disease in plants under natural conditions is more the exception than the rule and, also, that particular pathogens are able to parasitize only a very small proportion of the plant species available to them.

The relative importance of a particular resistance mechanism varies according to the nature of the pathogen. Structural barriers such as the cuticle and epidermal cell wall provide effective obstacles against those pathogens incapable of direct penetration. Mechanisms involving histological changes in the host will only restrict those pathogens which colonize the host tissue at a rate slow enough to be impeded by these mechanical barriers. The basis of this chapter is the study of disease resistance mechanisms. Most of the examples are the results of investigation at the individual plant level. However, in practical terms, disease must also be considered on a crop basis and attention is also given to resistance mechanisms which either reduce the losses due to disease, restrict the development of the epidemic through the crop, or both.

Disease escape

To escape disease is not to resist disease in the literal sense but, nevertheless, escape does represent a valid approach to the problem of reducing disease incidence in crops. The classical example of escape in cereals is that of wheat and barley to the ergot pathogen (*Claviceps purpurea*). Rye, an outbreeder, is particularly susceptible, the pathogen entering through the stigma surface after a brief period of about 20–30 minutes when the florets are open and receptive to pollination. Wheat, although an inbreeder, opens its florets for about a similar period but, by this time, the fertilization process has been completed and the stigma is very much less receptive. Barley, with its closed flower habit, escapes the disease almost completely.

The flowering behaviour of different varieties of wheat and barley also influences their susceptibility to loose smut (*Ustilago nuda*) and there is always a danger that this escape mechanism may be lost to new varieties if breeders incorporate an open flowering habit.

It has also been suggested that the growth habit of cereals affects their susceptibility to airborne pathogens, a prostrate habit being considered to be more prone to
spores settling from the atmosphere than varieties with more erect habits. Leaf hairs
have also been implicated by pathologists as means of keeping spores away from the

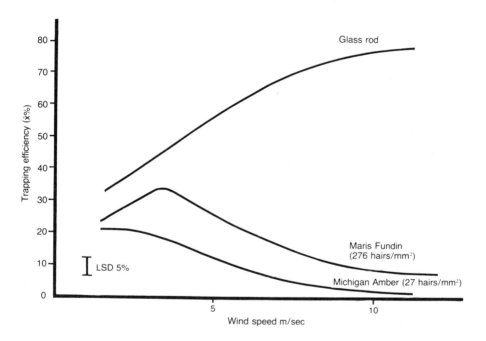

Fig. 3.1 *Trapping efficiency of wheat varieties for uredospores of* Puccinia recondita.

leaf surface. However, an opposite point of view suggests that hairs trap spores from
the atmosphere and render the leaf more disease prone than glaucous leaves. An
example of the spore trapping efficiency of plants is shown graphically in Fig. 3.1.
Disease escape does not figure prominently in the stratogy of modern plant breeding
programmes but It is obvious that insufficient precise information is available
regarding many potentially useful mechanisms.

Tolerance

Where two varieties appear to be damaged equally by the same pathogen, measured conventionally as disease symptoms, yet one variety suffers a greater yield or quality loss, then the reaction of the least affected variety is described as **tolerant**. The evidence for tolerant varieties of cereals dates back to the 1920s when it was demonstrated that certain wheat varieties, for example Fulhard, outyielded other varieties in the same trial although being more severely infected with leaf rust (*Puccinia recondita*). A similar observation was made of the selection Kansas 2627 which gave a relatively high yield although heavily infected with leaf blotch (*Septoria tritici*).

The concept of tolerance is based on the assumption that disease and damage are not synonymous. If we accept this assumption then tolerance cannot be expressed in plants where loss is a direct function of disease severity. For example, with *Ustilago nuda* on barley, the grain in the infected plant is directly replaced by the fungus and there is obviously no scope for tolerance. It is for this reason that reports of tolerance have mainly involved foliage diseases on grain-producing plants.

The proof of the existence of tolerance lies in the establishment of the equivalence of disease on varieties and on a non-equivalence of resulting yield. It is necessary to prove that a tolerant variety is at least as susceptible as a less tolerant variety but the error involved in disease assessment is high, particularly so in comparisons which may approximate. In addition, there are likely to be many misinterpretations of assessment data associated with single observations with no reference to the rate of infection up to the time of assessment.

The mechanics of tolerance are not fully understood although several hypotheses have been advanced. It has been suggested that tolerant plants have a reservoir of unused yielding capacity and this absorbs the impact of the disease. This implies that there would be no yield loss until the reservoir was exhausted. There is also the possibility that tolerant plants have the ability to divert plant nutrients from infected to healthy parts, or they may have the capacity for increased root growth when infected, or they may have the ability to compensate in terms of the components of yield. **Compensation** is now a recognized phenomenon and certain wheat varieties have been shown to compensate for disease damage by increasing the number of grains produced per ear.

Tolerance is clearly a complex phenomenon and appears to be useful irrespective of what might be subsequently found to be the biological explanations. It has the particular advantage over some resistance mechanisms in that it does not place selective pressure on the pathogen. However, critics point to the potential inoculum hazard of the tolerant variety and suggest that its superior performance is due to resistance of a nature and magnitude which cannot be detected by our present methods.

Genuine disease resistance

The concept of disease resistance can be studied both in functional and genetical terms. From the functional viewpoint, the actual mechanisms through which resistance operates must be fully understood and this must be considered alongside the range of pathogens or pathogen races resisted by these mechanisms. Resistance can be described as being major gene or polygenic, the characteristics of both types being listed in Table 3.1. A third category, general resistance, enables the plant to resist attack from a range of pathogen species. In genetic terms, resistance can be inherited in a very simple or a highly complex manner and the relationships between the genetic control of resistance and the genetic control of pathogenicity and virulence in the pathogen must be considered.

Resistance mechanisms

To achieve the best understanding of resistance mechanisms it is necessary to have a complete knowledge of the healthy plant. It is then possible to categorize each step of the infection process and subsequent stages in the development of the disease or its containment. The starting point of this study should, logically, be the arrival of the pathogen propagule on the host plant surface. In airborne foliar diseases, this does not present too many problems but the observations will be after the event in the case of soil-borne pathogens. Very often, resistant reactions are the result of a pathogen-invoked stimulus rather than a pre-existing state in the host plants. The former resistance category has been named active and the latter passive.

Active resistance mechanisms

In the case of active resistance, the plant's reaction is analogous to physical wounding where repair responses might involve the production of substances which act either by sealing off the infected area by initiating cell divisions or by repairing damaged tissues. In the sequence of events, resistance reactions may begin before any observable activity can be detected in the pathogen. This reaction may be expressed as the suppression or delay of spore germination and is likely to be the result of normal plant secretions. Such substances may also have been produced in response to the contact stimulus received from the fungal spore.

	Major gene	Polygenic
Expression	Usually clear cut; expressed from seedling stage to maturity, or may be expressed in mature plants only	Variable response; not usually expressed in seedling stage; resistance increases as plant matures
Mechanism	Generally an immune or hypersensitive host reaction	Reduced rate and degree of infection, development and/or reproduction of pathogen
Efficiency	Highly efficient and specific against certain pathogen races. May mask extreme susceptibility to other races	Variable, but operates against all races of the pathogen
Genetic control	One or few genes with major effect	Many genes with small but additive effect
Stability	Liable to sudden breakdown by new pathogen races	Not affected by changes in virulence genes of the pathogen
Commonly used but not strict synonyms	Vertical, race-specific, seedling, differential	Horizontal, race non-specific, mature plant, adult plant, field, uniform

(After Hayes & Johnston, in Diseases of Crop Plants, *Editor J. H. Western, Macmillan, 1971).*

Table 3.1 *Characteristics of major gene and polygenic resistance.*

The distortion of germ-tubes is a common resistant reaction and this reduces the success of spores in penetrating the host. The abortion of the germ-tube may occur at any time prior to or during penetration. Recent work on oats (Carver and Carr, Ann. appl. Biol. **86**; 29, 1977) describes a resistance to powdery mildew (*Erysiphe graminis avenae*) which prevents primary penetration by a proportion of spores (Fig. 3.2). Penetration was most frequently arrested at the infection peg stage, implicating the

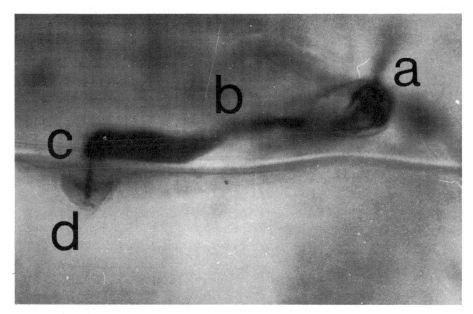

Fig. 3.2 *Conidial germination in* Erysiphe graminis avenae. a – *conidium,* b – *germ-tube,* c – *penetration peg,* d – *papilla (WPBS).*

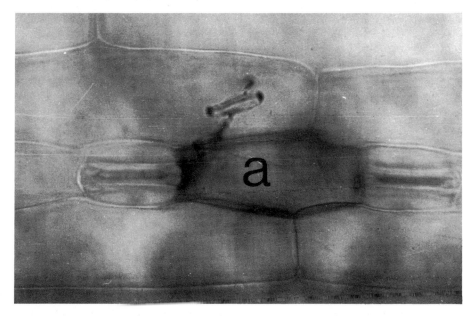

Fig. 3.3 *The hypersensitive response of barley cv. Vada to* Erysiphe graminis hordei. a – *the dead invaded cell (WPBS).*

41

papilla, which was formed by the host beneath the appressorium, as a defence mechanism. As none of the varieties possessed specific genes for resistance to the particular race used in this work the resistance must be classified as race non-specific. This resistance mechanism was also more strongly expressed in the fifth than in first formed leaves and thus is placed in the **mature plant resistance** category.

There are many examples of active resistance which are facilitated by the production of wound barriers, suberized cells, **lignitubers** or **tyloses**. They all have the effect of retarding the infection process or decreasing the rate of progress of the pathogen through the plant. When a cell is being penetrated by the penetration peg the cell wall may swell and become lignified or suberized resulting in the retardation, hinderance or complete prevention of the infection process. Such outgrowths of the host cell are known as lignitubers and are responsible for the resistance to the take-all fungus (*Gaeumannomyces graminis*) in certain wheat varieties.

Active structural resistance does not appear to be of great importance in cereals but it is as well to be aware of the possibility. However, one active resistance mechanism, which may be classified as structural, has been noted in wheat, oats and barley in response to invasion by the take-all fungus. Here, the response is an increase in root growth away from the point of invasion, the success and extent of which depends largely upon the nutrient status of the plant as a strong plant growing in a nutrient-rich environment will be better able to produce such additional growth.

Some plants also possess the capacity to resist disease by the production of chemicals which act in an antibiotic manner against the invading pathogen. These substances were first reported in potatoes by Muller and Borger (Arb. Biol. Reichsamstat. Land-u-Forstwirtsch, Berlin **23**, 189, 1940) who named them **phytoalexins**. Their presence has been established in many crop species but, to date, their production in cereals appears to be very limited although they have been reported in maize infected with *Helminthosporium turcicum*, in wheat infected by *Septoria tritici* and in certain rice varieties infected with *Piricularia oryzae*. The importance of phytoalexins in disease resistance is a most controversial topic. Much of the argument is based on the fact that, in many plants, the concentration of the phytoalexin is too low, it is suggested, to account for the observed resistance. There is evidence, however, that the highest concentration of phytoalexins is in the cells immediately surrounding the infection site and it is here that they would have a large effect.

Mostly, phytoalexins are considered as antifungal substances but they probably also account for some of the resistance to bacterial plant pathogens. It may well be that these substances play a part in the resistance of some cereals to some of the more economically important pathogens but, as yet, the evidence for their presence and activity has come mostly from pathogens other than the obligate parasites.

The hypersensitive response   The hypersensitive response is yet another active resistance mechanism which operates after penetration and it is a common resistance mechanism in many cereal varieties. In these varieties, the processes of spore germination, appressorium formation and penetration are completed as in susceptible varieties. The phenomenon of **hypersensitivity** commences once the pathogen breaches the cell wall in the resistant host. Whereas in compatible host-pathogen combinations tissue colonization continues without restriction, in the plants exhibiting the hypersensitive response, the pathogen's progress is arrested and colonization is limited to one or a very few host cells. At the host cell level, the cytoplasm of these few cells first becomes discoloured and granular, especially around the invading haustorium. The cells then become necrotic and rapidly die (Fig. 3.3). In cereal diseases caused by biotrophic fungal pathogens, the death of the cells is a highly successful resistance mechanism as the fungus is denied the necessary living cells from which to extract its nutrient supply. The manifestation of hypersensitivity in cereals is commonly a necrotic flecking of the leaves. There is some controversy over the causal relationship of hypersensitivity and resistance. It has been suggested that this phenomenon is merely the manifestation of resistance which has operated through an undetected mechanism. This view is partly substantiated by some evidence in cereals resistant to rust fungi in that the pathogen growth rate slows down prior to cell penetration and that the cell necrosis is the effect of a resistance mechanism rather than its cause.

Passive resistance mechanisms
Active resistance mechanisms restrict the development of many plant diseases, many more are restricted by passive mechanisms. A passive resistance mechanism is one which exists normally in the healthy plant and is not produced as a result of a stimulus from the invading pathogen. Again, it is convenient to divide them into structural or chemical categories. However, it is very difficult to establish the exact role of passive mechanisms as much of the evidence is circumstantial.

Passive mechanisms act against the infection process or the subsequent spread of the pathogen in the plant. The cuticle normally provides the first structural barrier and cuticle thickness has been implicated in resistance. Early evidence of the relationship between cuticle thickness and resistance was provided by Melander and Craigie (Phytopathology **17**; 95, 1927) who showed that young leaves of barberry, with their thin cuticle, were more susceptible to basidiospore infection by *Puccinia graminis tritici* than older leaves in which the cuticle had thickened. The resistance of rice plants to rice blast (*Piricularia oryzae*) has also been shown to be related to the silicon content of the leaves. It has been shown to be possible to alter the silicic acid content of rice leaves by planting in flooded soils or by applying the chemical directly. Increasing the availability of silicon leads to a higher level of an organic silicon complex in the epidermal cell wall which is resistant to the enzymes secreted by the pathogen.

Some pathogens enter the plant through the stomates and it has been suggested that stomatal structure and behaviour could have an effect on the infection process. Stomatal exclusion was proposed by Hart to explain the resistance of Hope wheat to *P. graminis tritici*. She suggested (Hart, J. Agri. Research, **39**; 929, 1929) that late morning opening of the stomata allowed time for the dew to evaporate from the plants causing desiccation of the infection apparatus before penetration. This assumed that the rust uredospores can penetrate only open stomates but she later showed that penetration can occur through closed stomates. However, work on infection of wheat by *P. recondita tritici* (Romig and Caldwell, Phytopath., **54**; 214, 1964) has shown that the resistance of wheat peduncles and sheaths, relative to leaf blades, was due to stomatal exclusion, resistance decreasing as the plants approached senescence. This resistance mechanism is not possessed by all wheat varieties and, in the varieties most susceptible to *P. recondita*, abundant uredosori are produced on the peduncles and sheaths. The exclusion mechanism operates as a structural barrier at the guard cells of the stomates but it is clear from the decrease of stomatal exclusion with senescence that function of the stomates is also involved. The resistance of some wheat varieties to loose smut (*Ustilago nuda*) has also been shown to be related to the length of time the glumes are open and the extent of this opening during the flowering period. This mechanism can also be categorized as a disease escape mechanism.

Once within the plant, resistance can act either against the spread of the pathogen through the tissues or by reducing the degree of sporulation. *Puccinia graminis tritici* fails to progress through lignified sclerenchyma tissue but finds a relatively easy passage through the unthickened chlorenchyma. The distribution of the two tissues in the wheat stem affects the development of the pathogen and its containment between the sclerenchyma ribs of the stem, giving a vertical striping effect, is a characteristic symptom of this disease (Plate 1.2). The production of enzymes and toxins by cereal pathogens is well documented but very little attention has been given to the degradation of such products to implement host plant resistance. Toxin inactivation has been demonstrated in resistant varieties of oats subjected to the toxin produced by the Victoria blight pathogen (*Cochliobolus victoriae*) and, although contradictory evidence suggests that host differences are not due to inactivation but to differences in the number of receptor sites which can accept the toxin, both mechanisms would be classified in the passive category. Enzyme production has been reported in several cereal pathogens such as the eyespot pathogen (*Pseudocercosporella herpotrichoides*) but there have been no reports of enzyme inactivation by the cereal host.

Physiological resistance

From an epidemiological standpoint, a reduction in the rate and degree of sporulation would have a retarding influence on the rate of the epidemic. The **latent period** is the time which elapses between penetration and the appearance of visible symptoms. The **incubation period** is the period between infection and sporulation. If either or both periods are increased then the number of cycles of infection and sporulation over a given period will be reduced. Such physiological resistance mechanisms will slow down the development of a pathogen within a host plant but, just as importantly, the rate of epidemic development will also be reduced. There is a growing literature on host variety differences in respect of such characters. The differential interaction between pathogen isolates of *Puccinia striiformis* and wheat varieties can be more clearly demonstrated by measuring spore production than by visual assessment of infection types. (Johnson and Taylor, Nature **238**; 105, 1972). This interaction is governed by genes conferring race-specific resistance but it has been shown that spore production differences between certain varieties are of the race non-specific type. However, the rate of spore production, or such characters as *slow rusting* are not themselves, a guarantee of non-specificity. (Johnson, Specificity in Plant Disease: NATO Adv. Stud. Inst., 1976.) Resistance of the slow rusting type has been demonstrated in wheat and barley to be specific and it has been shown that it is often conditioned by genes which confer a low infection response which acts from the seedling stage onwards. Differences in spore production observed in seedlings have also been correlated with differences in percentage leaf area infected in the field. It has been suggested that a gene conditioning a visually measurable low infection type may have an effect on the epidemic similar to that attributed to race non-specific resistance. Race-specificity has its disadvantages but there are also many examples of cereal varieties which have been widely grown for many years without becoming seriously diseased. There is little evidence to suggest that their resistance is not race-specific or that it would be permanent and this type of resistance has been called **durable resistance**.

In the United Kingdom, the resistance of the wheat variety Cappelle Desprez to yellow rust (*P. striiformis*) has remained effective for over 25 years despite its widespread cultivation and genetic uniformity. However, this resistance is not stable in its expression in different environments and commercial crops occasionally become heavily infected. Changes in resistance level from year to year are not due to the advent of more virulent races and, as this variety has been shown to also possess seedling resistance of the race-specific type, it emphasizes the point that durable resistance need not be of the race non-specific type (Wolfe, Ann. Rep. P.B.I. Camb. p. 106, 1976). Differences in epidemic patterns due to spore production can now be elegantly demonstrated theoretically by the use of computerized epidemic models. The best known of these is EPIMAY, a simulator of a Southern corn leaf blight epidemic. (*Cochliobolus heterostrophus*) (Waggoner, Horsfall and Lukens, Bull. Conn. Agric. Exp. Sta. **729**, 1972). Primarily intended to act as an epidemic simulator to aid in the forecast of epidemics, it is sufficiently precise to enable changes in inoculum production to be incorporated into the computer programme and their effect on the epidemic evaluated. Since this exciting pioneering work, a simulator, EPISIM, has been produced for a yellow rust epidemic (*P. striiformis*), Zadoks, Proc. Eur. Mediterr. Cereal Rusts Conf. Prague, 1972) and for a glume blotch epidemic (*Septoria nodorum*) of wheat (Rapilly and Jolivet, Revue de Statistique Appliquée, **24**, (3) 31, 1976.

Genetics of resistance

There have been numerous reports in the literature going back many centuries which have commented upon differences in disease reaction between varieties of the same plant species. The variation in the type of resistance mechanism operating has been discussed above and studies of the inheritance of these mechanisms have revealed an equally large range of genetic control.

Major gene resistance

In many instances, resistance has been shown to be controlled by a single gene. This was the exciting discovery by Biffen from his studies on the resistance of some wheat varieties to yellow rust (*Puccinia striiformis*) (J. Agri. Sci. **1**; 4, 1905). Biffen was able to demonstrate the simple Mendelian nature of resistance by crossing the susceptible Red King variety with the resistant Rivet. The F_2 generation exhibited the classical segregation ratio of 1 resistant : 3 susceptible and in the F_3 the progeny segregated 1 homozygous resistant : 1 homozygous susceptible : 2 heterozygous segregating lines. In this example, resistance was recessively inherited but, since this pioneer experiment, it has been found that there are many more examples of resistance being dominant.

Taking yellow rust of wheat as an example of resistance which is under the control of single genes, Lupton and Macer (Trans. Brit. Mycol. Soc. **45**; 21, 1962) proposed the symbol *Yr* for alleles determining yellow rust resistance. At that time, four loci, Yr_1 to Yr_4 were identified; at two of these (Yr_3 and Yr_4), three and two resistance-determining alleles, respectively, were found whereas only a single resistance allele was identified at each of the loci Yr_1 and Yr_2. Lupton and Macer found resistance to be inherited most frequently as a dominant character, although a few cases of recessive inheritance was found. It is now known that at least eight loci are involved and in an investigation of the yellow rust resistance of *Aegilops comosa* Sibth. and Sm., Riley, Chapman and Macer (Can. J. Genet. Cytol. **8**; 616, 1966) found that a single chromosome designated 2M, conditioned the resistance. There has only been a very limited amount of work carried out to identify the wheat chromosomes associated with the loci with alleles conditioning resistance to yellow rust but it has been shown that several chromosomes are involved which facilitates recombination in a breeding programme with relative ease. Similar information is now available concerning the inheritance of resistance to many cereal pathogens. In particular, the genetic control of resistance in some barley varieties to powdery mildew (*Erysiphe graminis hordei*) is well understood (Moseman, Ann. Rev. Phytopath., **6**; 264, 1966) with many alleles being involved, some of them operating at the same locus on a single chromosome.

These examples of monogenic or **oligogenic** resistance are probably the best documented due to the importance of the rusts and mildews and the amount of research time devoted to their study. It is apparent that the resistance to many other pathogens is controlled in the same way. Monogenic resistance is usually easy to detect, even at a seedling stage and is normally very specific, each resistance gene acting against one or a few physiologic races of the pathogen. This specificity gives the advantage of a high level of resistance against the designated races but, if by mutation, hybridization, heterokaryosis or parasexuality a new race appeared, this resistance would be overcome.

Major gene resistance, being mostly race-specific, has several important uses, not the least being to counteract a new disease problem by the rapid development of resistant varieties. Both *Rhynchosporium secalis* and *Puccinia hordei* provided 'new disease' problems in the United Kingdom in the 1960s and 1970s. The development of varieties incorporating major gene resistance was certainly pertinent at that time. Major gene resistance may also provide the most efficient control measure where the spread of new pathogen races may be slow, a situation likely to occur with soil-borne pathogens. It may also be used as the basis for **multiline**, **multigene** or **composite mixtures** of varieties. In these instances, the resistance of individual plants is utilized to reduce the rate of an epidemic through the crop either by a dilution process or by the physical effect caused by the isolation that exists between genotypes with the same resistance gene which limits the movement of compatible pathogen spores between them. There may also be a reduction in epidemic rate due to one or more of the races present in a crop having superfluous factors governing virulence and these may decrease their competitiveness. In consequence, multilines and mixtures might well result in the differential survival of races and this phenomenon is another which is an advantage of the use of major gene resistance. The whole topic of resistance diversification is discussed more fully in Chapter 5.

The gene-for-gene concept   The specificity of most types of monogenic resistance suggests that there is some relationship between the physiologic races of the pathogen and the host varieties incorporating different resistance genes. There is much evidence that, in certain plant/pathogen interactions, a gene for resistance in the host corresponds to and is directed against a gene for virulence in the pathogen. This relationship was first proposed by Flor (Advan. Genet. **8**; 29, 1956) working with the flax rust fungus (*Melampsora lini*). The hypothesis makes the interaction very orderly but has sinister implications for disease resistance. This is due to the mutability of genes and the fact that for every gene governing resistance in the host plant there is a gene in the pathogen capable of mutation to endow the pathogen with the ability to overcome the resistance. Unfortunately, such mutations appear to have occurred regularly in varieties of cereals incorporating major-genes or race-specific resistance with the consequential withdrawal of the varieties after very few years. The extent of the 'gene-for-gene' relationship in cereal diseases has yet to be determined although it is known to operate in the resistance of barley to powdery mildew. It is, arguably, the best available model for a number of plant/pathogen systems but if it was to be demonstrated that virulence was not under the control of a single gene then the concept would have no basis. Certainly, the hypothesis has helped to provide a better understanding of the genetical basis of resistance in cereals and, ultimately, should lead to a more efficient utilization of the resistance genes. Bearing in mind the limitations, the hypothesis does allow for a prediction of the number of physiologic races of a pathogen that a set of resistant varieties incorporating different resistance genes will differentiate (**differential varieties**). There are two phenotypes for each resistance gene, resistant or susceptible. Given a situation where there are 'n' genes for resistance in the host varieties there would be a possible 2^n different races. If the varieties incorporate more than one gene for resistance, such simple differentiation is not possible.

Polygenic resistance

Many plants possess resistance which is conferred against all races of a given pathogen. The level of this resistance will vary with host plant genotype and it is very much likely to be influenced by environmental factors. This race non-specific type of resistance is not normally detectable at the seedling stage and usually becomes apparent as the plants mature. For the screening of plant populations for resistance the breeder is forced into the field to study the disease in terms of the development of an epidemic rather than the reaction of individual plants as under glasshouse tests. This type of resistance is variously described as 'mature plant' or 'field' resistance but is not necessarily synonymous with these resistance types. Investigations have shown that, in many instances, it is quantitively inherited. The indication is that a number of genes at different loci are involved and that each has a small individual but, in combination, additive effect. In studies at the Welsh Plant Breeding Station (Ann. Report, W.P.B.S., p. 105, 1970) after crosses between the oat varieties Creme (Cc4761) and Milford, there was considerable variation in the progeny for resistance to oat powdery mildew (*Erysiphe graminis avenae*). In observations of single plants of F_2, F_3 and F_4 progenies, the observed frequencies of plants with varying levels of infection could not be ascribed to a simple system controlling resistance. The between-generation heritability was high suggesting quantitative control of the observed resistance, which was of the race non-specific type and originated from Creme, in which sporulation is both delayed and reduced. This suggestion of polygenic inheritance is further supported by the apparently continuous variation of resistance between genotypes. This multiplicity of genes makes genetic analysis very complicated and, if the number of genes involved and their dominance status is to be determined, complex biometrical techniques have to be utilized. There are indications of exceptions to the rule of polygenic control of race non-specific resistance. The resistance of Vada barley variety to powdery mildew (*Erysiphe graminis hordei*) and of Vulcan to leaf blotch (*Rhynchosporium secalis*) is thought to be monogenically controlled. It is thus a little unwise to conclude that all monogenic resistance is race-specific and, similarly it should be emphasized that polygenically controlled resistance is not necessarily synonymous with race non-specific resistance.

Under field conditions, race non-specific resistance can be expressed by:

(a) delaying and/or reducing entry into the host,
(b) limiting growth after invasion,
(c) delaying and/or reducing sporulation.

These mechanisms have been discussed previously in this book but it is as well to emphasize that their effects should not be judged solely at the individual plant level but rather within the crop as a whole, in particular, their effect on the rate of an epidemic.

General resistance
The concept of multiple disease resistance is not new and there are examples of wheat varieties which combine resistance to leaf rust (*Puccinia recondita*), stem rust (*Puccinia graminis*) and loose smut (*Ustilago nuda*) going back thirty years (Ausemus, Bot. Rev. **9**; 207, 1943). It implies that resistance is not specific to races of a particular pathogen but against many pathogens. It is a highly desirable attribute in a crop variety but is not encountered very frequently. The best known example in the United Kingdom in the past two decades was Proctor barley and it was this general type of resistance that enabled this variety to remain popular over many years. There are practical problems involved in breeding for general resistance especially if the resistance to the various pathogens is controlled by independent polygenic systems. On a random basis, if the progeny of a cross to combine resistance to four pathogens produce 10^{-1} plants with satisfactory resistance to one disease then only 10^{-4} will show satisfactory resistance to the four diseases. Where monogenic resistance is involved, the situation is more simple and there are several examples of varieties which combine resistance to two or three pathogens and often include resistance to nematodes in addition.

Further reading

Plant Pathology and Plant Pathogens *by C. H. Dickinson and J. A. Lucas, Blackwell Scientific Publications, Basic Microbiology, Volume 6, Oxford, 1977*

Physiological Plant Pathology *by R. K. S. Wood, Blackwell, Oxford, 1967*

Fungal Pathogenicity and the Plant's Response *Editors R. J. W. Byrde and C. V. Cutting, Academic Press, London and New York, 1973*

A Discussion on Disease Resistance in Plants *Editors P. W. Brian and S. D. Garrett* Proceedings of the Royal Society, Series B, 181; *211, 1972.*

Defence Mechanisms in Plants *by B. J. Deverall, Cambridge University Press, 1977.*

Disease Resistance in Plants *by J. E. van der Plank, Academic Press, London and New York, 1968*

Plant Diseases – Epidemics and Control *by J. E. van der Plank, Academic Press, London and New York, 1963*

Current Status of the Gene for Gene Hypothesis *by H. H. Flor, in* Annual Review of Phytopathology, 2; *275, 1971*

Chapter 4 **Pathological techniques**

Disease diagnosis

A plant may be considered to be diseased when its growth, development or appearance deviate significantly from normality. The effects of most pathogenic organisms leaves this distinction clear although the diagnosis of many environmentally induced disorders is often more difficult as their effects may be less clear cut. The symptoms of disease, which are the visible or measurable effects, are often similar for different causal agents. For example, a leaf spot may be due to a fungus, a genetic abnormality, a mineral deficiency or a chemical spray. This may be better understood when one considers that the same physiological processes in the host may be affected.

As a first step to diagnosis the investigator should be aware of the range of diseases of the crop in question and of descriptions, photographs or drawings of the diseases and causal organisms that may be available. He should also be familiar with the normal growth, development and senescence of the crop in question. Wherever possible, the disease should be examined *in situ* but, if this is not practicable, as much information as possible should be obtained from a sample of the diseased plants or plant parts. This sample should ideally include whole plants with intact root systems together with any particularly affected plant part. A recommended procedure for diagnosis in the field is as follows:

1 Observe individual plant symptoms on heads, stems, leaves and roots, both externally and internally, and look for signs of parasitic attack such as bacterial ooze from cut leaves or fungal mycelium and fruiting structures on and within the plant tissues. Peel back glumes, husks, leaf sheaths etc. and cut open stems, grains or leaves. Two basic tools of the field pathologist are a sharp penknife and a hand lens (magnification × 8–10). Inexpensive field microscopes are now available for more precise on the spot diagnosis. Soil pH often provides a clue and is easily checked using pH test papers.

2 Consult the farmer or grower about previous cropping practices, cultural procedures (particularly fertilizers, fungicides, insecticides, weed killers etc.) and obtain information on the local weather. Have there been any unusually hot or cold spells, hailstorms, soil waterlogging or droughts etc.? For example, yellowing symptoms in cereals may result from low soil nitrogen or lack of uptake in dry weather, soil waterlogging, cold weather or yellow dwarf virus.

3 Observe the pattern of disease in the field as this often provides a clue to the cause. Is it most severe along headlands, in tractor wheelings, where spray

booms overlap or in random patches? Do symptoms decrease to the edge of the patch? Are weed grasses or volunteer plants present in the crop? Are other plant species affected? In the compendium of cereal diseases, an attempt has been made to put together photographs of diseases that give similar symptoms so that comparisons can be made. Examples are the lens-shaped lesions on barley leaves which can be caused by a genetic abnormality, *Septoria nodorum* (normally a wheat pathogen) and *Cochliobolus sativus*. Manganese deficiency and *Pyrenophora avenae* also illicit similar responses in oats.

Isolation of fungal and bacterial pathogens

The majority of fungal and bacterial pathogens of cereals can be isolated from their host and grown on artificial media. It may also be necessary to isolate the obligate parasites, the rusts, downy and powdery mildews, onto fresh host plants. For diagnostic purposes it may be unnecessary to obtain pure cultures of a parasite as the presence of spores or fruiting bodies on diseased material may be easily discerned by direct observation. However, it is often necessary to obtain pure cultures and the method to be adopted will be determined by the nature of the organism and the host tissue affected. Contamination by saprophytic fungi and bacteria is a major difficulty and this can be minimized by the careful selection of initial material. Tissue with vigorous 'clean' lesions should be selected and should be used as soon as possible as material stored in polythene bags etc. will soon be over-run with saprophytes. If necessary, material should be stored dry and refrigerated prior to use. The kind of surface disinfectant used may affect the outcome of an isolation attempt as may the temperature at which the material is incubated and the culture medium used.

Basic methods of isolation

1 Direct The simplest procedure is the direct isolation of an organism from host tissue and its transfer to an artificial growth medium. Spores or fruiting bodies are transferred with a sterile needle, using a stereoscopic microscope, to an agar plate. Spores may be streaked out direct or in a drop of sterile water to obtain isolated colonies or for single spore transfers (see below). Fruiting bodies may first be placed on a flamed slide in sterile water, crushed and the drops streaked onto agar

2 Induction of sporulation This method is commonly used for fungi attacking aerial parts of plants. Pieces of stem, leaf, sheath etc. are cut less than 1 cm in size to include portions of the edge of the lesion. The pieces may be surface sterilized in 1% sodium hypochlorite for different times from a few seconds up to 1 minute. This may be preceded by a dip in 70% ethanol or a detergent to aid wetting of the surface. The pieces are then rinsed in sterile water and plated onto water agar. If sporulation does not begin after 7 days or so, fresh tissue pieces should be washed in running tap water for 15 minutes, rinsed in sterile water and plated out. Spores produced are transferred to a growth medium such as potato dextrose agar acidified with a drop of 25% lactic acid (APDA) to reduce bacterial growth, V-8 juice agar or similar medium. Small agar blocks containing hyphae which have grown out from the lesion may be cut with a flamed platinum needle (flattened and sharpened) and transferred to a growth medium.

3 Induction of Mycelial growth These methods are useful for deep seated infections and for fungi which sporulate poorly and, in particular, for stem and root infecting fungi. For stems, pieces should be dipped in 1% sodium hypochlorite and then the outer layers of tissue pared away or peeled back. Small pieces of tissue are then dug out using a flamed forceps or scalpel, plated onto APDA or similar medium, incubated and edges of hyphal colonies transferred to fresh plates. For fine roots or small seedlings, 1 cm pieces of material should be washed in running water for 15 minutes, rinsed in sterile water or 1% sodium hypochlorite and plated onto water agar. After incubation, agar pieces containing mycelium (from the edge of colonies) are transferred to plates of PDA which should not be acidified if damping-off organisms such as *Pythium* spp. or *Rhizoctonia* spp. are to be isolated.

4 Dilution methods These methods are of particular use for organisms which sporulate profusely and also for bacteria. The typical isolation of a bacterial pathogen from leaves or stems first involves cutting a young lesion in water and observing under the microscope if bacteria ooze out. If bacteria are present, material bearing lesions may be either briefly surface sterilized or placed directly in sterile water in a petri dish. The material is then chopped finely with a flamed scalpel or razor blade and, after waiting a few minutes for the bacteria to ooze out, a few loopfuls are transferred with a flamed loop to another dish containing 1 ml of sterile water and mixed. This procedure is repeated for 2 or 3 more plates to give further dilutions. Cooled agar (e.g. beef peptone) is added to the plates which are gently swirled, cooled, inverted and incubated. In a similar procedure, the initial inoculum suspension is added to 10 ml of sterile water and 1 ml of this is transferred to a tube containing 9 ml of sterile water. This procedure is repeated to give decimal dilutions. One ml from

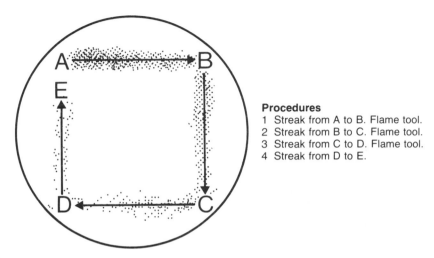

Procedures
1 Streak from A to B. Flame tool.
2 Streak from B to C. Flame tool.
3 Streak from C to D. Flame tool.
4 Streak from D to E.

Fig. 4.1 *Method of streaking agar plates with bacteria or spore suspensions.*

each of these tubes is then added to agar plates or tubes as above. More simply, loopfuls of bacterial cells may be streaked onto agar plates, the surface of which should be dry for single colonies to develop (Fig. 4.1). To obtain dry agar plates, the agar should be poured as cool as possible, i.e. about 45°C. and the plates kept at 25°C.

5 Isolation from soil There are many methods for isolating fungi from the soil detailed by Johnson, Curl, Bond and Fribourg (Methods for Studying Soil Microflora-Plant Disease Relationships. Burgess Minneapolis, 178 p. 1959) but only the methods more commonly used for cereal pathogens are mentioned here. A dilution method similar to that described above is commonly used but the initial inoculum consists of a soil suspension. A direct plating method involves crushing a small piece of soil (about 100 mg) in a drop of water in a sterile petri dish. About 10 ml cool (45°C.) Czapek plus 0·5% yeast extract agar, acidified to pH 4·0 with phosphoric acid, are added (Warcup, Nature, **166**; 117, 1950). 'Baiting' methods are particularly useful for Phycomycetes, which have motile zoospores. The bait, which usually consists of host plant material, is placed in the soil and samples are withdrawn at intervals. The bait sample is then well washed and transferred with fresh bait to a container of ⅓ pond and ⅔ distilled water which has been autoclaved. The culture from this bait is then transferred to agar for purification (see below). Another method involves placing a soil sample inside an apple which is then sealed and the fungus can later be isolated from the apple tissue. Baiting can also be carried out by growing susceptible plants in infected soil and the fungus then isolated from the root tissue using normal plating methods for fungi such as *Gaeumannomyces graminis* or by placing the well-washed root samples in baited water for the isolation of zoosporic species.

6 Host inoculation Diseased material, collected from the field, may be contaminated with saprophytic organisms that cannot be eliminated by the methods described above. In this case, fresh host plants are inoculated either by making a spore suspension, placing diseased tissue directly in contact with fresh host plants or shaking dry spores onto the plants. A highly susceptible host variety should be selected and grown under conditions conducive to disease development. These methods are also suitable for the isolation and maintenance of obligate parasites. Occasionally, mixed infections of parasitic species may be encountered in which case differentially resistant hosts can be used to isolate the target organisms. For example, mildew-resistant host varieties are commonly used to culture *Puccinia* spp. on wheat, oats or barley. Barley varieties resistant to *Rhynchosporium secalis* have been used to isolate the fungus from mixed infections with *Pyrenophora teres.*

7 Purification Obligate parasites growing on host plants may become contaminated with other obligate parasites. Separation of different genera has been discussed above and separation of different species can be achieved by similar means. For example, *Puccinia striiformis* and *P. hordei* may contaminate each other on barley. A low temperature (8°C.) during the dark dew period required for penetration will favour *P. striiformis* and a higher temperature (20°C.) will encourage *P. hordei*. The generation time is shorter for *P. hordei*, thus spores that first appear will mainly be of *P. hordei*. Selective hosts resistant to one or the other species may also be used. Purification of different physiologic races of *Puccinia* spp. or *Erysiphe* spp. is achieved by using selective hosts; complex races being isolated from simple races by using varieties resistant to the simple races. The purification of simple races from more complex races is more difficult as the former will only grow on host varieties without specific resistances and single spore isolations may be necessary.

The purification of cultures growing on artificial media can be achieved by various methods. Bacterial contamination of fungal cultures can be minimized by adding antibiotics such as streptomycin or aureomycin to the medium, by acidifying the medium or by using low temperature incubation. Single spore isolations or host inoculation may be necessary. A method for *Pythium* spp. which are fast growing but do not tolerate low pH, is to cut 'L' shapes in a stiff (3%) water agar plate, lift the flaps of agar thus formed and insert pieces of contaminated culture under them. Bacteria-free mycelium can be isolated from the upper agar surface after several days. *Diplodia maydis* can be separated from *D. macrospora* in culture as the latter has a requirement for biotin in the growth medium and this difference is used to distinguish the species.

8 Single spore isolation   Culturing from single spores ensures species purity but not necessarily genetic purity as the initial spore may be heterozygous. Also a **clone** developed from a single propagule may not be representative of the species and one may need to compare a number of isolates to determine the range of variation within the culture. A mass of spores would be more representative of the species. One approach to single spore isolation is a statistical one and is used for bacteria, the individual cells of which are extremely difficult to manipulate. A method is described by McNew (Phytopath. **28**; 387, 1938) in which broth cultures are agitated, suspended in cool melted agar and poured onto plates. Single colonies are selected and the procedure repeated five times. In another method, drops of very dilute bacterial suspensions are observed on microscope slides divided into grids and drops containing one cell only are transferred. Single fungus spores are normally trans-ferred direct using mechanical or semi-mechanical means which involves the location of individual propagules and their selection and transfer to an artificial growth medium or a host plant. The first step is the physical separation of the spores on an agar medium. A stiff (3%) water agar should be poured thinly (8–10 ml) onto petri dishes and seeded with spores. For dry spores this seeding may be achieved by gently tapping, or blowing a culture or infected plants over the agar, blowing a spore : talc mixture with an insufflator or by using a settling tower, the object being to obtain an even, sparce scattering of spores. These procedures are useful for rusts and mildews. Alternatively, spore suspensions may be streaked onto agar. For example, lesions of *Rhynchosporium secalis* on barley are placed in a drop of water on a cavity slide and left for 40 hours to stimulate sporulation. A wire loopful of spore suspension is then streaked onto agar (see Fig. 4.1). After seeding, sufficient time should be left to allow spore germination so that only viable propagules are transferred. The problem of bacterial contamination can be overcome by acidifying the medium or by adding an antibiotic.

The next step is to locate the spores for transfer and various methods are available. In one, the spore is located in the centre of a low power microscope field and the area illuminated in a darkened room by closing the diaphragm. The area is cut around with a suitable tool and transferred to a fresh agar plate or tube. A platinum needle, flattened and sharpened to make a spear, is a popular tool as is a 'biscuit cutter' made by flattening and rolling the end of a platinum wire to make an open cylinder. The tools are mounted in metal or wooden holders. A number of microscope attachments have been devised for spore location. One, described by Georg (Mycologia. **39**; 368, 1947), is a glass tube drawn out to a cone and fixed around the lens of a low power objective. The smaller end (1.8 mm approximately) is racked down into the agar to cut a circular plug on which a single spore has been located. A similar method uses a biscuit cutter mounted below an old objective and centred. This is swung into place and lowered to cut a disc of agar. The discs of agar thus cut are transferred by needle to fresh agar plates or tubes.

Direct inoculations of plants may be carried out for obligate parasites using settling towers or spore : talc mixtures to obtain sparse uniform inoculation. It has to be assumed (often incorrectly) that resulting pustules of rusts or mildews developed from monospore infections. For many purposes, conidial chain isolations of *Erysiphe graminis* are adequate and the transfer of single chains to plants is much more practicable than single spores. Similarly, single pustule cultures of *Puccinia* spp. can be obtained by a method described by Leath and Stewart (Plant Disease Reporter, **50**; 312, 1966) for *P. graminis*. Leaf segments containing single pustules are washed in Tween 20, rinsed in distilled water and placed on benzimidazole (60 ppm) agar in the dark for 3–4 hours and then in light for 2 hours. Any spores present will thus germinate and desiccate. After 48 hours, spores are collected with a Tervet cyclone collector.

Culture and inoculum production

A wide range of more or less defined artificial media are available for the culture of fungi and bacteria which may be used as a liquid broth or solidified with agar. Although recipes are available for making media from basic ingredients such as potatoes, carrots, sugar etc., most are manufactured in a convenient powder or tablet form. Specific requirements, where they exist, are given in the compendium of diseases. Some common media for growth and sporulation of fungi include potato-dextrose, corn meal, oat meal, nutrient and malt extract, whereas for bacteria, beef peptone is widely used. Clarified agar is available for nutritional studies and for single spore isolation techniques where granular or opaque media can cause problems. To limit bacterial growth in fungal cultures the media can be acidified with 25% lactic acid or a broad spectrum antibiotic such as streptomycin may be added. Some ingredients may be denatured by heat and so should be added to the medium after autoclaving.

Culturing the so-called obligate parasites is done normally on host plants and the general rule is that the plants should be in a vigorous, healthy state at a susceptible growth stage. For example, seedling plants of wheat or barley do not support *Puccinia striiformis* very well whereas juvenile plants provide more leaf tissue that is susceptible. The plants should be grown under optimum conditions of light, temperature, water and nutrition. In the glasshouse, in winter, artificially supplemented light may be required and nutrients may need to be added to the soil or water. Plant nutrient formulations containing major, minor and trace elements are commercially available or they may be made up from recipes, e.g. Hoagland's solution. Cereal rusts and mildews are commonly cultured on detached leaves either by floating the leaf segments on a solution of 20–100 ppm benzimidazole, which retards senescence, or on the same solution solidified with agar. In the latter case, a weak agar (0·5%) may be preferred to allow good surface contact or the cut leaf ends may be inserted in the agar in petri dishes or compartmented polystyrene boxes. For rusts, the host reaction may be modified on benzimidazole but good correlations between reactions of intact plants and detached leaves have been obtained for powdery mildews. (Jones and Hayes. Ann. appl. Biol. **68**; 31, 1971). However, leaf senescence and infection are affected by photoperiod and light quality. More recently, rusts have been successfully cultured axenically on defined media and the success rates have been improved by the production of sterile uredospore inoculum of uniform maturity for *P. recondita tritici* (Raymundo and Young. Phytopath. **64**; 262, 1974). Culturing rust fungi is reviewed by Scott and Maclean (Ann. rev. Phytopath. **7**; 123, 1969).

Spore production by fungi growing on artificial media is often affected by both the amount and quality of light. Sporulation by some, e.g. *Septoria* spp. and *Helminthosporium teres* is enhanced by near ultra violet ('black') light. Fluorescent lamps which use standard light fittings can be obtained for this purpose. Plastic petri dishes should be used, as N.U.V. light is transmitted poorly by glass. Some fungi respond to photoperiod and exhibit **circadian rhythms** of spore production. Conditions for the production of asexual and sexual spores are often different. For example, conidia of *Cochliobolus sativus* are produced abundantly on sucrose-asparagine-yeast extract agar whereas mature perithecia are produced on maize seeds, surface sterilized, boiled and immersed in Sach's agar. Ascus production by the heterothallic *C. carbonum* and *C. heterostrophus* requires the pairing of compatible isolates on opposite sides of a sterilized maize leaf on agar.

Maximizing spore production by rusts and mildews means maintaining the host in a viable condition for as long as possible. A method for the production of large quantities of *P. recondita tritici* uredospores in a controlled environment 'rust factory' and their collection onto V-shaped paper strips inserted between rows of seedling wheat plants has been published by van der Wal and Zadoks (Cereal Rusts Bulletin **4**; 9, 1976). The production of teleutospores for studies of the sexual phase of the rust fungi varies somewhat with environment and host variety although it has recently been observed that the systemic fungicide oxycarboxin enhances teleutospore production of *P. coronata avenae* on oats when applied at marginally fungicidal rates.

Methods for the collection of fungal spores fall into two categories. Firstly, there are those concerned with the collection of dry spores, particularly of rusts and powdery mildews. Powdery mildew conidia are delicate and ephemeral and should be handled accordingly. Rather than collect spores, it is often best to inoculate plants by growing them in association with mildew-infected plants or to shake the infected plants gently over the test plants. Spores may be collected by gently shaking plants over sheets of paper and collecting the spores with a cyclone suction collector or by tapping them directly into storage tubes. Uredospores of *Puccinia* spp. are similarly collected by shaking onto paper or by use of a cyclone collector (Cherry and Peet. Phytopath. **56**; 1102, 1966). A small cyclone collector for collecting spores from single pustules has been described (Tervet *et al.,* Phytopath. **41**; 282, 1951). Larger quantities of uredospores may be collected in the field using a modified car vacuum cleaner run from a 12 volt battery but the spores once collected may need to be sucked through a fine wire or muslin screen to remove plant debris, aphids, dust etc.

The second method involves the collection of spores of fungal cultures or bacterial cultures on agar by flooding the dish with water and gently rubbing the agar surface with a rubber-covered glass rod to dislodge spores. If required for immediate use the suspension of cells may be adjusted to the required concentration by dilution and a surfactant added to aid dispersal. If required for storage a 15% solution of glycerol may be substituted for water as the suspending liquid.

Preservation and storage

It is necessary to maintain reference cultures of fungi for type collections, to preserve experimental isolates for future use, to maintain physiologic races for reference and use and for a number of other reasons. Culturing fungi continuously on artificial media may cause them to lose pathogenicity, sporulation capacity and other characteristics and is often laborious, time consuming and wasteful of equipment and facilities and there is always the problem of contamination during transfer. For these reasons storage becomes necessary and the procedures followed will depend on the organism involved, the length of the storage period required and the equipment available. The main methods available are outlined below.

1 Culture on agar   Cultures are grown on agar slants in test tubes or medical flats poured and placed on their sides. Media should be clear and usually consist of natural ingredients, e.g. V-8 juice, potato dextrose etc. Cultures are stored at 5°C. in domestic-type refrigerators or cold rooms and transferred to fresh media every 6 months or so. Culture mites, contamination and loss of identity of the culture are problems with this widely used method.

2 Under mineral oil   The culture is grown on an agar slant in a test tube and then overlaid with sterile pharmaceutical grade mineral oil to a depth of 1 cm above the top of the slant. Cultures should be refrigerated at 5°C. and can thus be stored for 1 to 10 years. It is inexpensive, prevents drying of cultures and excludes culture mites.

3 Refrigeration   Storing infected plant parts (roots, leaves, etc.) at between −10 and −60°C. is successful for some pathogens, particularly bacteria and some obligate parasites. Even conidia of *Erysiphe graminis*, if produced under conditions of low relative humidity, will survive freezing on barley leaves at −60°C. and remain viable for 1–2 years (Hermansen, Friesia X, **1–2**; 86, 1972). However, the normal method for *Erysiphe* spp. is to maintain infected leaves floated on 50 ppm benzimidazole at 5°C. with an 8 hour photoperiod provided by fluorescent light. Cultures still need to be transferred every 14 days and many workers prefer to maintain cultures on whole plants.

Fungus cultures in broth with 15% w/v glycerol and bacterial cultures in phosphate buffer plus 15% glycerol can be stored at −20°C.

Dry spores of rusts can be stored without treatment in a domestic refrigerator for periods up to 1 year (Clifford, Cereal Rusts Bulletin, **1**; 30, 1973) but the success varies with different *Puccinia* species, for example *P. coronata* does not survive well. Conditions under which the spores are produced also affect the outcome of storage.

4 Cryogenic methods Liquid nitrogen at $-196°C$. is the storage medium and insulated canisters are manufactured for the purpose. The temperature does not rise above $-100°C$. even in the vapour phase above the liquid. Bacterial cells and fungus cultures are commonly suspended in a protective solution of 10–15% glycerol in ampoules prior to freezing. Rust spores placed directly in ampoules and sealed are commonly stored by this method. The use of gelatin capsules or cellophane packets avoids the risk of explosion of cracked glass ampoules when removed from the nitrogen. Stepwise cooling via a domestic fridge and deep freeze and then into liquid nitrogen is said to be beneficial. Dormancy may be induced by the low temperature but this is broken by a post-storage heat shock at 40–60°C. for 2 minutes (Loegering and Harmon. Plant Dis. Reptr. **46**; 299, 1962).

5 Freeze-drying and lyophilization Cultures are dried rapidly under vacuum (lyophilization) either with or without prior freezing. Centrifugation is used with liquid cultures to prevent frothing and after this the tubes are evacuated again on a manifold and sealed. Dry spores are evacuated and sealed directly without freezing and this is the preferred method for storage of rust uredospores. Cotton wool may be soaked in liquid cultures of bacteria and placed in ampoules for freeze drying. Rehydration of rust spores after storage is commonly carried out. Spores will survive storage periods of up to 10 years but differences in survival between *Puccinia* species have been observed, *P. coronata* surviving for only 2–3 years but much depends on the condition of spores prior to storage.

6 In soil Small quantities of soil (c 5g), usually sandy clay loams are placed in test tubes and autoclaved for 1 hour. Suspensions of the organism, usually spores, in 2 ml of sterile water are added to the soil and the tubes are then shaken and stoppered and stored either at room temperature or at 4°C. in the dark. *Fusarium* spp. are maintained in this manner and recently Shearer, Zeyen and Ooka (Phytopath. **64**; 163, 1974) have described a method for 5 *Septoria* spp. from cereals in which single spore isolates were successfully maintained for more than 20 months.

7 On dried host tissue Diseased leaf tissue may be dried in a plant press and stored for a year or more and *Helminthosporium maydis* and *H. turcicum* on maize have been successfully stored in this way. The method is also applicable to cereal rusts. Similarly, the leaves may be dried between sheets of blotting or filter paper over calcium chloride prior to storage in envelopes in a refrigerator. Field-collected samples of *Puccinia hordei*, *P. striiformis* and *P. recondita* store well for several months in envelopes in a refrigerator but *P. coronata* loses viability rapidly.

8 Dry preservation of agar cultures Discs of sporulating cultures on agar have been preserved for 4 years on filter paper or aluminium foil placed over dry self-indicating silica gel in screw cap vials or bijou bottles. (Seaby, Bull. Brit. Myc. Soc. **11**; 55, 1977). The method is of value for sporulating fungus cultures bearing mature spores. Malt agar (2%) is the best medium as it stimulates sporulation. Bacterial cultures grown on nutrient agar were also successfully stored for 4 years by this method.

Inoculation and infection

The establishment of an organic union with its host represents a crucial phase in the life cycle of a pathogenic organism. Basically, the object of artificial inoculation for experimental purposes is to simulate the optimum conditions for infection that occur in nature. Inoculation may be defined as the transfer of infective propagules (fungus spores, mycelium, bacteria, etc.) from their source to the host's **infection court**. The subsequent germination or growth of the propagules to the point where they establish an organic relationship with the host is generally considered as **infection**. The **latent period** encompasses the subsequent growth and development of the pathogen to the appearance of visible symptoms. The **incubation period** is the period between infection and the reproductive phase in the pathogen's life cycle, i.e. spore production. The delineation of these phases is somewhat arbitrary although it serves a useful purpose as, broadly speaking, the environmental conditions necessary for infection and incubation are often different. Infective propagules such as spores or mycelium are relatively unaffected by environmental conditions whereas germ tubes and other structures involved in the infection process are often delicate and therefore sensitive to unfavourable environments. Similarly, once established within the host the parasite is protected from environmental variations. It is therefore most important that, in establishing infection artificially, careful attention is paid to environmental conditions during the early stages of the process – usually the first 24 to 48 hours.

The specific procedure to be adopted is often determined by the experimental objective. This objective may be the assessment of host resistance or of the effectiveness of a fungicide treatment. It may be that a qualitative assessment of the presence or absence of resistance is sufficient, in which case, uniform inoculation will not be required whereas, if a quantitative assessment of resistance is needed, then a more precise method of inoculation will be necessary to ensure uniform and reproducible distribution of inoculum. Generally speaking, the experimenter has more control over his material in the laboratory or greenhouse than in the field although it may be difficult to simulate field conditions artificially.

The major requirements for a successful inoculation and infection are those classically given by the disease triangle – a susceptible host, a viable pathogenic organism and a favourable environment.

Susceptible host Susceptibility or resistance may vary quantitatively with the age of the host and with the individual host : parasite combination. Some pathogens will only infect certain organs at specific stages of host development. For example, spores of the loose smut organism, *Ustilago nuda*, will only infect barley at flowering time when the flowers are open and are thus receptive to the invading organism. The conditions under which plants have been grown will affect their susceptibility. Conditions of high fertility and good moisture and light tend to result in plants being more susceptible to the obligate parasites, or biotrophs, such as the rusts, powdery mildews and viruses whereas stress conditions tend to favour the development of the facultative parasites or necrotrophic organisms such as *Septoria* and *Fusarium* spp. Wounds due to wind action or the passage of machinery may result in easier entry of bacterial and virus pathogens.

Viable inoculum A minimum level of inoculum may be necessary to obtain satisfactory infection and disease development but too much inoculum may inhibit infection. It has been reported that root-infecting fungi such as take-all (*Gaeumannomyces graminis*) require relatively large amounts of inoculum to cause infection. With most fungal pathogens, spores should not be used straight from storage but wherever possible fresh inoculum from young vigorously sporulating cultures should be used. Organisms grown on artificial culture media may become attenuated and lose pathogenicity which may be recovered by a cycle of infection through a susceptible host. It is advisable therefore to use freshly produced inoculum wherever possible. Where physiologic specialization exists within a pathogenic species, a virulent strain must be used.

Suitable environment It is generally true that pathogenic organisms are most sensitive to their environment during the infection process. Temperature and humidity are the most important environmental variables with humidity being particularly critical. Fungal germ-tubes, for example, are very sensitive to desiccation. Clues to these environmental requirements are gained from a knowledge of the pathogen's life cycle and disease cycle. Rusts require a dark period of free moisture for uredospores to germinate and penetrate into their host and nights of heavy dew satisfy this requirement in nature. Temperature also affects this process and different rust fungi have different temperature optima. *Puccinia striiformis* uredospores require a relatively low temperature (8°C.), *P. recondita* is intermediate with an optimum about 12°C. and *P. graminis* penetrates best at 15°C. With *P. graminis* the development of substomatal vesicles is enhanced by light but this may not be a requirement for other rusts, e.g. *P. hordei*. A period of free moisture is required for the splash-borne pathogens such as *Septoria* spp. and *Rhynchosporium secalis* but free moisture is inhibitory to *Erysiphe graminis*, the powdery mildew fungus.

Inoculation methods

Any difficulty in artificially obtaining infection can usually be minimized by studying the field conditions that are conducive to disease development and from a knowledge of the disease cycle.

1 Direct application These methods are particularly suited for fungi that can be artificially cultured. Fungi such as *Rhynchosporium secalis*, *Septoria* spp. and *Helminthosporium* spp. may be cultured on agar and small segments applied to leaf surfaces. Pieces of filter paper or cotton wool may be dipped in a spore or mycelium suspension and applied directly. Cotton wool pieces dipped in dry spores such as uredospores of rusts may be similarly applied. The method allows point inoculations to be made and several different cultures can be applied to a single leaf. In this way the reaction of a plant to several different physiologic races may be determined. Blocks of agar containing single spores can be cut from agar plates that have been uniformly seeded with spores using a settling tower (Fig. 4.2) and these can then be applied to leaves. Seeds may be infected by placing them, after surface sterilization, on agar plates containing actively growing cultures as with *Pyrenophora graminea* on barley seeds.

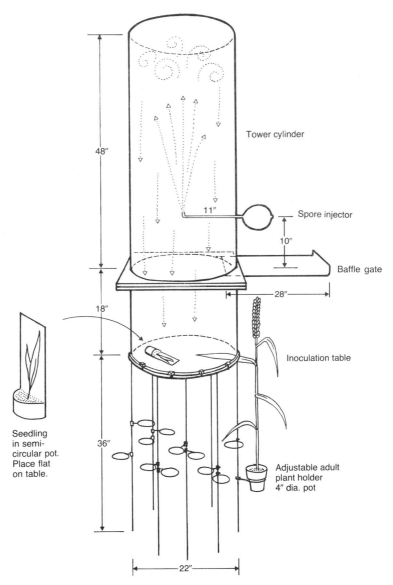

48"

Tower cylinder

11"

Spore injector

10"

Baffle gate

28"

18"

Inoculation table

Seedling
in semi-
circular pot.
Place flat
on table.

36"

Adjustable adult
plant holder
4" dia. pot

22"

Fig. 4.2 *Schematic representation of a spore settling tower (after Eyal, Clifford & Caldwell. Phytopath 58: 530, 1968).*

2 Diseased host material   Plant material to be infected is grown or placed in close association with diseased material. With air-borne foliar pathogens, such as rusts and mildews, infected plants may be placed in amongst test plants in the greenhouse and shaken to deposit spores evenly. For field experiments pots of infected plants may be transplanted either directly in association with test plants or, more commonly, at intervals along rows of a susceptible variety (spreader beds). The spreader variety serves as a source of inoculum which may be spread onto test plants. Disease can develop in the field from infected volunteer plants and plant debris from a previously infected crop. Such debris should be mechanically spread to ensure uniformity of inoculum. Seed harvested from infected plants, for example wheat glume blotch (*Septoria nodorum*), barley leaf blotch or scald (*Rhynchosporium secalis*) or barley leaf stripe (*Pyrenophora graminea*) can be sown to produce inoculum for the subsequent experimental planting. Similarly, infected straw chopped and spread amongst test plants will provide a source of inoculum, for example with the wheat or barley eyespot pathogen (*Pseudocercosporella herpotrichoides*). In experiments to assess individual wheat or barley plants for resistance to eyespot, infected hollow culm pieces about 30 mm in length are placed over the emerging coleoptiles of the test plants.

3 Dry inoculum application   In these methods spores are dusted, brushed or blown onto plants using mechanical aids. Spores may be diluted to give sufficient bulk by using talc, dead spores of the same organism or *Lycopodium* spores, usually in the proportions 1 part spores to 30 parts diluent. Dry spores can be applied to leaves or floral parts using an artist's paint brush, simple powder puffers or insuflators. A cyclone spore collector can also be used with a suitable air compressor to blow spores out. More precise dry spore methods are aimed at achieving uniformity of inoculation. The 'rolling' method (Nair & Ellingboe, Phytopath. **52**; 714, 1962) for inoculation of cereals with conidia of *Erysiphe graminis* consists of shaking infected leaves to remove old spores, waiting 6 hours and then tapping the freshly produced spores onto glass slides. Gentle blowing on the slides removes clumps and chains. A cotton-swab is then gently rolled across the slide and then across the leaf. This results in a uniform distribution of single spores. Settling towers have been developed to uniformly inoculate cereal leaves with uredospores. In one (Eyal, Clifford & Caldwell, Phytopath. **58**; 530, 1968), single adult leaves are inserted onto the inoculation table (Fig. 4.2) or seedlings grown in semi-circular pots with plastic backs are placed directly on the table. Spores are injected by an air blast and clumps which settle first are caught on a baffle gate which is then opened to expose the test plants to a uniform spore shower. Other towers have been developed in which plants are placed on a turntable and spores are injected by air blast or in liquid suspension (see below). Fans may be used to agitate the air to aid uniform spore deposition on all plant surfaces. Simple towers can be constructed using cardboard or plastic tubes, gramophone turntables and domestic fans.

4 Liquid suspensions These methods are commonly used for the water dispersed (splash-borne) foliar pathogens but dry spore inoculum can be prepared as a liquid suspension for ease of application. Spores and mycelium are collected from plants or from artificial growth media and made into liquid suspension. Normally such suspensions will need to be diluted but they may be concentrated by centrifugation or filtering and adjusted to the correct concentration. Some spores contain self inhibitors and may require prior washing. As a rule of thumb, a concentration of 10^4 to 10^6 spores per ml of liquid is about right. Distilled or deionized water should be used at a neutral pH as dissolved salts, for example of copper or zinc, may be inhibitory. Surfactants such as sodium oleate, Tween 20 or Tween 80 may be added to give a more uniform suspension of spores that will spread more evenly over the plant surface. Gelatin or agar may be added to help the spores to stick to the surface and to reduce desiccation. Light paraffinic mineral oils have been used successfully especially for inoculating with uredospores. A spray chamber in which cereal seedling pots are placed on a turntable and are then sprayed with a suspension of uredospores in mineral oil has been developed (Rowell & Olin, Phytopath. **47**; 650, 1957).

A whole range of sprayers which have been developed for liquid spray applications is available for use. These include domestic perfume sprayers, finger operated spray caps which screw onto 200 ml medical flats, small hand and pump sprayers of the garden type and larger portable and tractor mounted agricultural sprayers. A precise and reliable method of inoculating with a suspension of uredospores, especially spreader beds in the field, makes use of a hypodermic syringe which automatically dispenses pre-set quantities of liquid from a reservoir. A quantity of 0·5 ml of a suspension containing 0·5 mg uredospores per ml of deionized water plus Tween 20 is injected into the lower leaf whorls of cereal plants as soon as they are large enough to stab easily.

Micropipettes may be used to deliver single drops of a spore suspension onto leaf blades, floral parts or into leaf axils for example. Spores in suspension may be drawn into inaccessible plant parts such as floral parts or seed coats by a partial vacuum method. The plant part is immersed in a spore suspension in an air-tight container, for example, a desiccator. The air is exhausted and then the vacuum abruptly broken thus drawing the spore suspension into what were air spaces in the host. This method has been used successfully for *Ustilago maydis* (Rowell & De Vay, Phytopath. **43**; 654, 1953) and barley and oat smuts (Fischer & Holton, 1957. Biology & Control of the Smut Fungi. Ronald Press Co. N.Y.).

5 Wounding and physical methods These techniques are particularly useful for weakly parasitic organisms, where prior wounding may be required, or for pathogens such as bacteria or viruses which normally gain entrance through natural openings such as stomata, through insect punctures or with the aid of other minor organisms. Inoculum may be mixed dry with an abrasive dust such as carborundum and blown with force against plant parts, e.g. the stigmas of wheat and barley have been successfully inoculated with chlamydospores of the loose smut fungi by blasting the florets at anthesis (Moore and Munnecke, Phytopath. **44**; 499, 1954). When mixed with water, carborundum makes an abrasive paste which may be rubbed over plant surfaces prior to spraying or wiping on suspensions of bacterial or virus pathogens. Other artificial aids to damaging plant surfaces include tooth and nail brushes and a screw capped vial with a roughly punctured cap which is used as a self-feeding device for inoculating leaves. Maize is commonly inoculated with *Xanthomonas stewartii*, the bacterium which causes Stewart's disease, by cutting off the leaf tip prior to dipping or swabbing with a bacterial suspension. The insertion into maize stems of a toothpick, previously infested with *Diplodia zeae*, has been used with success as a means of inoculation. However, the method may have limited use in assessing resistance to the disease as plants that were resistant following natural field inoculations were susceptible when inoculated by the toothpick method (Hooker, Phytopath. **47**; 196, 1957). This cautionary note applies to many of the wounding methods described above.

6 Vectors Viruses and bacteria in particular may be introduced into host plants by vectors such as aphids, leafhoppers, nematodes and fungi. Bacteria are generally non-specific in their vector relationships, being transmitted to plants following chance encounters with various pests and even casual visitors. There are exceptions, for example in the specialized relationship that exists between *Erwinia stewartii* and its insect vector, the corn flea beetle (*Chaetocnema pulicaria*). Cereal viruses have, however, evolved specific relationships with various fungal and insect vectors.

Although wounding (see above) is often a substitute for insect vectors, most circulative viruses such as BYDV, are not mechanically transmitted and rely entirely on vector transmission. To artificially inoculate cereal plants with BYDV the appropriate aphid vectors must be fed on infected plants for 24–48 hours before transferring them to test plants where they should be allowed to feed for 12–24 hours at least. Inoculation of plants with disease agents transmitted by soil-borne vectors requires the use of infested soil techniques (see below). For example, oat plants would normally be inoculated with OMV by growing plants in soil known to carry the fungus vector, *Polymyxa graminis.*

7 Soil infestation   These methods are used to inoculate plants with root-infecting pathogenic fungi and fungal vectors of virus diseases. Naturally infested soil may be used directly or a natural or artificial growing medium may be inoculated with the organism either in pure culture or on crop debris. The technique used depends on the experimental objective. For example, the artificial inoculation of sterilized soil would be inappropriate to study the ecology of an organism in the soil as survival and growth will depend on competitive relationships with the soil microflora. If the object is to obtain an infested growing medium to compare the response of a range of varieties to infection then the method would suffice. The growing medium may be inoculated with infected plant debris such as chopped leaves, seeds or root tissues. Such material may be derived from naturally infected plants or from artificially inoculated seed or straw. Accurate placement of inoculum in the soil may be obtained by dipping string in a liquid culture and placing the string in the soil. A liquid culture or a macerated agar culture may be added to the growing medium but it is difficult to obtain uniform mixing with liquid cultures. In small pot experiments, standard aliquots can be dispensed in this way. A common method with *Cochliobolus sativus* and *Gaeumannomyces graminis* is to grow the fungus on a sand and corn meal medium and then to incorporate this into white silica sand at a rate of 1 part : 9 parts sand. The problems of soil infestation methods increase with the scale of the experiments and uniformly infested field nurseries are hard to maintain. Cultivations should be aimed at thorough mixing and movement of soil within the nursery where experiments comparing chemical control methods or resistant and susceptible varieties have been conducted or a patchy infestation will result. A break where a highly susceptible variety is grown in the entire nursery area will help restore uniformity and a high level of inoculum. Such field nurseries are used to good effect for soil-borne viruses, e.g. wheat and oat mosaic viruses, cereal cyst eelworm and various fungus diseases.

Incubation and symptom expression

The most important factors that affect the rate and degree of symptom expression are temperature and light during the incubation period whereas the early stages of infection are most influenced by moisture. Many fungi require free moisture during infection especially foliar pathogens such as the rusts, *Helminthosporium* spp. and the splash-borne pathogens, e.g. *Septoria* spp. This requirement may be met by simple moisture chambers made from polythene bags, glass jars or other water-tight containers (Cooke & Jones, Pl. Path, **19**; 72, 1970).

Spores may be sprayed in suspension or water may be sprayed on after inoculation. Non-toxic mineral oils have been used for rusts and these help prevent desiccation. Inoculated plants under polythene bags may then be placed in a refrigerator or in a cold room to induce dew formation on the leaves. More sophisticated variable dew point chambers are available which develop dew at the required temperature. An inexpensive chamber which has been used successfully with various cereal rusts, *Septoria* spp. *Rhynchosporium secalis* and *Helmintho-sporium* spp. and has been described by Clifford (New Phytologist, **72**; 619, 1973). Following infection, the incubation or latent period is affected mainly by temperature, light and the nutritional status and vigour of the host and, of course, the interaction between these factors. The formation of sub-stomatal vesicles of *Puccinia graminis tritici* is enhanced by light but with other rusts this is not a requirement. Temperature probably has the greatest effect on the host : pathogen encounter affecting it both quantitatively and qualitatively. Resistance governed by temperature sensitive major genes is known for *Puccinia graminis* and *P. recondita* on wheat, *P. coronata* on oats and *P. hordei* on barley. Such resistance may operate at either high or low temperatures and the 'switch' temperature range may be very narrow. Environmental lability may be manifested by quantitatively inherited and expressed resistances and by those which have an ontogenetic component. The expression of certain adult plant resistances in winter wheat to *P. striiformis* may be modified by the degree of vernalization of the host and certain adult tissue resistances of oats to *P. coronata* have their highest expression at relatively low temperatures. Quantitatively expressed resistance to rusts and mildews may be more apparent under host stress conditions of nutrient imbalance or low fertility. It is generally true that with biotrophic pathogens the more healthy and vigorous the host, the more compatible the host : pathogen relationship, whereas with noorotrophic organisms, the converse is often the case. The amount and duration of sporulation is affected by the factors discussed above but is also affected by humidity or free moisture. High humidity stimulates spore production by many foliar pathogens and free moisture or alternate wetting and drying is essential for spore production or discharge by many splash-dispersed organisms.

Observing host : parasite relations

Simple techniques are often adequate for diagnosis or observation of host : parasite relations but, for more detailed qualitative and quantitative studies, more precise detailed methods are required. The preparation of material involves several clear cut steps: fixing, clearing, staining, differentiation and mounting and many procedures have been developed for these specific purposes. Only the most widely used and successful methods are referred to here but it should be stated that these are only guides and that the outcome of a procedure will depend on the nature of the specific material under study. Timing of exposure, stain concentrations, temperatures used etc. will need to be modified to obtain the best results.

1 Surface observations Probably the best method for observing pre-penetration processes on plant surfaces involves the use of incident light optics, which are now available with most microscope systems, coupled with the spray staining method of Anderson and Rowell (Phytopath. **52**; 909, 1962). Quantitative assessments of spore germination and penetration of *Puccinia hordei* on barley leaves have been carried out by this method (Clifford. Proc. Europ. and Medn. Cereal Rusts Conf., **1**; 75, 1972) in which leaf segments, mounted on glass slides, are gently spray stained with acid fuchsin/cotton blue in acetic alcohol. This gives the minimum disturbance of surface structures. Scanning electron microscopy has been used recently to give information on the detailed architecture of host surfaces and pathogen structures.

There are various methods which involve making replicas of infected leaf surfaces for studies of pre-penetration processes. In one, a thin layer of coloidin or clear nail varnish is spread over the dried leaf surface, allowed to dry, peeled off carefully and mounted in clear lactophenol on a glass slide with a cover slip over. Lactophenol/cotton blue or lactofuchsin may be used instead. A similar method involves first making silicone rubber imprints of the leaf surface and collodion impressions are then made from the silicone rubber 'negative' (Sampson, Nature, **191**; 932, 1961). A number of silicone rubbers developed for dental work are now available which give a finely detailed replica. The method has the advantage of allowing the experimenter to store the replicas for repeated analysis.

Stripping of the leaf epidermis can be accomplished with a scalpel by a skilled technician after practice (Zimmer, Phytopath. **55**; 296, 1965) but damage to fungal structures may occur. Stripping can also be achieved by folding clear adhesive tape around a leaf, grasping the two ends and pulling sharply apart to leave the epidermis adhering to the tape ready for mounting (Leather, Bull. Brit. Myc. Soc. **11**; 54, 1977) in lactophenol/cotton blue.

2 Internal observations   Several whole leaf methods are available which allow observations to be made without sectioning the host tissue. Two are of particular value for general use. In the method of Shipton and Brown (Phytopath. **52**; 1313, 1962) infected leaf pieces are boiled for 2 minutes in alcoholic lactophenol/cotton blue, left in the stain for 48 hours at room temperature and immersed in saturated chloral hydrate for 30–50 minutes for differentiation. The leaves are then mounted on glass slides in 50% glycerine or clear lactophenol. This method is successful for rusts and powdery mildews and a modification for *Rhynchosporium secalis* on barley has been described in which leaves are cleared in glacial acetic acid in 95% ethanol and stained in 0·1% trypan blue in lactophenol for 25 minutes in a steam bath. Another method of particular value for observing rust haustoria is that of McBride (Am. J. Bot. **23**; 686, 1936) in which leaves are cleared in saturated chloral hydrate (5 g in 2 ml water) and stained in a 2% solution of acid fuchsin in chloral hydrate and alcohol. The destaining, differentiation and counterstaining with picric acid steps are not always necessary and the leaf pieces may be differentiated and mounted directly in chloral hydrate (Littlefield. Physiol. Plant Path. **3**; 241, 1973). A method in use for observing root infections involves boiling the roots in saturated chloral hydrate containing 0·01% acid fuchsin and mounting in clear lactophenol.

It may be necessary to section host tissue and this can be done crudely with a scalpel or razor blade. Alternatively, free hand sections of host tissue held in carrot or elder pith may be made with a safety, or preferably open, razor. Vibrating microtomes are available which cut sections of fresh plant tissue but for precise serial sectioning a rotary microtome should be used with wax-embedded material. A modification to a rotary microtome has been described (Popp, Phytopath. **48**; 19, 1958) for sectioning wheat embryos to examine them for mycelium of *Ustilago nuda*. For electron microscopy, ultra thin sections are required for the study of ultra structural relationships botwoon host and parasite. Rust and mildew relationships with their hosts have been studied in great detail by this technique (Bracker and Littlefield In 'Fungal Pathogenicity and the Plant's Response'. Ed. Byrde and Cutting. Academic Press 1973).

3 Quantitative measurements   It is becoming increasingly important to quantify infection especially in relation to characterizing host resistance mechanisms and in assessing the effectiveness and mode of action of fungicides. Micrometer eyepieces are used for linear measurements in one plane and grid micrometers may be used to estimate area. A linear measurement method of estimating hyphal density of *Gaeumannomyces graminis tritici* has been described by Wildermuth and Rovira (Soil Biol. Biochem. **9**; 203, 1977). If a fungal colony is of a regular shape, i.e. circular or ellipsoidal, measurements along one or two axes will allow an estimate of the area to be made. This is adequate for colonies restricted primarily to one plane, e.g. a surface or sub-cuticular colony. For colonies developing within tissue an estimate of the volume may be attempted. Estimates of volume using measurements in three dimensions are difficult to accomplish but a possible alternative is a chemical estimation of mycelial mass in infected tissue. Such a method has recently been

Fixatives (fixing and clearing)

Formol-acetic-alcohol (FAA)		Ethyl alcohol (95%)	Chloral hydrate (saturated)	
Formalin	13 ml		Chloral hydrate	5 g
Glacial acetic acid	5 ml		Water	2 ml
Ethyl alcohol (50%)	200 ml			

Stains

Lactophenol/cotton blue		McBride's stain		Andersen and Rowell's spray stain	
Anhydrous		Acid fuchsin (2%) in		Cotton blue (Trypan or	
lactophenol	67·0 ml	ethanol (70%)	0.5 ml	aniline)	2 mg
Water	20·0 ml	Sat. chloral hydrate	6·0 ml	Acid fuchsin	5 mg
Cotton blue (Trypan or		Ethanol (95%)	4·0 ml	Glacial acetic acid	0·2 ml
aniline)	0·1 g			Ethanol (95%)	35 ml
				Water	23 ml

Mounting media

Glycerol (50%)	Lactophenol		Lactic acid (20%)
	Phenol crystals	20 g	
	Lactic acid	20 g	
	Glycerol	40 g	
	Water	20 ml	

described by Harrower (Trans. Br. Mycol. Soc. **69**; 15, 1977) as a means of estimating resistance of wheat to *Septoria tritici.*

Disease Assessment

The accurate assessment of disease forms the fundamental basis of many aspects of cereal pathology. Firstly, disease survey data is essential to breeders, fungicide manufacturers, economists and government agencies in determining the importance of disease so that priorities can be given in allocating resources and in forecasting yield losses. Secondly, growers, marketing organizations and advisers require such information to facilitate the choice of crop and variety to be grown and to determine the type and timing of fungicide applications. Thirdly, researchers and extension workers concerned with the development of new or improved disease control practices require precise methods for assessing their experiments. Finally, breeders require to assess potential resistant parents, segregating material and new varieties for level and type of resistance.

The quality and quantity of disease data and the precision with which it is collected will vary with these different basic needs and, therefore, the objects of assessment must be clearly defined at the onset. The procedure adopted is often a necessary compromise between what needs to be done and what can be done with the available time and resources. The balance of this compromise will depend on the nature of the specific disease and the assessment objective.

In the past, methods for recording plant disease have been either too descriptive, too subjective or not standardized. The inadequacy of these methods has led to much activity in the production of pictorial and standardized assessment keys. This has resulted in improved methods for assessing certain types of disease, particularly fungal diseases of above ground plant parts but adequate methods are still lacking for root diseases and systemic virus infections.

Sampling methods

In small experiments, the entire material may be assessed but normally observations are made on a sample of the material. The number of samples taken relates to the standard deviation but, most importantly, the procedure must be random, representative and objective. In a field situation it is recommended that at least 50 tillers are sampled at random along one diagonal or other appropriate line. Where disease is non-uniform, as in surveys of natural field infections, especially of diseases with a scattered distribution such as take-all, more samples may be required than in experiments where diseases may be uniformly distributed. In the assessment of disease spread from a point focus in a field crop, samples may be taken on a polar co-ordinate grid. Where repeated assessments are made the plants may be marked by coloured tags, canes or aerosol paint sprays.

Sampling may be destructive or non-destructive. However, destructive sampling should not be carried out if the removal of diseased tissue or plants affects the progress of disease or the subsequent plant yield or its quality. In assessing root diseases, destructive sampling will be necessary, the entire root system being harvested for assessment. This may pose problems in the field but is facilitated in pot experiments.

Timing of assessment

This depends on the requirements of the test and on the epidemiology of the disease. **Simple interest diseases** may be assessed on one occasion but, with **compound interest diseases**, the rate of progress as well as the absolute levels of disease may be important. Similar considerations hold for **monocyclic** and **polycyclic** inoculation tests. A fungicide or cultural treatment effect may be appraised by assessing before and after treatments. Assessments should be related to the stage of plant development which in turn, should be related to an important physical function, e.g. grain filling. Growth stage can be determined from the Feekes scale of cereal growth stages (Fig. 4.3) which has been illustrated by Large (Plant Pathology. **3**; 128, 1954). An alternative scale has recently been introduced by Zadoks, Chang & Konzak, Weed Research, **14**; 415, 1974) (Fig. 4.4) which facilitates computerized data processing and has recently been described and illustrated by Tottman, Makepiece and Broad (Pub. by BASF United Kingdom Limited) (Fig. 4.5). The assessment of host resistance depends on its time of expression, e.g. seedling resistance, adult plant resistance, resistance to head infection etc.

Assessment methods

These may be direct or indirect. The simplest direct methods are for foliar pathogens that cause discrete lesions.

Disease may be assessed quantitatively or qualitatively. It may be adequate to assess either the presence or absence of disease, infected vs non-infected or resistant vs susceptible as for example with head smuts, but, more commonly, it is the amount of disease that is of importance. A widely used qualitative assessment is that of the host

Stage
1 One shoot (number of leaves can be added) = 'brairding'
2 Beginning of tillering
3 Tillers formed, leaves often twisted spirally. In some varieties of winter wheats, plants may be 'creeping' or prostrate
4 Beginning of the erection of the pseudo-stem, leaf sheaths beginning to lengthen
5 Pseudo-stem (formed by sheaths of leaves) strongly erected
6 First node of stem visible at base of shoot
7 Second node of stem formed, next-to-last leaf just visible
8 Last leaf visible, but still rolled up, spike beginning to swell
9 Ligule of last leaf just visible
10 Sheath of last leaf completely grown out, spike swollen not yet visible
10.1 First spikes just visible (awns just showing in barley, spike escaping through split of sheath in wheat or oats)
10.2 Quarter of heading process completed
10.3 Half of heading process completed
10.4 Three-quarters of heading process completed
10.5 All spikes out of sheath
10.5.1 Beginning of flowering (wheat)
10.5.2 Flowering complete to top of spike
10.5.3 Flowering over at base of spike
10.5.4 Flowering over, kernel watery ripe
11.1 Milky ripe
11.2 Mealy ripe, contents of kernel soft but dry
11.3 Kernel hard (difficult to divide by thumb-nail)
11.4 Ripe for cutting. Straw dead

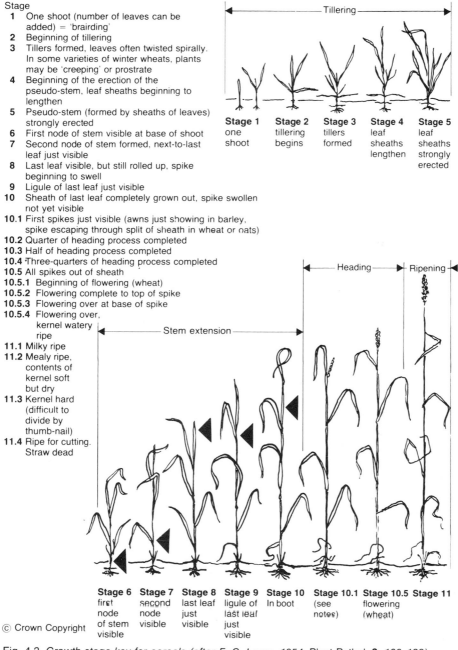

Stage 1 one shoot
Stage 2 tillering begins
Stage 3 tillers formed
Stage 4 leaf sheaths lengthen
Stage 5 leaf sheaths strongly erected

Tillering

Stem extension

Heading

Ripening

Stage 6 first node of stem visible
Stage 7 second node visible
Stage 8 last leaf just visible
Stage 9 ligule of last leaf just visible
Stage 10 In boot
Stage 10.1 (see notes)
Stage 10.5 flowering (wheat)
Stage 11

© Crown Copyright

Fig. 4.3 *Growth stage key for cereals (after E. C. Large, 1954,* Plant Pathol. **3**, *128–129).*

response or interaction, especially for rusts and mildews, where compatability and incompatability is often governed by simple genetic systems.

Standard reaction type symbols have been devised by rust workers, for example:

Symbol	Host : parasite interaction
Oi	Immune. No visible signs of infection.
Oc	Highly resistant. Minute chlorotic flecks.
On	Highly resistant. Minute necrotic flecks.
1	Resistant. Small pustules with necrotic surrounding tissue.
2	Moderately resistant. Medium-sized pustules with necrotic surrounding tissue.
3	Moderately susceptible. Medium-sized pustules with chlorotic surrounding tissue.
4	Susceptible. Large pustules with little or no chlorosis.
X	Mesothetic reaction. Mixed reaction types on one leaf.

Plants which exhibit O, 1 or 2-type responses are normally classified as resistant and 3 and 4-types as susceptible. The conventions are commonly used in genetic studies and breeding programmes conducted in the glasshouse where these responses are expressed most clearly compared with the field.

Recently, a four partite coding system has been devised for infection-type data for *Puccinia recondita* on wheat in which the first numerical element characterizes the amount of sporulation, the second describes relative lesion size and the third, which is mnemonic and alphabetic, describes the nature of the host tissue response (see Browder and Young. Plant Dis. Reptr. **59**; 964, 1975). A fourth element may be included to indicate the amount of mixtures in host line samples used in obtaining infection-type data.

Various quantitative assessments can be made. Colony or lesion numbers may be counted either by eye or with an automatic electric probe linked to a digital counter. A standard-sized frame may be placed on the leaf to assess disease per unit area. Alternatively, leaf area may be assessed by leaf area meters, graph paper or a planimeter, lesions counted and lesions per unit area are thus calculated. Sophisticated machinery is now available that will assess diseased and healthy proportions of cereal leaves using an electronic scanning procedure. Spore production can be assessed by various methods. Whole infected plants or individual leaves may be

Code

0 Germination
00 Dry seed
01 Start of imbibition
02 –
03 Imbibition complete
04 –
05 Radicle emerged from caryopsis
06 –
07 Coleoptile emerged from caryopsis
08 –
09 Leaf just at coleoptile tip

1 Seedling growth
10 First leaf through coleoptile
11 First leaf unfolded*
12 2 leaves unfolded
13 3 leaves unfolded
14 4 leaves unfolded
15 5 leaves unfolded
16 6 leaves unfolded
17 7 leaves unfolded
18 8 leaves unfolded
19 9 or more leaves unfolded

2 Tillering
20 Main shoot only
21 Main shoot and 1 tiller
22 Main shoot and 2 tillers
23 Main shoot and 3 tillers
24 Main shoot and 4 tillers
25 Main shoot and 5 tillers
26 Main shoot and 6 tillers
27 Main shoot and 7 tillers
28 Main shoot and 8 tillers
29 Main shoot and 9 or more tillers

3 Stem elongation
30 Pseudo stem erection
31 1st node detectable
32 2nd node detectable
33 3rd node detectable

Code

34 4th node detectable
35 5th node detectable
36 6th node detectable
37 Flag leaf just visible
38 –
39 Flag leaf ligule/collar just visible

4 Booting
40 –
41 Flag leaf sheath extending
42 –
43 Boots just visibly swollen
44 –
45 Boots swollen
46 –
47 Flag leaf sheath opening
48 –
49 First awns visible

5 Inflorescence emergence
50 ⌉ First spikelet of
51 ⌋ inflorescence just visible
52 ⌉
53 ⌋ ¼ of inflorescence emerged
54 ⌉
55 ⌋ ½ of inflorescence emerged
56 ⌉ ¾ of inflorescence
57 ⌋ completed
58 ⌉ Emergence of inflorescence
59 ⌋ completed

6 Anthesis
60 ⌉ Beginning of anthesis (not
61 ⌋ easily detectable in barley)
62 –
63 –
64 ⌉
65 ⌋ Anthesis half-way
66 –
67 –
68 ⌉
69 ⌋ Anthesis complete

Code

7 Milk development
70 –
71 Caryopsis water ripe
72 –
73 Early milk
74 –
75 Medium milk (Increase in
76 – solids of liquid
77 Late milk endosperm
78 – notable when
79 – crushing the the caryopsis between fingers)

8 Dough development
80 –
81 –
82 –
83 Early dough
84 –
85 Soft dough (Finger-nail impression not held)
86 –
87 Hard dough (Finger-nail
88 – impression held,
89 – inflorescence loosing chlorophyl)

9 Ripening
90 –
91 Caryopsis hard (difficult to divide by thumb-nail)
92 Caryopsis hard (can no longer be dented by thumb-nail)
93 Caryopsis loosening in daytime
94 Over-ripe, straw dead and collapsing
95 Seed dormant
96 Viable seed giving 50% germination
97 Seed not dormant
98 Secondary dormancy induced
99 Secondary dormancy lost

* Even code numbers refer to crops in which this stage is reached by all shoots simultaneously and odd numbers to unevenly developing crops when 50% of the shoots are at the stage given.

Fig. 4.4 *Decimal code for the growth of cereals. (Zadoks, Chang & Konzak, 1974* Weed Research **14**, *415).*

First leaf through coleoptile,
Growth stage: 10

First leaf unfolded,
Growth stage: 11

2 leaves unfolded,
Main shoot only,
Growth stage: 12, 20

3 leaves unfolded
Main shoot and 1 tiller,
Growth stage: 13, 21

4 leaves unfolded,
Main shoot and 2 tillers,
Growth stage: 14, 22

Winter wheat – 5 leaves unfolded,
Main shoot and 3 tillers,
Growth stage: 15, 23

Spring wheat – 5 leaves unfolded,
Main shoot and 2 tillers,
Growth stage: 15, 22

Winter wheat – 6 leaves unfolded,
Main shoot and 4 tillers, Pseudostem erect,
Growth stage: 16, 24, 30

Fig. 4.5 *Identification of cereal growth stages. Illustrated by Tottman and Makepeace (1977)*
(after Zadoks, Chang and Konzak, Weed Research, **14***; 415, 1974).*

enclosed in clear plastic or glass tubes and spores collected and weighed or counted. Leaf segments infected with rusts or powdery mildew can be floated on a solution of 20–100 ppm benzimidazole in enclosed containers such as plastic boxes or petri dishes. The leaves are then immersed, agitated to remove spores into the solution and the spores counted using a haemocytometer. Leaf area of the segments can be measured and numbers of pustules counted (see Clifford and Clothier, Trans Brit. Mycol. Soc. **63**; 421, 1974). The incubation time, or time from inoculation to onset of sporulation, is often a useful measure of the host : pathogen interaction.

Blotches, stripes and mosaics may be more difficult to assess visually but there are various field keys available (see Figs. 4.6 and 4.7) that enable the experimenter to match observed symptoms with standard diagrams representing known levels of disease. These keys may be in absolute terms and refer to actual percentage area of tissue affected or they may be in relative terms based on a theoretical maximum infection which is designated as 100%. The method is to assess the percentage area visibly affected by disease on individual leaves, sheaths, stems or flowering parts. If more than one disease is present separate assessments are made. The amount of green tissue remaining may also be assessed and then the percentage dead tissue not associated with the disease can be calculated by subtraction.

Three basic components of disease can be measured: the prevalence or number of plants or plant parts infected, the severity or degree of infection of diseased plants or plant parts and the response or reaction of the plant to infection. One or all of these components may be required to be assessed.

In the field the assessment of reaction type is often difficult as interactions can be modified by environment especially by temperature and surface wetting. For example, sporulation of *Puccinia striiformis* in leaf stripes on a susceptible host may be curtailed by high temperatures or in cold wet conditions where the spores are washed from the leaf. The stripes may then become necrotic and the resulting lesions appear incompatible. Under these conditions the infection can also be confused with *Septoria tritici*. Disease prevalence and severity are more readily assessed in the field and accuracy is often improved if an assessment is split into these two components rather than taking a simple measure of percentage infection. The first step is to assess the percentage of leaves of the plant or group of plants that are infected. Next, the mean percentage infection on these infected leaves is calculated and the two values multiplied together to give the overall percentage infection.

The assessment of cereal root diseases requires destructive sampling. In the case of eyespot disease of wheat (*Pseudocercosporella herpotrichoides*), tillers are taken

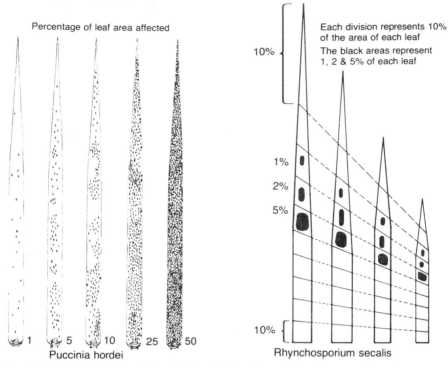

Percentage of leaf area affected

Each division represents 10% of the area of each leaf

The black areas represent 1, 2 & 5% of each leaf

10%

1%
2%
5%

10%

1   5   10   25   50

Puccinia hordei

Rhynchosporium secalis

Fig. 4.6 *Disease assessment keys for* Puccinia hordei *and* Rhynchosporium secalis.

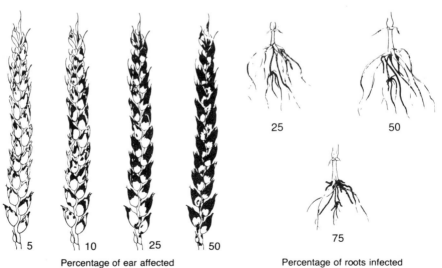

5   10   25   50

Percentage of ear affected
Septoria nodorum

25   50

75

Percentage of roots infected
Gaeumannomyces graminis

Fig. 4.7 *Disease assessment keys for* Septoria nodorum *and* Gaeumannomyces graminis.

Cereal diseases: notes on assessment
Fig. 4.6 Notes

To assess leaf diseases on cereals estimations should be made of the leaf area affected by each of the diseases present on appropriate leaves.

For recording:

(a) disease incidence up to the start of jointing, assess infection on the *lowest green leaf.*

(b) disease development and early differences in susceptibility from jointing to flowering, assess infection on *leaf 3*.*

(c) infection likely to be related to loss in yield, assess infection at the milky-ripe growth stage (usually 10–14 days after flowering) on *leaf 2* and flag leaf.

ALWAYS NOTE GROWTH STAGE AND LEAF RECORDED.

It is suggested that samples for assessment at or after jointing should be:

> for plots: 10 fertile tillers selected at random
>
> for fields: 25 fertile tillers taken on each of 2 diagonal traverses of the crop

To aid assessments a series of keys is provided illustrating specified percentage leaf areas affected by different types of disease symptom. Use whichever set of diagrams is most appropriate and score individual leaves for percentage area affected by each disease: include any chlorosis or necrosis associated with pustules. Interpolate between the levels depicted if necessary. It is also useful to record the area of dead leaf tissue not apparently associated with any specific disease or green leaf area.

*At jointing leaf 3 arises from the second lowest node in wheat and the third lowest node in barley; from flag leaf emergence it is the third from the top of the plant.

Fig. 4.7 Notes
S. nodorum

Crops may be examined at any growth stage after 10.1 if glume blotch has appeared. The precise assessment date will be governed by the aims and requirements of individual experiments.

In plots up to 1/50th acre assess 30 ears selected at random. For field assessments select 25 ears at random along each of two diagonals, totalling 50 ears.

Assess the % ear affected on both sides of the ear and record a mean figure for that ear. Interpolate if necessary, e.g. if an ear falls between 10 and 25% give it a score in between, say, 15–20%.

G. graminis

Infected *plants* should be recorded in one of these categories:

Slight: Root lesion(s) present on less than 25% of the roots.

Moderate: Lesions present on 25% to less than 75% of the roots.

Severe: Lesions present on 75% or more of the roots. Stem base is often blackened.

For sampling plots it is recommended that 10 samples each of 1 foot of drill should be taken using a stratified sampling procedure.

Sampling should be done at about flowering.

Before assessing the roots they should be washed and then examined under water in a shallow white container.

For assessing attacks likely to affect yield the *percentage of plants* with *moderate or severe* infection is most likely to be the most appropriate figure.

at random and assigned to one of the following classes (Scott and Hollins, Ann. App. Biol. **78**; 269, 1974).

Symbol	Host : parasite interaction
O	Uninfected.
1	Slight eyespot (one or more small lesions occupying in total less than half the circumference of the stem).
2	Moderate eyespot (one or more lesions occupying at least half the circumference of the stem).
3	Severe eyespot (stem completely girdled by lesions – tissue softened so that lodging would readily occur).

A disease index can then be calculated from the formula:

$$\text{disease index} = \frac{\text{(tillers in class 1)} + 2 \text{ (tillers in class 2)} + 3 \text{ (tillers in class 3)}}{\text{(total tillers in sample)}} \times \frac{100}{3}$$

For the take-all pathogen (*Gaeumannomyces graminis*), the roots must be examined and assigned to classes. A 0–5 scale for disease severity based on the presence and degree of vascular discolouration has been devised by Deacon (Trans. Brit. Mycol. Soc. **61**; 471, 1975).

Indirect methods of assessment include spore trapping over infected crops or trapping of insect vectors of a virus to estimate the degree of crop infection. A more recent innovation is the use of aerial or satellite photography using infra red film or colour filter combinations to enhance the differentiation between healthy and diseased tissue. At present, only the presence or absence of disease can be determined from such methods but, if the technology can be developed, it offers exciting possibilities for disease surveys over entire regions. Other indirect methods include the effect of disease on the host, i.e. the host response is assessed. This may include measures of stunting, increased or decreased tillering, premature or delayed ripening and reductions in ear numbers, grain numbers, size and quality.

Data format

The precision of data depends on the objective of the experiment. Simple classification into resistant or susceptible, diseased or healthy may be adequate. Mainly, it should be quantitative and standardized either in absolute terms or relative to control varieties. Comparisons may be required between experiments or within experiments. Where comparisons between years or locations are required for example, standard quantitative keys should be used and control varieties should be included to monitor interactions between genotypes and environment.

Data analysis

Often disease data needs to be transformed before analysis. Percentage data may require an arcsine transformation to satisfy the requirements of normality and independence of mean and variance in the analysis of variance. Disease progress curves may follow a sigmoid function and thus require probit, logit or log transformations for comparative analysis (see van der Plank, 1963). Original data may correspond to absolute scales as for example with the James keys (Can. Pl. Dis. Surv. **51**; 2, 1971) or may incorporate a transformation as with the modified Cobb scale (Cobb, Agric. Gaz. N.S.W. **3**; 60, 1882) where 100% scale reading corresponds to 29% actual disease cover of the leaf or stem.

Confounding factors

In the field, the disease being monitored rarely occurs alone. Diseases interact and the presence of one may enhance or suppress another. The environment may modify the disease response. For example, unduly high or low temperatures, non-uniform soil conditions resulting in uneven plant growth and the use of chemical treatments for weed or pest control may affect the host's response to the target disease.

Whilst in general terms the assessor should be objective in his measurements and assignations into severity classes, on some occasions it is necessary to incorporate an element of subjectivity. In a disease such as leaf blotch of barley (*Rhynchosporium secalis*) for example, an individual lesion on a leaf may be assessed as destroying 5% of the leaf area. Such damage would be considered of little significance. However, if the lesion was situated at the base of the leaf, as is often the case, it would eventually destroy the functioning of the whole leaf and should therefore be scored accordingly.

Crop loss appraisal

Disease assessments often need to bo linked with the effects of disease on yield and quality. In order that predictive statements can be made from disease data on the effects of given amounts of disease on yield, the value of a fungicide control measure, when to apply a fungicide etc., detailed experimental data must first be obtained relating disease incidence to crop losses. With some diseases this is simple, for example the number of barley heads infected with loose smut is directly proportional to the yield loss. With most diseases, the yield loss relates to the duration and severity of exposure to disease and also to the sensitivity of the host to disease. This sensitivity may differ between varieties and also within a variety at different stages of growth. Formulae have been derived that relate infection to yield loss for barley and oat mildew by Large & Doling (Plant Pathology, **11**; 47, 1962) where yield loss equals $2.5 \times \sqrt{\text{Mildew infection}}$ on the flag leaf at growth stage 10·5 for barley and $3.5 \times \sqrt{}$ for oats. Other workers consider that the area under the disease progress curve is a better measure than the critical point method described by James (Ann. Rev. Phytopath. **12**; 27, 1974). Relative sensitivity or tolerance must also be taken into account (Schafer, Ann. Rev. Phytopath. **9**; 235, 1971).

Monitoring pathogen populations

Many cereal pathogens exist in physiologically specialized forms which are characterized by their virulence on specific host genotypes. This characteristic of the major cereal pathogens, particularly the rusts, smuts and mildews, has frustrated the early promise of a permanent solution to the disease problem by the use of simply inherited host resistance. It is now commonly expected that virulent forms of the pathogen will emerge in the pathogen population in response to the introduction of resistance into the host cultivars. It is therefore necessary to monitor pathogen populations to determine the presence and frequency of specific virulences and virulence combinations relating to host resistances which are being used and are planned for use by plant breeders. The principal objective of such virulence gene (race) surveys is the early detection of previously unknown virulences so that farmers can make the best choice of available varieties and so that plant breeders, by using these physiologic races, may select new resistant varieties. There are several ways in which these surveys can be carried out.

Trap nurseries
Sets of genotypes are assembled which carry specific resistances to the pathogen in question. These nurseries, co-ordinated from a research centre, are grown by co-operators in different geographic locations. Standard methods of planting and assessing the nurseries are employed and the results are collected, compiled and distributed to the co-operators or published in scientific journals such as the Plant

Disease Reporter or the Canadian Plant Disease Survey. These nurseries provide information on pathogen populations and are a source of resistant genotypes for local breeding programmes. Several cereal nurseries are co-ordinated by the United States Department of Agriculture and, in Europe, by the Institute for Phytopathological Research and the Foundation for Agricultural Plant Breeding in Wageningen, Netherlands. The nurseries should ideally be located within or near a crop of the host variety susceptible to the disease in question and disease samples from the differentially resistant genotypes sent to a testing centre for virulence identification.

Testing centres

The traditional and standard race testing procedure has been to collect field samples of diseased material and send them to testing centres where the individual isolates are catalogued, multiplied and tested on standard sets of seedlings of differential varieties which carry specific resistances of interest. These sets may comprise internationally agreed genotypes to allow comparisons to be made between geographically isolated pathogen populations together with supplementary sets of varieties of interest to breeders and farmers within a region. Pathogen clones which carry specific virulence genes or combinations of genes are thus classified and named according to their spectrum of response on the differential varieties. A logical, simple and informative system of naming races has been proposed by Gilmour (Nature. **242**; 620, 1973) which makes use of the *octal system* of notation. One aim of these surveys is to estimate frequencies of virulences but this can only be achieved if sampling is random. A further complication is the recent increased use of host resistances which are quantitative in expression and are expressed only in mature plants. For these tests, it is necessary to grow the differential varieties to the adult plant stage in isolation nurseries in the field and to infect them with the specific pathogen isolates in question. In the Netherlands, such isolation nurseries for wheat yellow rust (*P. striiformis*) are grown widely separate from each other in crops of oil seed rape in the reclaimed polder regions. In the United Kingdom Cereal Pathogen Virulence Survey, the nurseries are isolated in farm crops or within polythene tunnels comprising a metal semicircular framework with plastic covering. Virulence is detected as an increase in the expected level of infection on the test varieties.

Mobile nurseries

A recently described method which combines features of the above two methods involves the use of mobile nurseries. This method was devised by Eyal, Hurman,

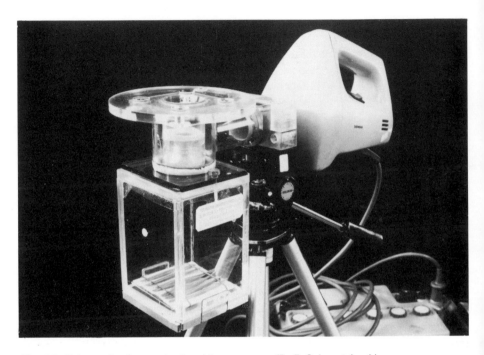

Fig. 4.8 *Schwartzbach sampler for airborne spores (Dr E. Schwartzbach).*

Moseman, and Wahl (Phytopath. **63**; 1330, 1973) for monitoring *Erysiphe graminis hordei* in Israel and involves exposing trays of barley seedlings for several days at selected sites across the country and then transferring them back to the greenhouse where they are incubated and assessed. The long field exposure time is necessary to ensure adequate levels of infection. A related method makes use of a suction apparatus which is made from a converted car vacuum cleaner and is powered by a car battery (Fig. 4.8). The exhaust agitates the crop thus releasing a spore cloud which is sucked into a deposition chamber containing a compartmented box in which are leaf segments on benzimidazole agar. The boxes are easily removed and replaced by others for sequential sampling. Although designed for barley mildew, the sampler may be used for a range of cereal foliar pathogens. (Schwartzbach, Phytopathol. **7**, 1978, in press.)

Fungicide insensitivity

A new dimension has been added to the monitoring of pathogenic variation following the detection of fungus strains that are insensitive to normal doses of certain fungicides. The first example of a cereal pathogen insensitive to a fungicide was *Pyrenophora avenae*, some strains of which tolerate high levels of organo mercurial fungicides. Similarly, relative insensitivity of some strains of *Erysiphe graminis hordei* to ethirimol has been reported and it is the potential evolution of insensitivity to such modern 'systemic' fungicides which gives cause for concern. For this reason it is becoming more common for workers involved in virulence surveys to include fungicide treated varieties in the sets of differential varieties to thus detect fungicide insensitivity.

Maintenance of physiologic races in isolation

One important service offered by surveying laboratories is the maintenance of type cultures and their supply to research workers, breeders etc. when requested. Various types of apparatus and facilities are available for the culture of physiologic races in isolation. A simple method uses a clear plastic cylinder which fits inside the rim of a plant pot within which infected seedlings are growing. Condensation inside the cylinder can be minimized by cutting several small holes in the sides and gluing muslin over them. The top is also covered with muslin. In an extension of this system, multiple units of plant pots with clear plastic covers are fed with filtered moistened air under positive pressure thus keeping the plants grown within them free from contamination (Jenkyn, Hirst and King, Ann. appl. Biol. **73**; 9, 1973). This same principle is used for larger plant isolators which may be necessary for the culture of larger quantities of spores. A portable, practical unit has been described by Emge, Melching and Kingsolver (Plant Dis. Reptr. **54**; 130, 1970). Taken to its conclusion, the principles of filtered air isolation chambers is seen in the design of sporeproofed glasshouses. In these, the main problem of cross contamination is by operators but this is minimized by using clean protective clothing and clean techniques. For critical work, it is often necessary to isolate cultures in small chambers within a large sporeproofed room. The spore-laden air which emanates from these positive pressure systems may present a potential hazard to local agriculture and, so, attempts are often made to filter this exhaust air but this can only reduce the risk as air will escape through access doors and leaks in the structure. The size of the problem must be balanced against the importance of the work being done. For work where escape of the pathogen strain cannot be entertained a negative pressure quarantine laboratory should be used similar to that described by Inman (Plant Dis. Reptr. **54**; 3, 1970).

Experimental design

This section is concerned mainly with experimental procedures and principles rather than with statistical analysis as an adequate treatment of this latter subject is beyond the scope of this book. As a general rule, unless the experimenter is a competent statistician or the design is simple, it is advisable to seek statistical advice during the planning stage so that the most meaningful analysis of the data can be made. Assuming the correct design, the experiment must be carried out in a technically sound and precise way. Correct design is not a substitute for poor experimental technique and all efforts must be made to minimize random variation and recognize non-random variation. Pathological experiments comprise three basic variables; the pathogen, host and environment and the experimental treatments may involve one, two or all three of these. Some can be controlled more easily than others. For example, pure seed stocks of the host genotypes should be aimed for and, similarly, pure cultures of the pathogen should be used. In pot experiments, extra plants can be grown so that uniform experimental material can be selected.

Environmental factors are more difficult to control but certain aspects are amenable to management by creation of artificial environments such as providing dew to ensure infection by rust fungi. Care should always be taken to uniformly apply treatments, e.g. to ensure thorough mixing of chemicals etc. In most experiments, space (glasshouse, field, controlled climate) is limited and limiting and, although adequate replication must be given, the more control there is over random variation, the more experimental treatments can be applied. Statistical advice should be sought on these aspects of design and a useful handbook for this is Statistical Methods in Agricultural Research by Little and Hills (University of California, Davis, California). Some of the pitfalls in pathological experiments that can be avoided are discussed below or, if not avoidable, should at least be recognized.

A first consideration is whether the variation to be assessed is quantitative or qualitative and, although less precise techniques may be necessary for qualitative data, even experiments of this type can benefit from quantification. For example, the assessment of different genotypes or segregating populations in the glasshouse or field for completely expressed resistance still requires reasonably uniform inoculation techniques to avoid misclassifying escapes and resistant plants. In another example, the uniform application of spores to plant surfaces facilitates assessments of spore germination and penetration by making scanning much easier for the operator and by minimizing interactions between spores which are clumped together.

Many potential errors in fungicide experiments both in the glasshouse and field can be avoided or minimized. One such source of error relates to inter-plot interference which can result in over- or underestimation of treatment effects. Such interference is most common in experiments with airborne foliar pathogens when spores are readily carried into and out of test plots and this is discussed for barley mildew by Bainbridge and Jenkyn (Ann. appl. Biol. **82**; 477, 1976). As a rule of thumb, plots should be isolated from each other by a distance of twice the plot size for experiments with airborne pathogens. Care must therefore be taken in extrapolating plot experiment results to field situations. Similar consideration must be given to experiments designed to assess partial resistance of varieties to foliar pathogens. Some fungicide treatments may exert a direct influence on adjacent plots as has found to be the case with triadimefon which has a strong vapour phase and this may result in the underestimation of the effect of such a fungicide.

Quantitative assessment of host resistance in the field is becoming more and more a part of the routine of the plant breeder and therefore the uniform inoculation of test plants becomes of considerable importance. The particular plot arrangement depends on the precision required. For routine screening of large numbers of segregating lines a spreader bed nursery should be employed which consists of drills of a susceptible variety with rows or clumps of test material on either side (Fig. 4.9 and Plate 16.3). Spreader rows of 3 drills spaced 15 cm apart gives an adequate plant density and a variety should be chosen which, if possible, is highly susceptible to the target disease and resistant to other locally prevalent diseases. Selective fungicides may be used to eliminate unwanted diseases and mixtures of varieties may be used to encourage specific combinations of diseases or pathogenic races. A useful planter for small nurseries is the Planet Jr. (Lloyd and Co., Letchworth Ltd, Herts, U.K.) which sows a single row from a seed box. In a modification the seed box is replaced by a straight-through funnel down which seed is dropped for sowing in short rows at right angles to the spreader bed (Fig. 4.10). Small clumps may be planted using a hand-held corn planter (Fig. 4.11) or, for larger clumps, a metal cylinder may be used as a guide. Small (30 cm) square plots may be hand sown in an impression made by a wooden 30 cm square template marker on the bottom of which are a number of triangular sectioned pieces of wood. The template has 1 m long vertical handles and

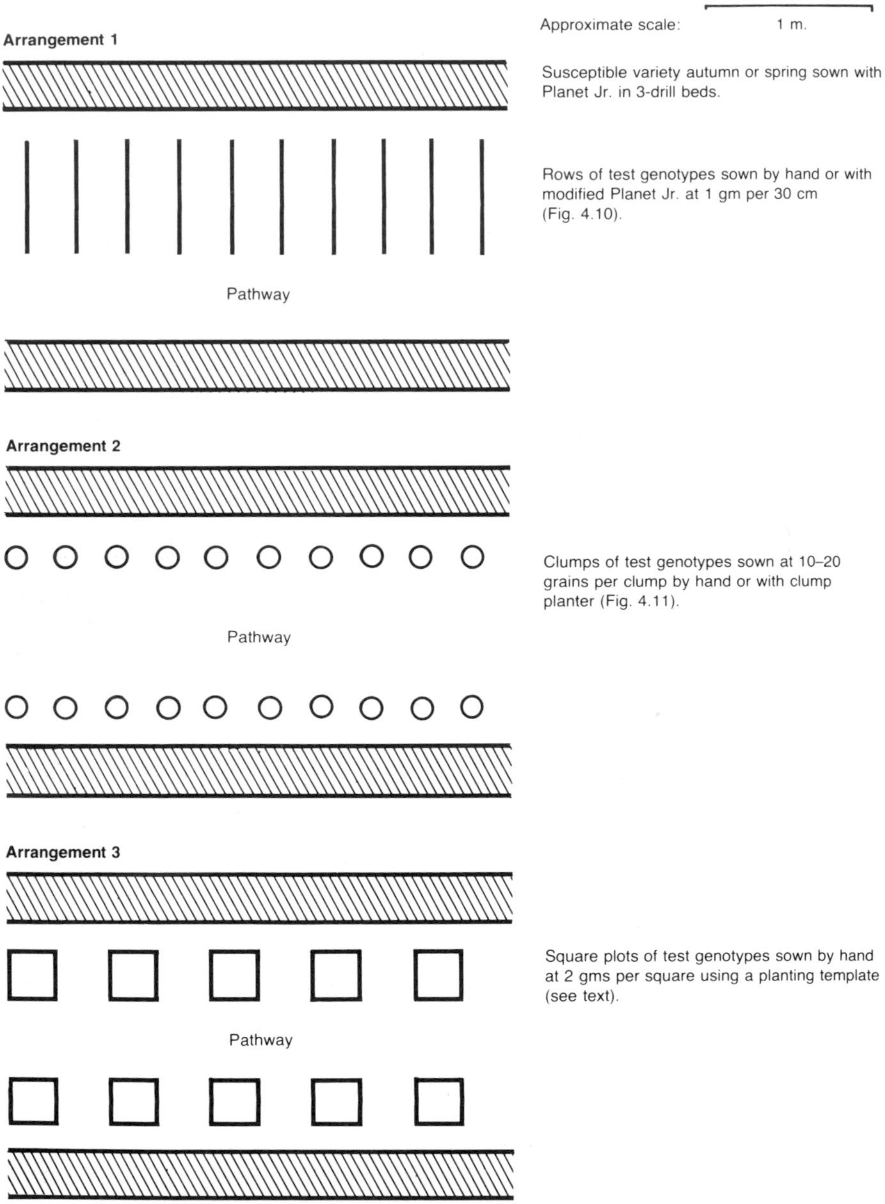

Arrangement 1

Approximate scale: 1 m.

Susceptible variety autumn or spring sown with Planet Jr. in 3-drill beds.

Rows of test genotypes sown by hand or with modified Planet Jr. at 1 gm per 30 cm (Fig. 4.10).

Pathway

Arrangement 2

Clumps of test genotypes sown at 10–20 grains per clump by hand or with clump planter (Fig. 4.11).

Pathway

Arrangement 3

Square plots of test genotypes sown by hand at 2 gms per square using a planting template (see text).

Pathway

Fig. 4.9 *Spreader bed nursery arrangements.*

the operator treads on the implement to make an impression in finely worked soil. The spreader beds in such nurseries are artificially inoculated with rusts or mildews but with splash-borne diseases, such as *Septoria* spp. and *Rhynchosporium secalis*, the disease nursery may be sown in an area previously grown with a susceptible crop. Alternatively, a susceptible winter variety which is seed infested (as with *R. secalis*) is planted and, in the spring, planting beds are sprayed with paraquat and ploughed or

Fig. 4.10 *Modified Planet Jr. for planting short rows (WPBS).*

Fig. 4.11 *Hand held planter for clumps of plants (WPBS).*

rotovated prior to planting. For soil-borne diseases such as soil-borne viruses, uniform inoculum is difficult to achieve and the same nursery arrangement may be employed except that the spreader bed will be of a susceptible variety that will act as a continual check for assessing the uniformity of soil infestation in the nursery.

More precise measurements may be required for many experimental purposes such as evaluation of fungicides, assessment of resistance of new varieties or potential resistant parents in breeding programmes etc. Some problems associated with fungicide experiments have been described above and a related problem area is the accurate assessment of quantitatively expressed host resistance. The level of such resistance may be underestimated in spreader bed nurseries due to the high level of inoculum and certain resistances may not be expressed at all. It may be argued that such resistance would be of no practical value but resistances of minor effect may be of value when combined with others and possibly with a fungicide treatment. The experimenter must choose a test which will allow expression of the resistance in question. Resistance to spore deposition is a good example of this. The question of test plot size relative to external inoculum density is important in assessing genotypes as the true level of resistance of a genotype is best assessed from plots which generate their own inoculum internally, i.e. are insulated from outside influence. Circular spread plots have been designed for this purpose in which the genotype is sown in rows in concentric circles 30 cm apart by means of a Planet Jr. The plots are centrally inoculated and spread of disease from the centre is monitored. This has been employed successfully for various cereal rusts. The plots are isolated from each other to minimize inter-plot interference and so the method is expensive in terms of land requirements and can only be used for correspondingly valuable experimental or breeding material.

Further reading
Measuring Plant Disease *by E. C. Large, in* Annual Review of Phytopathology, 4; *9, 1966*
Assessment of Plant Diseases and Losses *by W. C. James, in* Annual Review of Phytopathology, 12; *27, 1974*
Plant Pathologists' Pocketbook *Commonwealth Mycological Institute, Kew, England, 1968*
Statistical Methods in Agricultural Research, *by T. M. Little and F. J. Hills, Univ. of California, Davis, 1972*

Chapter 5 **Resistance breeding techniques**

Why breed for resistance?

The use of inherited host resistance is commonly the preferred method of control of cereal pathogens with the notable exception of those which are seed-borne where chemical seed treatments are standard practice. There are many advantages to the use of genetic resistance to control diseases including simplicity of use by the farmer and the low cost which at present relates only to the cost of varietal development. Until recently, the available protectant chemicals required repeated applications and were therefore uneconomic. In addition, they also contributed to residue problems in the environment. However, the recent development of systemic fungicides, which are much more effective, offers the possibility of their integrated use with host resistance. The design and development of a resistance breeding programme should, therefore, take into account other available control measures and their complementation with the kind of host resistance available.

The first step to be taken before embarking on a breeding programme for resistance is to assess the importance of disease in the region for which the variety is to be bred. This becomes important because, by discarding susceptible genotypes from a segregating population, there is a reduction in the number of plants on which selection for yield, quality and agronomic characters can be practised. This is illustrated in Fig. 5.1 which shows the number of plants remaining after susceptibles have been discarded from an F_2 population of 500 plants segregating for differing numbers of independent, dominant factors for resistance. This reduction would be even greater if resistance factors were linked in repulsion or if recessive factors were operating. However, the loss of potential yield from the cross may be relatively small as depicted in Fig. 5.2 which has been drawn from values calculated on the basis of an F_2 population of 500 plants in which yield is normally distributed and in which, it is assumed, there is no linkage between resistance and deleterious genes. These losses of potential yield are therefore minimum values in that deleterious genes are commonly associated with resistance factors introduced from unimproved genotypes and there is some evidence that yield factors are not distributed normally but are negatively skewed. Fig. 5.2 illustrates that selection for each resistance gene may carry only a small yield penalty and the benefit of that resistance can be expected to more than compensate for this. However, the yield penalty may well exceed these minimum calculated values and the importance of incorporating resistance must be weighed carefully.

In determining the importance of disease, use will be made of disease surveys, local knowledge and an appreciation of disease problems in similar geographic

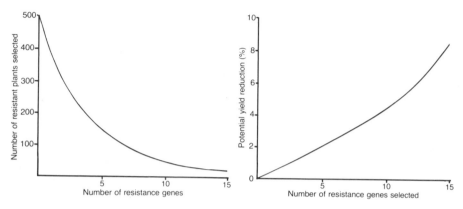

Fig. 5.1 *Effect of selection for resistance genes on F₂ population size.*

Fig. 5.2 *Reduction in potential yield improvement from an F₂ population of 500 plants resulting from selection for resistant plants only.*

regions. As much basic information on the biology, life and disease cycles and **epidemic potential** of the pathogen should be obtained as the recorded disease incidence may relate to the use of resistant varieties or unfavourable climate in which case the importance would be underestimated. Alternatively, current varieties may be highly susceptible, in which case, the importance may be overestimated. Once it has been decided that resistance must be incorporated the next question is, how much and what type of resistance should be used and what should be the strategy of use?

The type and level of resistance required will depend on the nature of the disease, whether it is seed-, soil-, or air-borne, whether it develops early or late in the season, whether it occurs regularly or occasionally etc. However, even though these are important considerations, the actual approach will depend on the availability of resistance and, therefore, the first stage of a breeding programme is the search for sources of resistance that will give effective and stable control of disease.

In this initial search, the net should be cast wide to include old indigenous varieties, exotic varieties, wild forms, related species and genera etc. and any expression of resistance should be investigated. Later, the most useful types will be selected. There then follows one of the most painstaking and most vital aspects of the work. That is the characterization of resistance. Because of the large plant numbers often involved, the initial screen for resistance may not be very precise but attempts to make the test as relevant as possible should be made. A seedling test and a field test of adult plants uniformly inoculated with a range of pathogen variants should be made. Following this initial screen, a number of promising types may be selected for more detailed characterization to determine the expression of resistance, genetic control, environmental lability etc. These results will determine how useful the resistance is and, of equal importance, whether it can be manipulated in a breeding programme. Once the breeder has decided what type of resistance to use he must then utilize it to the greatest effect and the way in which he does this will be governed by the overall strategies to be used in the deployment of that resistance in the cultivation of the particular crop.

This entire procedure is long and involved and, because of the ability of most major cereal pathogens to evolve forms capable of overcoming many host resistances, it has been a recurring effort. The central challenge in disease resistance breeding is the development of varieties with resistance that is both stable and effective over the lifetime of the variety.

Sources of resistance

In the case of many of the more common diseases of cereals, a range of resistance is to be found in cultivated varieties which has been assembled following years of observation and testing and many have not yet been exploited fully. Resistance from varieties of the same species is of most direct use to breeders as the introduction of undesirable 'wild' characters into the gene pool is minimized.

There are a number of world collections or germplasm banks to which breeders have access for sources of disease resistance and other characters. The most well established is that of the United States Department of Agriculture, Plant Genetics and Germplasm Institute, Beltsville, Maryland and more recently other regional centres have been founded. For small grain cereals there is the Institute Pflanzenbau FAL 33, Braunschweig, Bundesallee 50, West Germany and for the Middle East region the Agricultural Research and Introduction Centre, P.O. Box 9, Menemen, Izmir, Turkey has been founded. The centre for maize germplasm and also small grain cereals is CIMMYT, Apartado 61641, Londres 40, Mexico 6, D.F., Mexico. In addition there is the Consiglio Nationale delle Richarde, Laboratorio del Germoplasma, Via Amendola 165/A, 70126 Bari, Italy. Many different collections have been screened for resistance to various diseases and the selected genotypes assembled in disease nurseries which are available to be grown by co-operators thus giving information on the performance of resistance at different locations and providing breeding material for those locations. These nurseries are co-ordinated by various agencies. For example, the Plant Genetics and Germplasm Institute of the U.S.D.A. co-ordinates an International Oat Rust Nursery, International Spring and Winter Wheat Rust Nurseries and a Wheat *Septoria* Nursery. In Europe, the Institute of Phytopathological Research, Wageningen, Netherlands organizes a wheat and barley yellow rust (*P. striiformis*) nursery and the Foundation for Agricultural Plant Breeding at the same location co-ordinates European Barley Disease Nurseries. These collections form the vital basis for cereal improvement programmes and the need to conserve germplasm is becoming critical with the domestication and cultivation of the geographic regions which are the centres of origin and diversity of the cereals. These collections are valuable as sources of different types of resistance to common diseases and also for resistance to hitherto unimportant diseases.

In some situations, for example, where physiologic specialization in the pathogen has depleted the stock of available effective resistance, it may be necessary to search in related species and genera. In these instances there are often genetic and cytological barriers which prevent normal hybridization with the cultivated species and special techniques have to be developed to overcome these difficulties. However, one major difficulty is that resistance factors transferred from alien germplasm are often accompanied by undesirable genetic material. Also, in most instances where resistance has been successfully transferred, particularly into bread wheat (*Triticum aestivum*) with regard to rust resistance, the pathogen has subsequently been able to overcome the resistance. However, the techniques developed offer exciting possibilities of introducing new germplasm into cultivated species and more success may be achieved in future if different types of resistance are transferred.

If all these sources fail to reveal any satisfactory resistance there is one other alternative available and that is the artificial creation of novel resistance. Much attention has recently been given to attempts at artificially inducing mutations for resistance to disease especially by the International Atomic Energy Authority (IAEA). The results to date have not been particularly promising, but this is not perhaps surprising when one considers that natural host resistance is the result of thousands of years of evolution and the probability of emulating this process by the use of damaging physical and chemical agents must be fairly low. There is available a number of physical and chemical agents which will induce heritable genetic changes and these include the ionizing and non-ionizing radiations. Alpha particles and neutrons are densely ionizing and have a primarily mechanical action resulting in gross chromosome rearrangements and breakages. X-rays and gamma rays are less densely ionizing and produce fewer chromosomal alterations and more point mutations. Ultra-violet light is a non-ionizing radiation which has an even greater tendency to produce point mutations. Chemical mutagens include mustard compounds, alkylating agents and purines and their derivatives and some of these allow more precise point mutations to be effected. Ethyl methane sulphonate (EMS) is one of the most commonly used today. However, the amount of control is generally small.

The disappointing results of attempts to induce resistance artificially can be understood when one considers the mechanisms of host resistance to biotrophic pathogens. Resistance is commonly governed by dominant alleles, the biochemical products of which are believed to interact with the gene products of dominant avirulence alleles in the pathogen. The vast majority of artificially induced mutations cause loss of function (recessiveness) but to produce resistance would require the creation of a functional allele. However, the mode of action of mutagenic agents is destructive rather than constructive. It is significant that the successful induction of resistance to *E. graminis* in barley resulted from the creation of recessive (ml-o) mutants (Jørgensen, Induced Mutations for Disease Resistance in Crop Plants. IAEA Vienna, 1976) and one must conclude that the biochemical basis for resistance in this instance is different to that postulated from the gene-for-gene hypothesis. Similarly, Konzak (Brookhaven Symposia in Biology **No. 9**, 157, 1956) was able to induce resistance to *Helminthosporium avenae* in Victoria oats, the susceptibility of which was due to sensitivity to a toxin which was inherited as a simple dominant factor (associated with resistance to crown rust). Again, in this case resistance to the toxin was associated with a loss of genetic function. Conversely, susceptibility has commonly been induced by mutagenic agents and McIntosh has recently shown that a range of nonsense and mis-sense mutations were produced at the Lr 20 and Sr 15 locus in wheat by EMS (McIntosh R.A., The Use of Induced Mutations for Improving Disease Resistance in Crop Plants, IAEA Vienna, 1977).

Characterization of resistance

It is often convenient, if not necessary, to characterize resistance in two stages. Commonly, the initial screen involves large numbers of genotypes and so precise detailed tests are not possible. An initial field assessment and a greenhouse test on seedlings is desirable and the pathological techniques of inoculation and assessment are discussed in Chapter 4. The seedling greenhouse test should involve a number of different cultures or races of the pathogen to assess the specificity of resistance. Seedling tests are usually qualitative but some quantitative assessments can be made by, for example, measuring the generation time which often indicates **partial resistance** to foliar pathogens such as rusts and mildews. These tests are usually **monocyclic** and measure response to a single inoculation and as such do not measure the effects of resistance on rate of disease increase. Therefore, a field test should be carried out in conjunction with the seedling tests. For foliar pathogens, this will allow assessments of rates of disease increase and measurements of host resistance which change as the plant develops. For the **compound interest diseases**, at least two assessments should be made in spreader bed nurseries preferably on upper and lower leaves. Variable reactions on a given leaf should also be noted which, in the rusts, involve either a random distribution of different pustule types (X-reaction) or a gradation of decreasing compatibility from tip to base (Y-reaction) or *vice versa* (Z-reaction). At this stage, one hopes that new types and expressions of resistance will come to light and so the importance of open minded careful observation cannot be over emphasized. For the **simple interest diseases** such as the smuts, bunts and ergot, a monocyclic test is adequate and the assessment may be qualitative, as with the smuts, or quantitative, as with ergot. For compound interest diseases, resistance may be measured by the rate of disease increase, described mathematically as a regression coefficient or as the apparent infection rate (r) of van der Plank (Plant Diseases: Epidemics and Control. Academic Press. 1963) or by the actual amount of disease present at a given time.

These initial tests will allow selection of those genotypes which appear to show the best types of resistance for the particular breeding procedure in mind. They may in themselves be adequate but, more usually, further detailed characterizations will need to be carried out. This should at least involve inheritance studies and assessments of environmental lability of resistance. In particular, temperature can affect the expression of resistance not only of the partially expressed types but also of the **hypersensitive** types. This information, together with that gained previously on race specificity and expression of resistance at different host growth stages, is an essential preliminary to the necessary genetic studies. All of this information can then be used by the breeder when planning how to handle the resistance in a breeding programme.

Genetic information is essential to enable the resistance to be handled most effectively. Recessive genes are difficult to manipulate in backcross programmes and selecting for them also reduces the population size considerably in pedigree systems. Polygenic resistance also poses problems in breeding programmes. Allelic relationships also need to be elucidated as two different resistance alleles at the same locus cannot be combined into one true breeding line of an inbreeding species but they can be used in F_1 hybrid maize, wheat or barley varieties. Alternatively, allelic resistances may be combined in a heterogeneous multiline variety. Genetic linkages with undesirable characters or undesirable pleiotropic effects of the resistance genes should also be determined.

Detailed characterization of resistance mechanisms is often helpful in determining the best screening procedure to be adopted and also, histological and biochemical studies of resistance may bring an understanding of the basis of resistance that will allow predictions to be made concerning its stability and effectiveness. Much of the detailed analysis that has been carried out has been for the rusts and mildews. Resistance can theoretically operate at any stage in the infection cycle beginning with spore deposition. Wheat varieties have been found to differ in their efficiency in trapping uredospores of *P. recondita*, leaf hairs being associated with high efficiencies. Germination of spores on the leaf surface may be reduced and resistance to penetration of oats by *Erysiphe graminis avenae* has been described which is expressed more in upper leaves and therefore has an adult plant component (Carver & Carr. Ann. appl. Biol. **86**; 29, 1977). An adult plant resistance to *P. striiformis* has been described for some wheat varieties which is expressed more in the recently produced leaves. Colony growth rates were reduced and there was hypersensitivity and general necrosis and browning (Mares and Cousen, Physiol. Plant Path. **10**; 257, 1977). The **adult plant resistances** of oats and wheat to *E. graminis* have similar characteristics and appear to be **race non-specific**. However, other adult plant resistances to *P. striiformis* and *P. recondita* in wheat have proved to be highly race-specific. Resistance may express more in the older leaves of plants (mature tissue resistance) rather than in younger ones and some resistances to *P. coronata* in oats have proved to be of this former type. The majority of these host resistances appear to operate after spore germination and relate to reduced amounts or rates of penetration, establishment, colonization or sporulation. A *partial resistance* to *P. hordei* operates in some barley genotypes (Clifford Proc. 5th European and Medn. Cereal Rusts Conf. Prague. **1**; 75, 1972) resulting in the relatively slow development of fewer, smaller pustules of a compatible type from a given quantity of inoculum with little or no evidence of a necrotic host response. Such partial resistances are called *slow mildewing* or *slow rusting* types but these are not mechanistic concepts and only describe the epidemiological consequences of resistance.

The effectiveness of such partially-expressed resistances in preventing yield losses must be determined before they are used. For example, a disease that is damaging during the early development of the crop will not be controlled effectively by adult plant resistance. However, Shaner and Finney (Phytopath. **67**; 1051, 1977) concluded that the partial resistance to *E. graminis* in Knox wheat remained effective even under high nitrogen regimes and Jones (Ann. appl. Biol. **86**; 267, 1977) came to similar conclusions for oat mildew as did Statler, Watkins and Nordgaard. (Phytopath. **67**; 759, 1977) for *P. recondita* in spring wheat. Some types of resistance may not be expressed under the test conditions prevailing and, in particular, the expression of partial resistance may relate to the amount of external inoculum relative to the test plot size in a spreader bed nursery. If this balance is unfavourable, resistance may be swamped and only certain types of resistance may be expressed and these may not necessarily be the desirable ones. To obtain an accurate assessment of the level of resistance of a potential donor genotype, large field plots which generate their own inoculum may need to be used. Such tests should involve a number of locations and environments and a range of pathogen cultures should be employed. For all these above reasons, the identification of desirable resistance donors becomes more and more the province of pathological research which should function in close association with active breeding programmes.

In addition to true resistance, the response of a plant may be influenced by its morphology. The closed flowering habit of certain spring barley varieties prevents the entry of loose smut spores thus providing an effective escape mechanism. Some dwarf varieties of barley and wheat are particularly susceptible to *Rhynchosporium secalis* and *Septoria* spp. respectively because the splash-borne nature of the spores allows rapid movement of the pathogen up the plant. Similarly, a prostrate juvenile growth habit allows movement of the pathogen from plant to plant in surface water. Varieties that mature early may escape severe disease even though they are susceptible. The trend in cereal breeding has been for the development of early maturing varieties for ease of harvesting and in Britain this has resulted in stem rust becoming rare on wheat and oats as uredospores arrive from southern regions of Europe too late to infect the ripening crop. Mention should also be made of tolerance, the ability of a host to endure severe pathogenic attack without apparent yield loss. It is a character that is difficult to measure and manipulate and has the major disadvantage of not reducing field inoculum potential. However, as Schafer states in his review of the phenomenon (Ann. Rev. Phytopath. **9**; 235, 1971) it may be useful as an undergirding of true resistance.

The characterization of resistance should therefore be carried out as precisely as possible to ensure that the breeder will be using the best available resistance in the most effective way possible. The numbers of plants usually involved in a breeder's segregating population will mitigate against his selecting correctly for resistance, especially that of the partial type, on every occasion. Therefore, final precise tests must be carried out on his selected potential varieties as part of their general evaluation for agricultural use to ensure that the parental level of resistance has been recovered.

Utilization of resistance

Host breeding systems
Wheat, oats and barley species that are cultivated are inbreeding or self-pollinated and this results in offspring being genetically similar to the parent and, following artificial hybridization, in the segregation of a population into homozygous plants. Hybridization is effected artificially by the breeder through the removal of the anthers from the floret before they are mature (i.e. pollen bearing) and then transferring pollen from the ripe anthers of another plant to the feathery stigmas of the emasculated floret. The fertilized inflorescence is then covered with a transparent bag to prevent further unplanned pollination (Fig. 5.3). The procedure is similar for wheat, oats and barley.

Rye and maize are naturally outbreeding crops and cross-pollination is therefore the rule. A plant population is heterogeneous and the individual plants are heterozygous. If inbreeding is induced, loss of plant vigour or inbreeding depression results. In maize, the male and female flowers are separated on the same plant (**monoecy**) and so pollination can be artificially controlled by the physical removal of the male inflorescence and transfer of pollen to receptive female inflorescences. Alternatively, the growing together of genetically or cytoplasmically controlled male sterile plants with selected male fertile pollen donors is used to produce desired hybrids.

Cytotaxonomy
Wheat exists as an **allopolyploid** series with a basic chromosome number of $x = 7$. The most widely grown wheat is *Triticum aestivum*, the bread wheat, which is

Trimming tip of flower.

Detail of flower showing anthers (3) and feathery stigmas (2).

Removal of immature anthers (emasculation).

Ripe anther from pollen donor (male parent).

Pollination of emasculated female parent.

Developing hybrid seeds.

Fig. 5.3 *Stages in the artificial hybridization of spring barley.*

hexaploid with genomes designated AABBDD. *T. compactum* (club wheat) has a similar genomic composition but is less widely grown whereas the important macaroni or durum wheat (*T. durum*) is tetraploid, AABB. The genomic relationships of cultivated wheats and their related wild species are given in Table 5.1 which is based on Feldman (Wheats: in 'Evolution of Crop Plants', ed. N. W. Simmonds. Longmans, 1976). These relationships indicate the ease with which the species can be intercrossed and the expectancy of genetic exchange between species of the same or different ploidy.

Series	Wild	Cultivated	Genomes
Diploid $2n = 2x = 14$	*T. speltoides*		SS ($=$GG?)
	T. bicorne		S^bS^b
	T. longisimum		S^lS^l
	T. tauschii ($=$ *Ae squarrosa*)		DD
	T. monococcum		AA
	var. *boeoticum*	var. *monococcum*	
Tetraploid $2n = 4x = 28$	*T. timopheevi*		AASS(GG?)
	var. *araraticum*	var. *timopheevi* ⎫	
	T. turgidum		AA BB
	var. *dicoccoides*	var. *dicoccum* ⎬	
		durum	
		turgidum	
		polonicum	
		carthlicum ⎭	
Hexaploid $2n = 6x = 42$		*Triticum aestivum* ⎫	AA BB DD
		var. *spelta*	
		macha ⎬	
		vavilovii	
		aestivum	
		compactum	
		sphaerococcum ⎭	

Table 5.1 *Genomic relationships of cultivated wheats and related wild species.*

Oats also exist as an allopolyploid series with a basic chromosome number of $x = 7$. Cultivated forms occur at the diploid level ($2n = 2x = 14$) and include *Avena strigosa*, *A. brevis* and *A. nudibrevis*. The only cultivated tetraploid ($2n = 4x = 28$) is

A. abyssinica whilst, in the hexaploids ($2n = 6x = 42$), there are *A. nuda, A. byzantina* and *A. sativa*, the latter two being of greatest commercial importance. Wild relatives exist at the three ploidy levels and their genomic relationships are summarized in Table 5.2 although with some of these, the relationships have not been fully elucidated. The AABB tetraploids appear to have their origin in the diploid *A. wiestii – A. hirtula* group as evidenced by the homeology between the A, As and B genomes. The hexaploid species *A. fatua, A. sterilis, A. sativa, A. nuda,* and *A. byzantina* all share the same karyotype AACCDD. A detailed study, from which the data of Table 5.2 was abstracted, is to be found in Cytogenetics of Oats by Rajhathy and Thomas (Misc. Pub. Gen. Soc. Canad. No. 2, 1974).

Series	Wild	Cultivated	Genomes
Diploid $2n = 2x = 14$	*A. pilosa* A. clauda		CpCp
	A. ventricosa		CvCv
	A. prostrata		ApAp
	A. wiestii	*A. strigosa*	AsAs
	A. hirtula		
	A. longiglumis		A_lA_l
	A. damascena		AdAd
	A. canariensis		AcAc
		A. brevis A. nudibrevis*	AsAs
Tetraploid $2n = 4x = 28$	*A. barbata* A. vaviloviana*	*A. abyssinica*	AA BB
	A. magna A. murphyi*		AA CC ?
Hexaploid $2n = 6x = 42$	*A. sterilis* A. fatua*	*A. sativa* A. byzantina* A. nuda*	AA CC DD

Table 5.2 *Genomic relationships of cultivated oats and wild related species.*

Barley   In its cultivated form (*Hordeum vulgare*), it is a diploid with $2n = 2x = 14$. The wild form, usually designated as *H. spontaneum*, is cytogenetically indistinguishable from *H. vulgare* and they cross readily although it has the brittle rachis common in wild cereals. Crosses between *H. vulgare* and other *Hordeum* spp. are highly sterile, e.g. *H. murinum* and *H. bulbosum*.

Rye   Apart from artificial polyploids, all *Secale* spp. are diploid ($2n = 2x = 14$). The taxonomy is confused. There is a group of annual weeds including *S. ancestrale*, *S. dighoricum*, *S. segetale* and *S. afghanicum* which are cytologically similar to each other and to the cultivated *S. cereale* and a second group of wild perennials which are considered by some as variants of the single species *S. montanum* (see 'Rye' by G. M. Evans in Evolution of Crop Plants. ed. N. W. Simmonds, Longmans, 1976).

Maize exists only as the one species *Zea mays* ($2n = 20$) although some consider that the closely related teosinte is a subspecies designated *Zea mays* ssp. *mexicana* although it is more commonly referred to as *Euchlaena mexicana*. It has the same chromosome number as *Z. mays*, crosses readily with it and grows with it in Mexico and Guatemala where reciprocal introgression is thought to occur and this is borne out by the similar chromosome morphology of the two. *Tripsacum* spp. are thought to be related but their chromosome numbers are in multiples of $x = 18$ and although hybridization occurs, progeny of *Tripsacum* × *Zea* are variously sterile.

Breeding methods

The genetical principles and methods adopted in breeding for resistance to disease in cereals do not differ from those employed for any other trait. Indeed, in many instances, resistance is only one of many characters for which the breeder will be selecting in an integrated programme. These principles are discussed fully in plant breeding texts such as those of R. W. Allard (Principles of Plant Breeding, John Wiley, 1960) or W. Williams (Genetical Principles and Plant Breeding, Davis, 1964). The methods adopted are governed by the breeding system, either natural or imposed.

Self-pollinated species
1 Mass selection and pure line selection   These methods were practised on primitive populations or land race varieties which often consisted of heterogeneous mixtures of pure lines. It is not a particularly efficient method because natural selection would have resulted in the elimination of the most susceptible genotypes. However, even modern varieties are only pure for the characters for which they have been selected and they may comprise a mixture of types which differ quantitatively or qualitatively for resistance. This variation may be exposed by a pathogen or pathogenic race to which the variety was not subjected during breeding.

2 Bulk hybrid method   A bulk hybrid population is generated following the planned hybridization of two or more parents. The resulting F_1 progeny are treated as a bulk population on which selection is practised. Selected seed is again bulked and re-selected and this process is repeated for six to eight generations after which pure lines are selected. The populations are subjected to natural or artificially induced epiphytotics and selection of resistant plants made either by direct observations of disease levels or by harvesting and sieving the grain to discard small, light and shrivelled grain. This method allows the selection of tolerant types in a susceptible population.

This method may also be used to select for resistance in a **composite cross** population. In this case, a range of varieties are assembled, some of which are male sterile, which allows the population to perform like an outbreeder in which repeated cycles of hybridization occur in each generation. The method is particularly useful for polygenically controlled resistance where the accumulation of desirable resistance genes into one genotype is enhanced by selection of resistant lines under epiphytotic conditions in each generation. This method will be used more if polygenic resistance increases in importance in the future.

3 Pedigree method   This is the most common method of selection in a segregating population resulting from planned hybridization. The parents are selected for their disease resistance and other characteristics which, when combined, will produce a plant with the most desirable characteristics of both parents and possibly exceed them through **transgressive segregation**. The method allows the identification and selection of specific desirable segregants and allows their relationships to be traced. Following hybridization, selection is practised on individual F_2 plants, mainly for qualitatively expressed characters such as disease resistance, plant height etc. Seed of a single head from the selected F_2 plants is sown the following year in drills and the selection procedure repeated on the F_3 plants. Individual heads are selected and sown again in drills giving a head-row selection procedure. Homozygosity of selected progenies is reached by $F_7 - F_8$ and seed of these lines is increased so that larger replicated plots can be assessed for yield, disease resistance and other characters. Susceptible spreader varieties may be interspersed in the early generation breeding nurseries and in the later generations, sufficient seed is available for tests in disease nurseries. Potential new varieties will be assessed precisely in larger plots at different locations (see Fig. 5.4).

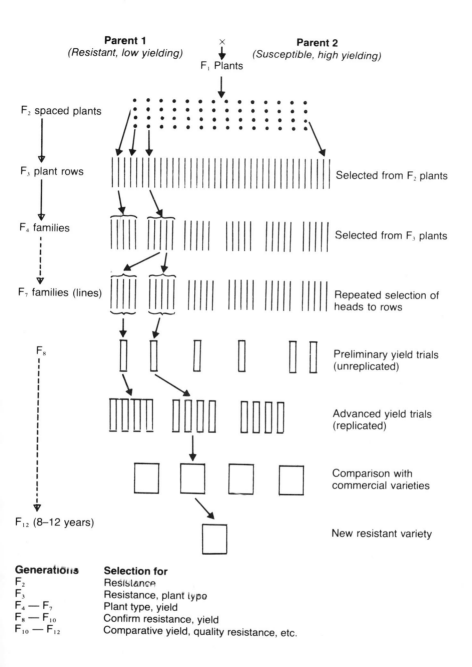

Fig. 5.4 *Schematic representation of pedigree breeding method.*

109

4 Backcross method   This method is of value for the incorporation of a specific simply inherited trait into an otherwise desirable variety. It is useful for the rapid incorporation of resistance as a 'fire brigade' measure but suffers from the disadvantage of conservatism in that no yield improvement above the recurrent parent can be made. To be successful it must therefore be executed rapidly. Where resistance is governed by a single dominant gene, the F_1 hybrid of the chosen parents is crossed with the agronomically desirable parent. The resulting F_1 plants are tested with the specific pathogen and the homozygous recessive plants are discarded. One of the heterozygous resistant plants is crossed again with the recurrent parent (the first backcross) and the procedure is repeated for from 6 to 10 backcross genera-tions. The rate of recovery of the quality parent genotype depends on linkage and selection for the quality parent's phenotype. If resistance is inherited as a recessive trait, the backcross F_1's must be selfed and progeny tested and the homozygous plants used for further backcrossing. This method is applicable to the development of near-isogenic lines of a variety differing only in specific resistance genes for development of **multiline** varieties. If two or more resistances are to be incorporated, single gene lines can be developed and then intercrossed to produce a **multigene** variety. It is also a method that has been used to transfer specific resistance genes to cultivated varieties from related wild species.

5 Alien gene transfer   Wild relatives of cultivated species represent a valuable source of resistance to diseases but the cytogenetic barriers to intercrossing that exist often make transfers difficult to achieve. There are several levels at which alien germplasm may be introduced to a cultivated species. An entire genome may be added as is the case with Triticale, which is an amphiploid derived from either tetraploid or hexaploid *Triticum* spp. crossed with *Secale cereale* resulting in either hexaploid or octaploid *Triticale* spp. Alternatively, individual alien chromosomes may be added to or substituted for specific chromosomes of the cultivated species. Rye chromosomes have been added to and substituted for *T. aestivum* chromosomes and the more stable forms involve a single pair of chromosomes. At a third level, only part of the alien chromosome is substituted for or added to the recipient chromosome (reciprocal or non-reciprocal translocation) and, finally, only specific genes are transferred to the cultivated species. The latter situation is the ideal to be aimed for because the uncontrolled addition of other alien genetic material usually leads to the disruption of genetic harmony in the cultivated species and the appearance of undesirable characteristics. The precision of genetic transfer is governed by the cytological and genetic relationships of the species involved (see Tables 5.1, 5.2 and 5.3) and various special techniques have been developed to overcome these barriers. The whole subject has been recently reviewed by Knott and Dvorak (Ann. rev. Phytopath. **14**; 211, 1976) and only a summary of this extensive and important area can be given here. Most work has been done on the transfer of disease resistance to the bread wheats (*T. aestivum*) and to a lesser extent to oats (*A. sativa*) and barley (*H. vulgare*) and examples of successful transfers are given in Table 5.3.

Bread wheats *Triticum aestivum* ($2n = 6x = 42$. AA BB DD)

Donor species	Ploidy	Resistance to
Aegilops speltoides	$2n = 14$ SS	*Puccinia recondita*
Ae. squarrosa	$2n = 14$ DD	*P. recondita*
Ae. umbellulata	$2n = 14$ C^{u}C^u	*P. recondita*
Ae. comosa	$2n = 14$ MM	*P. striiformis*
Ae. ventricosa	$2n = 28$ DD M^{v}M^v	*Pseudocercosporella herpotrichoides*
Agropyron elongatum	$2n = 70$	*P. recondita, P. graminis*
A. intermedium	$2n = 42$	*P. recondita*
Triticum turgidum dicoccum	$2n = 28$ AA BB	*P. graminis*
T. turgidum durum	$2n = 28$ AA BB	*P. graminis*
T. timopheevi	$2n = 28$ AA SS ($=$ GG)	*P. graminis*
Secale cereale	$2n = 14$ RR	*P. recondita, P. striiformis, Erysiphe graminis*

Oats *Avena* spp. ($2n = 6x = 42$ AA CC DD)

Avena strigosa	$2n = 14$ AsAs	*P. coronata*
A. hirtula	$2n = 14$ AsAs	*E. graminis*
A. ventricosa	$2n = 14$ CvCv	*E. graminis*
A. barbata	$2n = 28$ AA BB	*E. graminis*
A. abyssinica	$2n = 28$ AA BB	*P. coronata*
A. sterilis	$2n = 42$ AA CC DD	*E. graminis, P. coronata*, Cereal cyst nematode (*Heterodera avenae*)

Barley *Hordeum vulgare* ($2n = 14$)

Hordeum spontaneum	$2n = 14$	*E. graminis*
H. laevigatum	$2n = 14$	*E. graminis, P. hordei*

Table 5.3 *Disease resistance factors transferred to cultivated species from wild relatives.*

At its simplest, transfer can be effected from a related species with the same ploidy by backcrossing. In this way, *A. sterilis* has donated rust and mildew resistance to *A. sativa* through backcrossing and chromosome homology has allowed transfer of specific genes. Similarly, *H. spontaneum* and *H. laevigatum* have donated resistance to mildew and brown rust to *H. vulgare.*

Transfer is more difficult between species of the same ploidy but whose chromosomes have diverged. For example, no successful transfers of resistance between *Tripsacum* spp. and *Zea mays* or *H. vulgare* and *H. bulbosum* have been reported.

The most common transfers made have been between species of different ploidy levels and particularly transfers to hexaploid cultivated *Triticum* and *Avena.* Crosses between wheat and rye have resulted in the development of substitution and addition lines. Wheat lines carrying rye chromosome 1R substituted for the wheat chromosome 1B and also natural translocation lines involving 1B/1R have been used extensively in European breeding programmes for their resistance to mildew and rusts. (Zellar, Proc. 4th Intern. Wheat Gen. Symp. 209, 1973). By similar crossing and selection, early workers derived valuable resistant lines from interspecific hybridizations of *T. aestivum* with *T. turgidum* var. *durum* and *T. turgidum* var. *dicoccum.* These include the famous Thatcher, Hope and H44 rust resistant lines.

More sophisticated techniques have been used to improve the fertility of inter-specific hybrids and to increase the amount of genetic exchange between alien chromosomes. **Bridging species** are used to facilitate transfers from diploid to hexaploid forms and the spindle anaesthetic drug colchicine has been of immense value in the production of fertile amphiploids which act as bridging species. The fertile amphiploid is the first step in the development of lines carrying an additional alien chromosome or chromosome piece which is then subjected to irradiation, usually by X-rays or thermal neutrons, to induce translocation of the desired piece of alien chromosome into the recipient cultivated species genome. An irradiation technique was used by Aung, Thomas and Jones (Euphytica **26**; 623, 1977) to transfer resistance from *Avena barbata* ($2n = 28$) to *A. sativa* by the irradiation of a disomic addition line according to the scheme outlined in Fig. 5.5.

Irradiation results in random chromosome breakages and so the technique is imprecise and results in other disruptions and also in the transfer of large blocks of alien germplasm which may be detrimental. A more exciting future possibility is the discovery of genes controlling homologous pairing in hexaploid wheat and oats which should largely eliminate the need for irradiation and which allows more precise

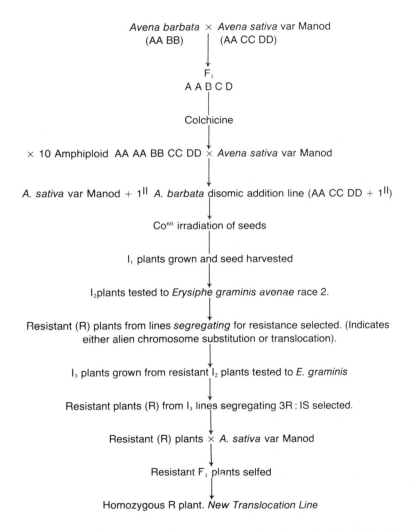

Fig. 5.5 *The transfer of resistance to* Erysiphe graminis *from* Avena barbata *to* A. sativa. *After Aung, Thomas and Jones, 1977.*

genetic exchange between homoeologous chromosomes. In wheat, the gene is located on chromosome 5B and a genotype of *Aegilops speltoides* has been found which suppresses its action. The 5B mechanism has been used to transfer resistance to *Puccinia striiformis* from *Aegilops comosa* to *T. aestivum* by Riley, Chapman and Johnson (Genetic Res. **12**; 199, 1968) and the procedure is outlined in Fig. 5.6. The system has been further developed by Sears (Proc. 4th Internat. Wheat Gen. Symp. p. 191, 1973) by using as the recipient parent, a *T. aestivum* line deficient for chromosome 5B which thus allowed homoeologous pairing between wheat and *Agropyron elongatum* and this resulted in the transfer of resistance to *Puccinia recondita* from *A. elongatum*.

Cross pollinated species
Maize is a naturally outbreeding species and most commercial varieties are derived by controlled interbreeding between desirable genotypes or, more commonly, through the production of specific F_1 hybrids from specific parents chosen for their combining ability as measured by the degree of heterosis exhibited by the F_1. Larger numbers of parents (eight or more) may be intercrossed to produce a synthetic variety which has the advantage of being genetically more complex and therefore more buffered against environmental changes particularly with regard to disease.

The discovery of genetic male sterility in wheat and barley has encouraged breeders to explore the potential of F_1 hybrid varieties but as yet they have very limited commercial use.

Hybrid cereals have certain potential advantages in the control of disease in that resistances which are allelic can be combined in one variety. There are, however, certain disadvantages, one being that if resistance is inherited as an additive character it must be introduced from both sides of the cross to get the full expression and this also applies if resistance is recessive. A disadvantageous side effect in hybrid wheat and barley is that the open flowered habit necessary in such varieties increases the risk of infection by flower-infecting pathogens such as ergot (*Claviceps purpurea*) and smuts (*Ustilago* spp.).

Strategies
In breeding for resistance to disease in cereals, the problems caused by the emergence of physiologically specialized populations of pathogens capable of overcoming such resistance are becoming more acute as larger areas of crops

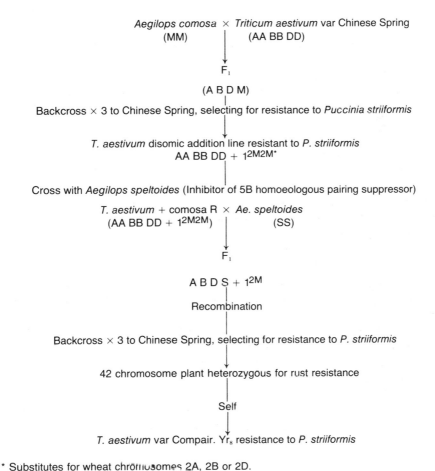

Aegilops comosa × Triticum aestivum var Chinese Spring
(MM)   (AA BB DD)

F₁

(A B D M)

Backcross × 3 to Chinese Spring, selecting for resistance to Puccinia striiformis

T. aestivum disomic addition line resistant to P. striiformis
AA BB DD + 1²M2M*

Cross with Aegilops speltoides (Inhibitor of 5B homoeologous pairing suppressor)

T. aestivum + comosa R × Ae. speltoides
(AA BB DD + 1²M2M)   (SS)

F₁

A B D S + 1²M

Recombination

Backcross × 3 to Chinese Spring, selecting for resistance to P. striiformis

42 chromosome plant heterozygous for rust resistance

Self

T. aestivum var Compair. Yr_8 resistance to P. striiformis

* Substitutes for wheat chromosomes 2A, 2B or 2D.

Fig. 5.6 *The transfer of resistance to* Puccinia striiformis *from* Aegilops comosa *to* Triticum aestivum. *After Riley, Chapman & Johnson, 1968.*

homogeneous for resistance are grown. Although it is an oversimplification, it is convenient to catalogue resistance into two types. Firstly, it is commonly accepted that there is a qualitative resistance, expressed as a hypersensitive host response governed by oligogenes and which is race-specific, differential or vertical. The alternative is a non-hypersensitive, quantitatively expressed resistance governed by polygenes and which is race non-specific, uniform or horizontal.

In this section we consider the breeding objective of stable, effective resistance to cereal diseases through the strategic use of so-called uniform and differential host resistances either singly or in combinations. The integration of host resistance with chemical and cultural methods is discussed in Chapter 6.

Exploitation of stabilizing selection

It has been suggested by van der Plank (Disease Resistance in Plants, Academic Press N.Y., 1968) that certain virulences, although they arise frequently in the pathogen population, confer lower fitness on their carriers which therefore do not compete and occur at lower frequencies than expected. This should confer stability on such host genes which he calls 'strong' genes. There is evidence that stabilizing selection may have operated in the barley yellow rust system in north-west Europe in recent years. There were two common races which occurred during the 1960s, namely, race 23 and race 24. Resistance to race 23 was common in popular varieties and yet the more widely virulent race 24 occurred at a low frequency. The severe epidemic of barley yellow rust in 1961 was caused by race 24 when conditions were particularly conducive to yellow rust build up. However, over a period of some 15 years *Puccinia striiformis* has been considered unimportant on barley. The wide cultivation of the partially resistant cultivar Proctor contributed to this situation, but it may also have been partly due to the lower vigour or aggressiveness of race 24. However, there is recent evidence that race 24 and variants of race 24 are now predominant even though varieties with resistance to race 23 are not now widely grown, suggesting that further changes have taken place in the pathogen population.

The evidence for the operation of stabilizing selection in cereal pathogen populations is limited and rather negative. The conclusion at this time must be that the concept is of little practical significance.

Use of differential resistance where disease spread is slow

Effective differential resistance is being used to control the cereal cyst nematode (*Heterodera avenae*) on barley in north-west Europe on soils where heavy infestations occur. Resistance to the common pathotypes 1 and 2 is effective in Britain because build up and spread of the nematode population is slow. A third pathotype has been detected but its emergence can be monitored and, because of the time scale involved, appropriate breeding action can be taken. The use of differential resistance would also be appropriate to other soil-borne pathogens but its value against splash-borne diseases is being questioned, as evidence emerges that such pathogens can be dispersed rapidly and over quite long distances presumably as aerosols created when rain is accompanied by strong winds, as commonly occurs.

Use of differential resistance as a 'fire brigade' measure
Occasionally, a situation arises where a previously unimportant pathogen increases significantly in severity. This may result from a virulence change in the pathogen population or in the introduction of highly susceptible varieties. Alternatively, a crop may be introduced into a new geographic region where the climate is particularly favourable to a given disease or where the pathogen is already endemic. In these situations, the most rapid way in which resistance can be incorporated is often by backcrossing major gene resistance into the best available varieties. However, the value of this method is doubtful in practice as it would take at least 3 years to develop the backcross lines, assuming that 3 generations per year can be produced, and then at least 3 more years will be required for seed multiplication and yield trials.

Multigene varieties
It has been hypothesised by van der Plank (loc. cit.) that the possession of unnecessary virulence genes causes a depression in fitness so that complex races, with many virulence genes, are at a selective disadvantage compared with simple races which possess few virulence genes. This does not appear to hold for powdery mildew (*Erysiphe graminis*) of wheat or barley where many virulence genes occur with a high frequency in the pathogen population in the absence of corresponding host variation. Similarly, surveys of variation in *P. hordei* on barley in Britain have shown that complex races occur most commonly and in the absence of corresponding host resistance genes and this is also the case in Holland and West Germany. However, the absence of a virulence in the pathogen population, associated with the absence of the corresponding resistance in the host population, does not necessarily imply that the virulence is 'weak'. There are examples of virulences that were readily detected only after the corresponding resistance was widely used and it was only then that these virulences increased rapidly and to a level which brought about the

demise of the variety. The gene Mlas which conditions reaction to *E. graminis hordei* in the spring barley cultivar Sultan is a case in point.

In breeding for resistance to stem rust (*P. graminis*) of wheat it was hoped that the assembly of two or more major genes for resistance into one variety would present the pathogen with a more difficult mutational barrier, but there is little evidence for this having occurred in Australia where the procedure has been vigorously pursued. During the period 1919 to 1938, most wheats were susceptible and the virulence genes corresponding to the resistance genes Sr_8 and Sr_{15} occurred commonly although these genes were not used. It is implied that Sr_8 and Sr_{15} are 'weak' genes although this characteristic is more positively attributed to the corresponding virulence which may be said to be strong. Between 1939 and 1964, varieties with single genes for resistance were common and from 1964 onwards two or three genes were commonly combined in single varieties. There has been a corresponding increase in widely virulent races according to Luig and Watson (Proc. Linn. Soc. N.S.W. **95**; 22, 1970).

In the State of Victoria, losses estimated at 25 million bushels occurred in the 1973–74 season (McCann, J. of Agric., Victoria, **72**; 197, 1974) due to a combination of favourable environment and susceptible varieties. Experience has shown that varieties with single and double gene resistance have quickly lost their resistance because of the appearance of strains of the rust organism which attack them. Perhaps, more significantly, there is also evidence that the growing of susceptible varieties and, in some cases, varieties with single, two- or three- gene resistance can lead to a breakdown in the multiple resistance of other varieties. This does not augur well for the prospects of controlling obligate foliar pathogens of cereals by such methods in the long term. In Canada, it is feared that the multigene resistance to *P. coronata* in oat lines being developed may be put at risk by the independent release of the three resistance genes in question further south in the United States. As a consequence, a system of regional deployment of resistance genes has been proposed and agreed by some oat workers along the 'North American *Puccinia* Path.'

Another dimension to the rational deployment of differential resistance genes has been added by the work of Wolfe (Ann. appl. Biol. **75**; 132, 1973). He has carried out detailed analyses of virulence gene frequencies in the barley mildew population in Britain over a number of years. Based on the observed frequencies of individual virulences, the expected frequencies of combinations of virulences can be calculated and compared with those actually observed. In most instances there is a close correspondence between the expected and observed frequencies of combined virulences but there are exceptions and it is these that are of interest. For example, in barley mildew the combination of virulence genes V-g and V-as occurs at a significantly lower than expected frequency.

The combination of the corresponding resistances should therefore impart stability for resistance to mildew on the varieties carrying those genes. A possible alternative explanation for the observed low frequency of the virulence combination is that the varieties carrying the corresponding resistance combination also have an additional effective gene for resistance which would depress the frequency of the carriers of the combination being analysed. Looked at in another way, the method of analysis could be seen as a way of detecting hitherto unknown resistance genes.

Resistance diversification

The object of diversification is to deploy the available different resistances in a logical manner to present the pathogen with new barriers to infection as it moves in space and time. One way in which this may be achieved is by the deployment of different resistances in winter and spring sown varieties where they are grown in the same agricultural region as is the case with wheat, oats and barley in north-west Europe. In principle, virulences against resistances in the spring sown varieties would be at a low frequency in the population coming from winter sown varieties and virulences against 'winter resistances' would decline in the summer population as they would have no selective advantage in that population. This should reduce the rate of build-up of complex virulences in the pathogen population and allow the resistances to remain effective longer than if used randomly. Such schemes would require co-operation between breeders similar to that which has resulted in the regional deployment of oat crown rust resistances in the U.S.A.

Spatial diversification of varieties has developed into a rational scheme of varietal deployment on a farm scale in England and Wales. Although the important air-borne pathogens are capable of movement over vast distances, the majority of inoculum moves only a limited distance from its source. For example, it is estimated that 99% of the uredospore inoculum of cereal rusts is deposited within a 100m radius of the source. This means that even farm crops are reasonably isolated from each other and if a range of varieties each with different specific resistances are grown on the farm, the migrant population will meet new resistance barriers to which it will carry virulence only at a low level, at least in theory. Bearing these considerations in mind, the National Institute of Agricultural Botany, which makes varietal recommendations for England and Wales, has devised a diversification scheme using wheat varieties for the control of stripe rust (*P. striiformis*) and of barley for the control of powdery mildew (*E. graminis*). Varieties are placed in groups based on their specific resistances and farmers are advised to select varieties from different groups for growing together on the same farm. Varieties from different groups should not cross-infect if the pathogen population is specialized on a particular variety and does not carry additional 'unnecessary' virulences.

Mixtures and multilines

A further development of diversification theory is seen in multiline varieties or varietal mixtures. A true **multiline variety** is developed from the objective of producing lines isogenic except for major disease resistance genes and these component lines are then assembled in varying proportions into a variety. A varietal mixture, on the other hand, is composed of varieties which differ both in disease resistance and other agronomic characters. In terms of the principles of control of the target disease they are similar and may be considered together but they differ significantly in the breeding methods by which they are developed and the consequences of those methods. They also differ in terms of agronomic performance and control of non-target diseases.

How then does such a heterogeneous plant population have its effect on reducing the rate of increase of disease in the population? If one assumes that the individual resistances in the host population are matched only by single individual virulences in specific carriers in the pathogen population (i.e. combinations of virulences are rare) then a multiline/mixture exerts its effects in several ways. Firstly, there is the physical effect caused by the isolation that exists between genotypes with the same resistance gene thus limiting movement of compatible pathogen spores between them, and secondly, there are physical barriers to this movement caused by host genotypes carrying other resistances which will trap the spores thus diluting the spore cloud. The physical effects are therefore of isolation and dilution. There are also physiological effects of the resistance genes themselves which occur where any given host plant is resistant to the majority of pathotypes in a simply structured pathogen population. It has also been suggested that cross protection may operate, in that normally susceptible genotypes acquire resistance following prior infection with avirulent pathotypes which trigger a general resistance response.

Experiments have shown that multiline effects do result in considerable reductions in disease and consequent yield increases but the critical questions regarding the use of mixtures and multilines remain to be answered. The most important of these relate to the evolution of complex races of the pathogen because, if they do evolve rapidly and become dominant in field populations of the pathogen, the multiline effects will be lost and the resistance will be no more stable than that currently used. It may be argued that if, for example, we have 10 major gene resistances each with an individual effective lifetime of 3 years, then a multiline variety of these resistances must have a potential lifetime of 30 years to be of value. The advantages of multilines must be seen to be considerable because of the great difficulties in producing them. The development of true multilines suffers from the conservatism inherent in the backcross method of breeding necessary for their production. There is also the pathological problem that they are otherwise genetically uniform and will be polarized for potential or actual susceptibility to other diseases. For these reasons, there is more current interest in mixtures of existing varieties which also retain diversity of resistance to other diseases and mixtures should certainly be made with these considerations in mind.

A disadvantage of mixtures is that the varieties may not complement each other for other characteristics such as quality, date of maturity, height, etc. and for these reasons a more productive breeding objective may be the development of line mixtures. A line mixture is developed from a cross or crosses involving parents which contribute specific resistances to the target disease or diseases and also desirable agronomic attributes. Selection is made for specific lines carrying the individual resistances and which conform to the desired agronomic type. The lines thus developed would be used to synthesize the line mixture.

The technical problems of multiline production are compounded by the difficulties of variety registration and performance testing but these problems have been overcome in the U.S.A. where multiline oat varieties developed for the control of crown rust (*P. coronata*) have been in use for a number of years following the pioneering work of Browning and Frey (Ann. Rev. Phytopathol. **7**; 355, 1969). More recently, the Dutch winter wheat variety Tumult has been released which is a multiline with regard to yellow rust (*P. striiformis*) resistance.

Use of uniform host resistance

The frequency of a specific virulence or combination of virulences in the pathogen population will depend on mutation rates, dissemination of the genes in the population, survival of carriers and selection pressure from the corresponding host resistance genes. In addition, the pathogenic effect of that virulence on the host population carrying the corresponding resistance will depend not only on these pathogen factors, but also on the residual or background resistance of the variety. It is inferred that such residual resistance, partial in expression, may be race non-specific or uniform. There is no *a priori* reason why non-specific resistance should have a particular genetic, mechanistic or ontogenetic interpretation. Non-specificity may well be found to result from diverse mechanisms in different host : pathogen systems. For example, it is often inferred that adult plant resistance is race non-specific and therefore stable. That this is not necessarily so was shown by the epidemic of *P. striiformis* which occurred on the winter wheat Joss Cambier in Britain in 1971 although the adult plant resistances of wheat and oats to powdery mildew (*E. graminis*) appear to be uniform and stable. The point that emerges is that it is dangerous to make generalizations concerning mechanisms of resistance from one host : pathogen system to another – each must be evaluated on its own merit. Stability may result from the use of certain types of adult plant resistance but not others.

Stability may be achieved through the assembly of components of resistance into one variety. Such components, if under separate genetic control, would be cumulative in action and would present a formidable barrier to the pathogen. Having identified resistances in the field as being potentially valuable, the refined analysis of the mechanisms involved, so that components can be identified and assembled into desirable genotypes, would seem to offer real possibilities for the development of cultivars with stable resistance. Such analyses have, for example, been made by Zadoks (In. Proc. 6th Congress of Eucarpia. Ed. Lupton, Jenkins & Johnson. Cambridge 1972) who has identified different components of resistance to *P. recondita* in wheat. He has carried out computer simulations of epidemics using as input the components of resistance identified and quantified in laboratory tests. The value of this technique is that it indicates which components of resistance will have the greatest effect on the development of the epidemic in the field. The value of a resistance lies not only in its stability but also in its effectiveness.

Experience tells us that the achievement of stable effective resistance to the major epidemic cereal pathogens is unlikely to be realized through the identification and deployment of a specific type of resistance. It therefore seems of increasing importance to combine resistances either into different components of the population or into single genotypes. The former is only now being attempted (mixtures and multilines) and the latter has been used for similar resistances but with limited success (multigene varieties).

The incorporation of hypersensitive resistance together with quantitative resistance may offer an additional means of achieving stability if the technical problems can be overcome. One criticism of the use of major genes of large effect has been that they mask the background response of the carrier. Cultivars with highly susceptible backgrounds will therefore be put at greak risk if the hypersensitive resistance is rendered ineffective by virulent races of the pathogen. To avoid this, differential resistance should be incorporated into cultivars with high levels of 'uniform' resistance. This could be done by backcrossing, but yield levels could not be improved at the same time. The feasibility of selecting for both types of resistance in a segregating population has been demonstrated by Clifford (Trans. Br. Mycol. Soc. **63**; 215, 1974) who showed that there was a correspondence between the number of incompatible or compatible infections sites that developed on barley genotypes inoculated with either avirulent or virulent races of *P. hordei*, i.e. the number of incompatible sites was a measure of the degree of cryptic susceptibility of the genotypes. The technique may have limited use in routine breeding programmes because of the need for precision inoculating equipment. Alternatively, selection could be made in F_3 and F_4 lines. Plants with the hypersensitive resistance could be selected from those segregating lines whose susceptible individuals gave low levels of infection.

How much resistance is required?

Instability of resistance, as measured by the emergence of forms of the pathogen physiologically specialized to grow on hosts carrying that resistance, often results when that resistance has a high degree of expression as is common with the hypersensitively expressed major gene resistances. The breeder and pathologist have focused their attention on this end of the host : pathogen interaction spectrum but one may need to consider partially expressed resistance as being more likely to offer stability. Major epidemics are generally caused by ultra susceptible varieties and if these can be detected and removed from cultivation major progress will have been made. A significant step in this direction has been made by the imposition of minimum standards of resistance to the major diseases of cereals by the National Institute of Agricultural Botany before they will be recommended for use in England and Wales. These minimum standards vary for different diseases in different geographic locations. For example, wheat brown rust (*P. recondita*) is of marginal significance in Britain but it has become more prevalent recently with the cultivation of highly susceptible varieties. An imposition of a standard of susceptibility of the level of earlier varieties would redress the balance and relegate the pathogen to its previous minor status. Undoubtedly, higher resistance levels are required for barley powdery mildew in north-west Europe where it is very well adapted but the problem arises that high levels of resistance mask the background resistance, or more importantly the lack of it, and such high resistance is likely to be overcome by the pathogen. More research is required to find ways of measuring background resistance in the presence of effective hypersensitive resistance and to determine the level of resistance required to reduce the pathogen population to economically insignificant proportions and which will not result in selection of physiologically specialized pathotypes which will render the resistance ineffective.

The identification and prediction of stability

One of the most important questions in plant pathology that remains to be answered is the prediction of how effective and stable a resistance will be when deployed in agricultural situations. It is not required that any resistance be permanent but only that it be sufficiently durable to remain effective during the commercial lifetime of a variety. There are several approaches to the solution of this problem.

Pathogen studies

Most of the above discussion has emphasized host resistance although stability of resistance naturally implies stability in the pathogen population. It is therefore necessary when studying host resistance to make parallel studies of pathogen variability in relation to that resistance. The concept of 'strong' and 'weak' resistance genes is really a concept of strong and weak virulence genes and, consequently, the rational use of such major genes will require knowledge of mutation rates of corresponding virulence factors and fitness of their carriers. Detailed studies of changing patterns of virulence genes, singly and in combination, as done by Wolfe (loc. cit.) will be necessary for the rational deployment of resistance genes in multigene and multiline cultivars. Studies of pathogen variation in relation to quantitative 'uniform' resistance will aid in predicting its stability. Techniques developed for the evaluation of quantitative resistance can be and have been utilized in such studies. Using such precise techniques, Zadoks (loc. cit.) concluded from a range of tests involving varieties of wheat and races of *P. striiformis* that there seems to be a fluid transition between instances with near-uniform resistance and those with extreme differential resistance, whereas the level of intermediate resistance was more or less race specific.

Quantitative techniques allowed Clifford and Clothier (Trans. Br. Mycol. Soc. **63**; 215, 1974) to identify variation for virulence in *P. hordei* on the non-hypersensitive resistant barley cultivar Vada. Pathogen isolates were detected which produced a similar number of spores per unit area on Vada as on the fully susceptible control cultivar Sultan. The latent period was, however, similar for adapted and non-adapted isolates indicating that this component of the resistance remained effective. This was confirmed when Vada adapted and non-adapted isolates were compared in 5 m circular field plots of Vada. The rates of spread from centrally inoculated foci of infection were similar, indicating that the component of resistance extending the latent period in Vada was sufficient to reduce the epidemic. This observation agrees with the computer simulations of Zadoks which showed variation in latent period to be critical in affecting the progress of the epidemic.

Host resistance studies
The more that is known about the basis of the mechanism of resistance being studied, the greater the probability of being able to predict its stability. Information must be brought together from biochemical, physiological, histological and genetical studies so that assessments of potential stability can be made. A particularly fruitful approach is to study known stable resistances if these can be positively identified as such. The resistance of winter wheat varieties to *P. striiformis* has shown the typical pattern of instability due to race specificity over the last 20 years or so. In contrast, some varieties, the best examples being Cappelle Desprez, have been grown widely for a long time and their resistance has remained stable or durable according to Johnson who has studied these resistances extensively from an historical and genetical point of view. Cappelle Desprez and Hybride de Bersee are susceptible as seedlings and resistant as adult plants to certain races of *P. striiformis* and Johnson and Taylor (Pathology and Entomology Dept. Rep. Pl. Breed. Inst., 1972) concluded that the resistance is durable. The resistance increases on successively produced leaves and is expressed as reduced colony growth rates, hypersensitive cell responses and more general necrosis and browning according to Mares and Cousen (Physiol. Pl. Path. **10**; 257, 1977). It appears to be governed by a relatively complex genetic system located on both arms of the 5BS-7BS chromosome (Johnson and Law. Ann. appl. Biol. **81**; 385, 1975). This entire chromosome can be transferred into other genetic backgrounds by appropriate cytological techniques and the performance of such derived varieties will be followed with great interest.

Assessment of the value of resistance

It has been implied above that much of the resistance which is potentially stable is incomplete in expression either on a single plant basis, e.g. adult plant resistance or on a host population basis, e.g. a multiline variety. Therefore, estimates of the effectiveness of resistance in controlling the disease and thereby conferring a yield advantage must be obtained. Final proof of the value may only come from the performance of the variety in agriculture, but earlier predictive assessments are necessary. For example, a circular spread plot technique was used by Clifford and Schafer to assess the development of *P. coronata* in oat varieties differing in type and composition of resistance.

Estimates of the effectiveness of resistance in controlling epidemics can be inferred from laboratory assessments of various infection parameters or components. Shaner (Phytopath. **63**; 1307, 1973) thus obtained a 'sporulation index' for mildew on Knox wheat. He concluded that the combined effect of reduced colony formation and reduced spore forming capacity indicated that mildew should spread one-third as fast on Knox as on Vermilion and this agreed with differences in infection rate observed in the field.

Conclusions

The incorporation of disease resistance into a varietal improvement programme imposes restrictions on the breeder's capability to select for yield potential parameters. These restrictions increase with the number of resistances being handled and with the complexity of the genetics of resistance. It is therefore of increasing importance that statements be made on the intrinsic effectiveness of the resistance in terms of yield benefit and on the stability of that resistance. The concept of stability relates to the lifetime of the variety.

It has been suggested that stability may be achieved in different ways each worthy of consideration in relation to the particular host : pathogen system in question. Although the use of major gene resistance has had limited success it may be more rationally used in future to better effect. Other types of resistance will, no doubt, come into wider use as they become more clearly understood. However, it would be dangerous to use too rapidly or too extensively, alternative empirical methods without sound knowledge of the mechanisms involved. Hypersensitive resistance which is race-specific has failed to give the results desired, although recent theory suggests a future potential through gene management. The examples cited in the foregoing make one raise questions about this potential. The biological limitations of such resistance are exacerbated by the technical problems associated with gene management to such an extent as to seriously impair their practicability. No doubt the near future will reflect the present trend in the intensification of the empirical approach to breeding for resistance, but a long-term solution to the problem would seem to lie in a better understanding of mechanisms of host resistance and corresponding mechanisms of pathogen variation. The achievement of this goal will be marked by our ability to make positive predictive statements on the stability of resistance.

Further reading

Annual Reviews of Phytopathology *Annual Reviews Inc., California*
Breeding Field Crops *by J. M. Poehlman, Henry Holt, New York, 1959*
Disease Resistance in Plants *by J. E. van der Plank, Academic Press, 1968*
Evolution of Crop Plants *Editor N. W. Simmonds, Longmans, 1976*
Genetical Principles and Plant Breeding *by W. Williams, Davis, 1964*
Principles of Plant Breeding *by R. W. Allard, Wiley, New York and London, 1960*

Chapter 6 **Control of plant diseases**

Objectives

The provision of efficient control measures against cereal diseases relies upon accurate information on both the pathogen life-cycle and the disease epidemiology. Existing control measures vary considerably depending upon the nature of the pathogen, the plant tissue affected and the site of application.

The sites of application are:

a the infected host, **b** the healthy host, **c** the environment.

The choice of method will depend upon preliminary investigation results which will enable the timing of the control measure to coincide with the most vulnerable period in the disease cycle. It is necessary to find out how the pathogen overwinters or how it exists in the intercrop period and how it is dispersed, how it infects and the effect of the many interacting environmental factors. Such information is essential if the control measure is to be precise and efficient. A lack of basic data about the pathogen and its subsequent infection of the plant means that the choice of control measure becomes arbitrary or a blanket approach is adopted with an inevitable reduction in efficiency. To illustrate this principle, differences in the rate of spread of disease can be used. With a disease that spreads rapidly, a chemical control method may be selected especially if any host resistance is liable to be quickly eroded by changes in the virulence in the pathogen population. Where a disease spreads slowly, a cultural method based perhaps on crop hygiene may prove effective although, in some instances, host resistance may be less ephemeral than in the rapidly spreading type of disease.

With such a variety of pathogens and disease situations, it follows that the control measures adopted will be correspondingly diverse. However, it is possible to group the measures according to their underlying objectives:

a exclusion of the pathogen, **b** inoculum reduction, **c** host plant protection, **d** pathogen eradication, **e** adjustment of the environment, **f** increasing host plant resistance.

Control by breeding for resistance has been described in a previous chapter and will be further discussed at the end of this chapter. The other objectives will be seen to be the basis of all the control measures described below which, for convenience, have been grouped according to the method of application:

a Regulatory, **b** Cultural, **c** Biological, **d** Physical, **e** Chemical, **f** Integrated.

There is a certain amount of overlapping between the two systems of classification in that more than one objective may be achieved, or partly achieved by the application of a single method.

In practical terms, control measures must be of economic benefit to the farmer and, it should also be emphasized, they are primarily intended to save crops rather than individual plants. They are applied to the host population as a whole and may be aimed at saving the crop even at the expense of a few individuals. In addition, except in the case of the absolute immunity of the host, control measures are rarely completely effective. In consequence, it may be necessary to embark upon an integrated control programme in which more than one method is used, the methods being complementary and yielding additive benefits. It may also be necessary to carry out the programme for more than one season before the disease is reduced to negligible and acceptable levels.

Regulatory methods

In some countries with a relatively recent history of agricultural development, as for example New Zealand, many of the diseases of major economic importance have been introduced accidentally by some means or other. On entering a country for the first time, a pathogen often encounters host plants which have evolved under conditions which exerted no selection pressure for resistance against the new pathogen. Disease quickly establishes on the very susceptible hosts and epidemics become of common occurrence.

In general, regulatory methods involve legislation to enforce quarantines and inspections. They may also incorporate certification schemes linked to purity, and viability of the seed. Regulatory methods first came into being in the 1870s when plant pathology was in its infancy and the pathogenic nature of some fungi and bacteria was still being elucidated. The overall objective of quarantines and inspection is one of exclusion sometimes to exclude a pathogen from a locality or region but mostly from a country. For example, in many countries, a special permit is required before any cereal seed is imported and all seed imports are subject to quarantine. In the U.S.A., Federal quarantine regulations require that an import permit be obtained from the U.S. Department of Agriculture's Animal and Plant Health Inspection Service because several very destructive pathogens have entered the country undetected on imported plant materials. Examples include black stem rust of wheat (*Puccinia graminis tritici*) and downy mildew of maize (*Sclerospora sorghi*).

The import of barley, oats and rye into the U.S.A. is only restricted from the standpoint of requiring an initial inspection for freedom from pests. Samples of these imports are, however, grown in a detention nursery. Wheat imports to the U.S.A. are prohibited from countries where flag smut (*Urocystis tritici*) is endemic unless a special permit is granted and samples grown in the detention nursery. From other countries, wheat imports are restricted as are barley, oats and rye.

There are no U.K. national plant health restrictions for import and export of cereal seeds although seed consignments leaving the country might need an International Phytosanitary Certification. This states that samples have been, '. . . examined by an authorized officer of the Ministry of Agriculture, Fisheries and Food and found, to the best of his knowledge, to be substantially free from injurious diseases and pests; and that the consignment is believed to conform with the current phytosanitary regulations of the importing country . . .' Within the E.E.C. (European Economic Community), certain minimum requirements exist for the maintenance of quality in seed but as far as health is concerned, the cereal seed directive simply requires that stocks are as free from diseases as possible.

Maize is prohibited from many countries because of certain diseases, downy mildew (*Sclerospora sorghi*) being an important example. Introductions from prohibited countries require a quarantine permit which specifies propagation under special controlled conditions. Most cereal growing countries have the complete spectrum of cereal pathogens already present and quarantines and inspections are

	Minimum	**Higher voluntary standard**
1 Wheat and Barley		
Pre-basic seed	Not more than 0·5% infection	—
Basic seed	Not more than 0·5% infection	Not more than 0·1% infection
Certified seed 1st generation	Not more than 0·5% infection	Not more than 0·2% infection
Certified seed 2nd generation	No standard	No standard
2 Oats		
All categories	No standard	No standard

Table 6.1 *U.K. seed certification standard for loose smut (*Ustilago nuda*).*

mainly precautionary. Inspection and seed testing of cereal grain consignments can still be a useful exercise in determining the level of seed-borne infection and contamination.

Seed certification schemes are now almost universal in Europe and in many other countries. They are mainly concerned with the maintenance of quality in terms of sample purity, minimal numbers of weed seeds, especially wild oats, and germination. They also are a safeguard that the buyer receives the variety he ordered. The U.K. Seed Certification Scheme contains statutory requirements which must be followed to obtain certification and these are listed in 'The Cereal Seeds Regulations, 1976' and 'The Seeds (Registration and Licensing) Regulations, 1974'. For example, it is stated that seed must meet certain standards for ergot sclerotia (*Claviceps purpurea*) and for loose smut (*Ustilago nuda*) infection (see Table 6.1).

For both Minimum and Higher Voluntary standards, the levels are checked by growing control plots. For barley, the embryo method for the detection of infection (Simmonds, Sci. Agric. **26**; 51, 1946) can be used for any grade of seed to obtain an indication of quality before sowing. In addition, for barley and wheat there are minimum requirements for isolation, with more stringent recommended standards and recommendations for seed treatment. For example, it is recommended that crops of a 2-row barley for the production of Pre-Basic, Basic and Certified seed, first generation, should be isolated by at least 50 metres from any crop of a 6-row barley variety and vice-versa; similarly 6-row seed crops of different varieties should be mutually isolated by the same distance. Crops of wheat and barley should be isolated by at least 50 metres from any possible source of infection from loose smut.

Grade of seed	No. samples examined	% loose smut infection			
		nil	0·1–0·4	0·5–2·0	2·0
Basic and Certified seed	400	77·2	22·3	0·5	nil
Multiplication and Field Approved seed	2364	75·8	22·4	1·5	0·3
Commercial and Farmers seed	4728	62·0	28·5	8·0	1·5

Table 6.2 *Embryo infection by loose smut in seed barley samples of eight susceptible varieties, 1970–71 to 1974–75.*

During the period 1970–71 to 1974–75, a voluntary cereal seed scheme was in operation in the U.K. with standards for barley loose smut similar to those now recommended. An indication of the effect of such measures on levels of barley loose smut is provided by the results of embryo tests during this period (Table 6.2). The results are based on 7,500 samples from known grades of seed of eight frequently grown susceptible varieties, examined at the Official Seed Testing Station for England and Wales (P. D. Hewett, personal communication).

Cultural methods

These are aimed primarily at reducing the inoculum and are concerned mostly with the destruction of plant debris which may be harbouring pathogens. The incorporation of such infected plant material into the soil before temperatures drop too low will usually accelerate decomposition and effectively starve out the pathogen. Such practices as early ploughing in of cereal stubble and volunteer plants should be carried out wherever possible even if only for precautionary reasons. This is especially so with such pathogens as *Septoria nodorum* and *S. tritici* on wheat trash and *Rhynchosporium secalis* on barley debris which are known to be able to exist on the host remains during the intercrop season.

For similar reasons, wheat stubble can be burned to destroy the overwintering cleistothecial stage of *Erysiphe graminis*. Crop hygiene also includes such practices as rogueing which takes place during the growing season. Rogueing is more often associated with crops grown for seed where a limit is placed on the number of infected individuals allowed in the standing crop. Such diseases as loose smut in barley (*Ustilago nuda*) and many virus diseases of cereals can be reduced in this way although this reduction may be aimed at seed certification rather than eliminating disease. However, the general practice of rogueing is one to be encouraged wherever possible if only to reduce the amount of potential inoculum.

Theoretically, crop hygiene can be carried out thoroughly and effectively but, unfortunately, removal of plants as they become diseased is often practised without due consideration as to whether the results will be worth while. In many cases, local sources of inoculum may be eliminated but the disease may still enter from distant sources if the pathogen is suited to long-distance dispersal. In addition, the 'law of diminishing returns' operates in respect of the sanitation of many crop diseases. Destroying 90% of the inoculum is no easy task in any situation but the effort to eliminate each additional unit increases alarmingly without a corresponding increase in the return and it must be emphasized that, with pathogens that can multiply rapidly, disease can reach epidemic proportions from very small amounts of inoculum given the right environmental conditions. With the splash-dispersed *Septoria nodorum*, it has been estimated that a severe epidemic can result from an initial sowing of about one thousand infected seeds per hectare (Griffiths and Hann, Trans. Brit. mycol. Soc. **67**; 413, 1976) and this represents only a minute proportion (0·03%) of the sown seeds.

Cultural methods of control also include the *eradication of the pathogen* by rotation. The length of the rotation will vary with the longevity of the pathogen in the absence of the host and may be as short as one year. In the case of the cereal take-all disease (*Gaeumannomyces graminis*), the pathogen is a poor soil competitor and once the host debris, upon which it was overwintering, has disappeared then it too will rapidly diminish. There will, in consequence, be a considerable reduction in the amount of this fungus present in the soil if a one-year rotation free of the appropriate cereal or grass host is practised.

The *eradication of alternative hosts* will also reduce the potential number of infected plants and hence the potential inoculum. Alternative hosts provide the pathogen with a means of overwintering when its economic host is an annual. Many virus diseases of cereals, e.g. barley yellow dwarf virus have weed grasses as alternative host species. Volunteer cereal plants also carry over inoculum of the powdery mildews, rusts and *Septoria* spp. during the 'inter-crop' period and, although this period may only bridge the gap between harvest and the subsequent autumn sown crop, great care should be taken to remove and destroy them.

The *eradication of alternate hosts* has also been recognized as being an efficient method of reducing inoculum. It also serves as a means of reducing the production of new races by genetic recombination in such pathogens as the rust fungi where the sexual stage occurs on alternate hosts. Even before the **heteroecious** nature of the black-stem rust fungus of wheat (*Puccinia graminis tritici*) was demonstrated by De Bary, wheat growers in Europe and America had realized that there was a connection between the barberry and the rust diseases. Many barberry eradication schemes have been introduced, the first in France in 1660, the latest being the continuing scheme which started with the eradication legislation in America in 1918 and which progressively expanded to include almost all the wheat growing states.

The American scheme was very expensive to operate due to the fact that barberry had become widely grown as a decorative shrub in domestic gardens. Even so, by 1942, it was estimated that about 60% of the wheat growing areas were free of barberry after destroying about 300 million bushes. Unfortunately, the scheme never attained complete success due, in part, to the incomplete barberry eradication and also to the long distance dispersal of uredospores from the south where they over-winter. The scheme was economically justified by the reduction in early spring inoculum which resulted in delaying the epidemic with an associated reduction in disease damage. Such schemes should be undertaken wherever possible.

The situation in the United Kingdom is not analogous as *P. graminis tritici* has never been isolated from aecidia on barberry in this country. Presumably, therefore, the alternate host has no epidemiological significance in this instance and eradication schemes would be of no avail. In the event, black stem rust is rarely a problem in the United Kingdom, such disease as does occur usually arriving late and resulting from uredospores blown in from south west Europe and north Africa.

The aim of any sanitation measure is eradication; cultural measures are only partly successful but they do significantly reduce the amount of disease inoculum.

Biological methods

As a practice, biological control is very much in its infancy in so far as few of the known examples have reached commercial significance. Simply defined, it is the reduction of inoculum density or the disease-producing activities of a pathogen or parasite by one or more organisms be they antagonistic or hyperparasitic. Biological control may also be accomplished through the manipulation of the environment to produce an indirect effect. This may be achieved by altering the environment to increase the ability of the host to resist, tolerate, or escape the pathogen. It may be achieved by increasing the capacity of the antagonist as a competitor, parasite or antibiotic producer. It may be achieved by weakening the ability of the pathogen to affect the host or resist the antagonist.

Within the soil, plant pathogens can normally be eliminated or greatly reduced by the superior competition from antagonistic microorganisms which may be at a disadvantage when competing with aggressive saprophytic soil inhabitants. The practice of green manuring, recommended for the control of take-all of cereals (*Gaeumannomyces graminis*) is believed to encourage such soil inhabitants at the expense of the invading pathogen. A reduction of this pathogen can also be produced by inoculating the soil with the hyperparasite *Didymella exitialis*. In this latter case, the hyperparasite not only invades the pathogen hyphae but also releases amino acids that inhibit growth.

Biological control has been primarily directed against soil fungi and root diseases. However, many pathogens which cause diseases of aerial plant parts also spend part of their life-cycle in or on the soil and there are many others which infect aerial plant parts and have no known connection with the soil. Biological control of such pathogens has received much less attention than those which have a subterranean habitat. It may well be that success in this direction will be achieved by the manipulation of epiphytic organisms which are present but do no damage.

Physical methods

Heat treatment is the most common physical control method used against cereal diseases and, even so, it is used only against a very few pathogens. Before the advent of the systemic chemical carboxin, the traditional method of treating wheat seed infected with loose smut (*Ustilago nuda*) was to immerse the seed in cold water for 4–6 hours, to ensure complete wetting, followed by a further immersion at 54°C. for 10 minutes. The timing and the temperatures are fairly critical as the success of the control method is a compromise between destroying the infecting pathogen and destroying both the pathogen and the seed's viability. An alternative to this method has been described by Sharvelle (The Nature and Uses of Modern Fungicides; Burgess & Co. U.S.A. 1961). In this method, the seed is soaked for 4 hours at 15–21°C., drained and then stored in air-tight containers for 70 hours at 21°C. or 30 hours at 32°C. It is then quickly dried before sowing. The mechanism of destroying the fungus is not fully understood but it is thought that during the anaerobic respiration of the wet seed, antibiotic substances are produced which account for the *eradication of the pathogen*. The only other physical method that has been used to any great extent has been the control of *Claviceps purpurea* by the flotation method. Here, the seed is immersed in brine and, with constant stirring, the very light ergots float to the top and can be skimmed off.

Chemical methods

The use of chemicals to control disease is not a recent development. In fact, the early writings of Homer indicate that the Greeks had discovered the beneficial effects of certain chemicals such as the 'all-curing' sulphur although they were unaware of the nature of the maladies of the plants they were treating.

The term control, in this context, requires a little qualification in that it implies that the object of the treatment is to eliminate a population of harmful plant pests whether they are insects, nematodes, fungi or bacteria. Such a sanitary measure would be of obvious value but this is not the major objective of the majority of the chemical control treatments used against cereal diseases at the present time. More often than not, the aim is to reduce the effects by such a degree that the increase in the harvested crop translates into a profit within the farming enterprise. The cost of the chemical, its application and any resulting harmful side-effects must be included when computing the overall return on investments.

Ideally, chemists and pathologists would like a chemical which could be applied as a seed-dressing or be rapidly absorbed by plant roots and which would then protect the growing plant throughout its susceptible period of development and which acts against a wide range of pathogens. A treatment of this nature would revolutionize agriculture although there are associated risks in terms of the possibility of selecting out mutant strains of the pathogen, insensitive to the chemical. This ideal may never be attained and, at present, farmers have to manage with chemicals very much inferior to the ideal. Alternatively, a foliar applied chemical which would be downwardly translocated and act systemically is very much desirable in the fight against disease.

The foundation for the agro-chemical industry was layed by Prévost in 1807 when he controlled bunt of wheat (*Tilletia caries*) by using copper sulphate as a seed treatment. The momentum gathered with the use of lime-sulphur in 1880 by H. Marshall Ward in an attempt to control coffee rust (*Hemileia vastatrix*) and by the discovery of Bordeaux mixture, a copper sulphate and hydrated lime suspension, for the control of vine downy mildew (*Plasmopora viticola*).

These developments, occurring almost simultaneously towards the end of the 19th century, led to a great surge of interest and research into alternative chemicals for use in disease control and into methods for applying such treatments. Very rapidly, by the early 20th century, the theory of seed protection was elucidated, chemical sterilization of soil became an accepted practice and new chemicals such as formaldehyde and mercury compounds entered the arena.

The next milestone was again the result of an accident or, more accurately, the bonus for carrying out a fundamental and painstaking research programme in an extremely thorough manner. In 1934, the Du Pont Company were screening chemicals for use in the vulcanization process of rubber. The theory was advanced that this industrial process had similarities to that of the action of sulphur on fungi. This led to many organic compounds being screened for fungicidal activity. One group of compounds exhibited excellent fungicidal properties. These were derivatives of the hypothetical dithiocarbamic acid and these fungicides still constitute a large proportion of our present-day protectant fungicides. They are known collectively as 'dithiocarbamates'.

This latter group of chemicals was indeed more practical and, in some cases, more efficient than the more traditional copper or sulphur compounds but still the search continued for fungicides with systemic properties. The discovery of such compounds in the 1960s and their rapid adoption by the grower constitutes the latest, and undoubtedly the most exciting milestone in the history of fungicides.

Basically, there are only three approaches to the chemical control of plant diseases:

a The *protection* of the healthy host (*Prophylaxis*).
b The *cure* or *therapy* of the diseased host (*Chemotherapy*).
c The *destruction* of spores or pathogen propagules on the host surface, e.g. seeds (*Disinfestation*).

However, disease control may also be achieved by applying chemicals to the environment. Thus it is that there are three categories of chemical used in plant disease control, the *protectant*, the *eradicant* and the *disinfectant*. There may be large differences between the three types of chemical in terms of molecular structure and constitution. There are also fundamental differences in time and place of application.

The protective value of any compound can be measured by its ability to prevent infections. To be most efficient, the chemical must be present in a high enough concentration of the active form when the inoculum arrives. With airborne pathogens it will not be known when or where the inoculum will land on the host surface. Protectants will therefore require properties of stability, initial retention and adherence and will need to be applied over the whole of the exposed plant surface.

The use of the eradicant (chemotherapy) entails killing the fungus after infection has occurred. The term eradicant is also used commonly to describe compounds which can inhibit the growth of a pathogen after infection has occurred. There are few of these chemicals available and these are limited to the systemic category. A distinction should be made here between the effects of different chemicals on fungi:

a **fungicidal** – the chemical kills the fungus,
b **fungistatic** – the growth of the fungus is inhibited,
c **genestatic** – sporulation of the fungus is inhibited.

Disease control on an agricultural level is concerned with the limitation of the epidemic in a crop rather than the elimination of disease on an individual plant within that crop. This leads to the possibility of using genestatic chemicals to prevent the spread of the pathogen from plant to plant and hence prevent the build-up of an epidemic.

Chemical disinfectants are often applied to the environment immediately surrounding the host plant but this is not yet a practical proposition for the control of cereal diseases. They may also be applied to the plants themselves or, more specifically to seed, in an attempt to inactivate contaminating pathogens. Seed treatments with copper sulphate, formaldehyde, organo-mercurials or a mixture of carboxin and thiram to combat bunt of wheat (*Tilletia caries*) can be considered in this category.

The application of fungicides

Fungicides and bactericides can be applied to the growing crop, to the seed or other planting material and to the soil. Apart from seed dressings, the majority of fungicides in widespread agricultural use are foliage protectants for the control of airborne diseases and the aim is to provide a uniform protective covering to the crop canopy ideally at a time prior to the arrival of the inoculum. The almost flat surface of a cereal crop canopy lends itself to be sprayed or dusted by a variety of machines which are either conventionally operated with ground vehicles or from some form of aircraft.

The progress of tractor and spraying machinery through a cereal field inevitably causes physical damage to the crop and, before the introduction of systemics, the loss of yield that would occur after several applications of a conventional protectant fungicide made this form of treatment uneconomical. The introduction of the 'tramline' system of cultivation has been described in Chapter 1. With the higher cash value of the cereal crop, the use of tramlines to facilitate the application of both herbicides and pesticides has now established this procedure as common practice in many countries.

Spraying is widely practised and is a proven success against many diseases. Dusting is generally less effective and is confined to small scale applications, such as in glasshouses, and is only used on a field scale where water is a factor limiting spraying or where it is inadvisable to use heavy machinery.

There are two kinds of spray machinery in common use. The *high-volume* sprayer is used most where there is plenty of water available as water is the most common carrier or diluent for the formulated product. The sprayer consists of a large tank, perhaps of about 500 l capacity, some method of agitation which will be necessary if the fungicide is insoluble, and a spray boom along which are placed many nozzle outlets. A pump will often be fitted to convey the contents of the tank to the nozzles. The machinery will normally be mounted on the rear of a tractor and will be adjusted to deliver between 400 l and 800 l/ha. The fungicide is applied in this way until the foliage is completely covered and the 'run-off' point achieved. On drying, this gives the characteristic 'drip-tip' pattern on the foliage.

The tendency in agricultural practice, however, has been to reduce the weight of machinery and lessen the problems of water transport by using *low-volume sprayers*. Here, the amount of active ingredient would be the same as with the high-volume sprayer but the volume of fungicide plus carrier is much smaller, perhaps 100 l – 250 l tanks delivering about 150 l/ha. Such applications involve the production of very small droplets by a pumping and pressurization process resulting in an atomization effect. The resulting deposit on the leaves is one of a pattern of discrete droplets of the chemical, very few droplets having coalesced and certainly no run-off reached. There is very little difference in the efficiency of control between either of these spray application methods. Low-volume fungicidal sprays are also often applied from light aircraft or helicopter where control may be achieved when as little as 20 l/ha is delivered.

Various substances can be added to water-based sprays to improve their efficiency. There are several objectives to be achieved. Good distribution and coverage are essential but adherence and tenacity of the deposit are also important. **Dispersing agents** such as water dispersible cellulose derivatives can be added to keep the fine particles of an insoluble fungicide in suspension. Similarly, additives are employed which facilitate contact between the spray and the sprayed surface. Such chemicals are known as **spreaders** and many types of detergents are used for this purpose. An apparent conflict then arises between the effect of the spreader and the loss of the chemical by the possibility of easier removal by rain in the presence of the spreader. In fact, many spreaders, especially those not easily removed by water, enhance retention by improving coverage. However, to aid retention **stickers** can also be added and such substances as oils, natural and synthetic adhesives and pastes fall into this category. It must also be mentioned that many factors affect the sticking quality of fungicides, fine particles being generally more tenacious than large particles.

Lastly, the timing of application of fungicides is of paramount importance. By definition, protectant fungicides must be applied prior to the arrival of the pathogen inoculum but if they are applied too soon they are subject to erosion and their effectiveness diminishes in inverse proportion to the interval between application and inoculum arrival. There are two basic approaches to the efficient timing of protectant or systemic sprays. The first is designed in conjunction with information derived from disease forecasting, the second a 'play-safe' routine schedule. Disease forecasting, discussed elsewhere in this book, has become very much a computerized science. A thorough knowledge of pathogen biology is required and the nature of the host, its resistance and the interactions between host, pathogen and environment must be elucidated. In most cases, disease forecasting has enabled a more efficient usage of fungicides by ensuring a better timing of application.

Forecasting systems are in their infancy and undoubtedly have some way to go to achieve perfection. The farmer has the problem of deciding when to begin his spray operations and he will be guided in the main by local knowledge of climate and records of disease outbreak. Where more than one application is necessary he will have to determine the intervals between each application. This will depend upon the amount of disease present, the prevailing weather and the economics of the situation.

Major groups of non-systemic agricultural fungicides

Copper

Copper compounds were among the first to be used in the chemical control of plant disease but it was Millardet's publicity of Bordeaux mixture that really launched copper as a fungicide. Copper fungicides are protectants and the object was to keep the foliage healthy for as long as possible. This was done by a series of spray or dust applications, 'insurance sprays', but copper has not been utilized to any great extent in the control of cereal diseases. In addition, protectants are not really suited to the cereal crop due to the physical damage which results from the repeated passage of machinery through the crop although the recent developments of 'tramline' farming has almost eliminated this source of damage.

Sulphur

This was the earliest recorded fungicide and has probably been more widely used than any other. It is best known for its effectiveness in the control of powdery mildews, receiving a great impetus in the 19th century when it was first used in England in 1847 for the control of powdery mildew of grapes (*Uncinula necator*). Originally, it was used as a finely divided dust or as a dispersible powder. The more finely divided the sulphur, the greater is its fungicidal properties. Its fungicidal action is difficult to explain but a generally accepted hypothesis suggests that sulphur acts as a hydrogen acceptor and thus interferes in the normal processes of hydrogenation and dehydrogenation.

Another sulphur compound in use is *lime-sulphur*. This is prepared by boiling together sulphur and lime-water. Traditionally, the preparation took place near the site where the spraying was to be carried out and just prior to application. Lime-sulphur consists mainly of calcium polysylphides which break down to release the toxic elemental sulphur. Proprietary, 'ready-made' preparations are now available but none are in commercial use against cereal diseases although some are used in small plot and glasshouse trials where reasonable control of powdery mildews can be achieved by regular spraying.

Mercury fungicides

Both organic and inorganic preparations of mercury are in use and are highly effective fungicides and bactericides. All formulations are extremely toxic to man, animals and birds and, as mercury will accumulate in the body and therefore proceed up the food chain, there is much public opposition to their use. In many countries, for example New Zealand, their use has been banned by legislation and throughout the world there is a major effort in progress to find less toxic substitutes.

Inorganic mercurials have generally been superseded by organo-mercurials for plant disease control. Organo-mercurials find two main uses in agriculture and horticulture: spray materials, such as phenyl mercury acetate, for the control of apple scab (*Venturia inaequalis*) and as cereal seed dressings. All the organo-mercurials have the general formula,

$$R - Hg - X$$

where R may be either an aryl or alkyl radicle and X may be an organic or inorganic acid group. In Sweden alkyl compounds have been widely used as seed dressings against seed-borne diseases. They are certainly effective against the pathogens but they also contribute, through mercury poisoning, to the death of many wild birds including the birds of prey which live on the seed-eating smaller birds.

Organic fungicides

The early fungicides were all inorganic chemicals but in 1913, Riehm discovered the value of organo-mercury preparations as fungicides for the control of bunt (*Tilletia caries*) on wheat. This stimulated research into the fungicide activity of many other organic compounds although, for the first 25 years, the aim was still confined to getting improved seed disinfectants.

It was not until the discovery and patenting of dithiocarbamates in 1934 by Tisdale and Williams of the du Pont Company that organic compounds for use as foliage fungicides began to be developed. There was an added impetus to their introduction with the shortage of copper and mercury during World War II. Sulphur was never scarce during that period and the screening of organic sulphur compounds for use in synthetic rubber production led to the discovery of the fungicidal properties of the derivatives of dithiocarbamic acid which are now collectively called the *dithio-carbamates*.

dithiocarbamic acid

The first of these compounds, tetramethylthiuram disulphide, now known as *thiram*, was used as an activator in the production of synthetic rubber and became the first of these compounds to be used commercially as a fungicide both as a foliar protectant of turf grasses and tulips and as a cereal seed dressing.

Thiram

In addition to the thiuramdisulphides, the dithiocarbamates in use as fungicides today are derivatives of two main groups:

1 Dimethyl-metal-dithiocarbamates Many metallic dithiocarbamates have been developed but only iron (*ferbam*) and zinc (*ziram*) dimethyl dithiocarbamates have been commercially successful.

Ferbam is a black solid and leaves an unsightly and undesirable deposit on the sprayed surface. *Ziram* is a skin irritant and induces dermatitis in some people. These factors, and the discovery of equally good alternative organic fungicides, have led to a marked decline in their use.

2 Ethylene-bis-metal-dithiocarbamates   These are formed by the joining of two dithiocarbamic acid molecules through the carbon atom.

Nabam	*Zineb*	*Maneb*

The sodium salt is called *Nabam*, the zinc salt *Zineb* and the manganese salt *Maneb*. *Nabam* was first used as a protectant under the trade name Dithane but it has been shown to be markedly improved if zinc sulphate and lime is added to the mixture. With zinc sulphate, when it is called *zineb tank mix*, it is best known for its use against tomato leaf mould (*Cladosporium fulvum*) and in many field trials involving *Septoria* pathogens of wheat where this protectant gives good control when applied regularly, albeit uneconomically.

Nabam has, however, been largely replaced by zinc ethylenebisdithiocarbamate, *Zineb*, and the manganese salt *Maneb*.

More recently, *Mancozeb* has been developed, a complex of zinc and maneb containing 20% manganese and 2·5% zinc. Nowadays, all the metallic bisdithiocarbamates are marketed as various types of *dithane*.

The dithiocarbamates are relatively harmless to mammals, they are either soluble, as is *Nabam*, or are formulated as wettable powders suitable for spray application as with *Zineb* and *Maneb*. They have a distinct advantage over copper, which they largely replaced, in that they are not phytotoxic.

Another successful organic fungicide which has rivalled dithiocarbamates is *Captan*. This is a member of the *heterocyclic nitrogen* group of compounds whose fungicidal activity was discovered by Kittleson in 1952.

Captan

It is widely used as a foliage and fruit protectant, it is very persistent and is somewhat specific in its action but although it has activity against certain cereal pathogens it is not generally recommended for this purpose.

Captafol is a non-systemic protectant with a very long persistency. It is closely related to Captan and has achieved considerable success against potato blight (*Phytophthora infestans*) and coffee berry disease (*Colletotrichum coffeanum*). It is sometimes used in mixtures with systemic MBC generating compounds for the control of certain foliar pathogens of cereals, for example *Septoria nodorum*.

Systemic fungicides

Any chemical that can penetrate the plant cuticle and then be translocated within the plant is a potential therapeutant. Such chemicals are termed systemic compounds and if they also confer a level of fungitoxicity on the plant tissue they are known as *systemic fungicides*. A chemical that is absorbed but not translocated can only confer fungitoxicity at the sites of application. These chemicals are termed topical *therapeutants* or, more often, *eradicant fungicides.*

The systemic fungicide has distinct advantages over the eradicant and the traditional protectant. Firstly, it can be translocated to remote plant tissues and afford a more efficient level of protection against invading pathogens. It is not subject to the processes of weathering, limitations in method of application or variation in plant surface. The systemic chemical may be applied after infection and consequently eliminates the costly wastage inherent in incorrectly timed insurance spray programmes against diseases where the start of the epidemic cannot be predicted with any degree of certainty.

Systemic fungicides can modify and be modified by the tissues of the plant. Some may demonstrate *in vivo* fungicidal activity which may not be apparent *in vitro*. In such cases, it may be the breakdown products of the chemical within the plant tissue that possess the fungicidal properties. Other systemic fungicides are fungitoxic *in vivo* and *in vitro*.

Several hypotheses have been advanced to explain the mechanism of chemotherapeutic action:

1 Direct toxic action   This is based on the accumulation of a sufficiently high level of the fungicide at the infection site. It may be the fungitoxic breakdown products that accumulate but, in either case, the compound must be selectively toxic to the invading pathogen and not phytotoxic.

2 Toxin inactivation   Toxins are known to be involved in the development of many disease symptoms and some systemic fungicides are thought to bring about a reduction in host symptoms by either the degradation or the immobilization of these toxins.

3 Enhancement of host resistance   Mechanisms ranging from a general alteration of plant metabolism to physical alterations of the host surface have been suggested but are difficult to demonstrate. In the case of bunt of wheat (*Tilletia caries*), resistance can be enhanced by a shortening of the susceptible phase, but this has only been demonstrated so far by the application of the systemic compound gibberellic acid.

The uptake and translocation of systemic fungicides
The cuticle is the initial barrier to the penetration by chemicals into the aerial parts of plants. Penetration depends upon the degree of separation of the wax platelets which are embedded in the cuticle matrix. In turn, the degree of separation of the platelets depends upon the amount of water imbibed into the cutin matrix. Water solubility seems to be the only absolute requirement for compounds to penetrate the cuticle.

The roots are more adapted for the absorption of solutes although, as the roots age, they become less permeable.

Once in the plant the chemicals first pass into free space between the cells and eventually enter the xylem vessels. In this way they can be passively transported upwards through the plant. A chemical which is absorbed by the root can be readily translocated to the leaves. In contrast, chemicals applied to the foliage will require transport in the phloem. The phloem is mainly involved with the transport of photosynthates from the leaves to the growing zones. Root applied systemic chemicals are therefore more efficiently distributed throughout the plant than foliage applied systemics.

The early systemic fungicides were all xylem translocated. *Benomyl*, for example, or *thiophanate methyl*, both of which produce the fungicidal metabolite MBC (the methyl ester of 2-benzimidazolecarbamic acid) can be used as seed dressings on barley to demonstrate xylem translocation. The effect is clearly shown in the foliage if dressed and undressed seeds are grown and later exposed to powdery mildew (*Erysiphe graminis hordei*). *Ethirimol*, one of the pyrimidine group of fungicides, is similarly translocated and is also active against powdery mildew. Evidence of xylem translocation in cereals has also been presented for the oxathiin derivatives, *carboxin* and *oxycarboxin* and for *tridemorph* and *triforine*, all of which will be discussed later.

The lack of phloem translocated systemics is a distinct disadvantage in that root diseases may not be controlled by foliar applications. Phloem transported systemics open up entirely different patterns of disease control in that roots are protected without the application of the chemical to the soil or the seed and young growing tissue could be protected by treating the foliage.

Systemic fungicides in present-day use

In the following account, systemic activity has been interpreted in the broadest sense and compounds showing only limited movement, such as trans-laminar activity, have also been mentioned.

1 Organophosphorous compounds

Substituted 1,2,4-triazoles

Following on the discovery of the insecticidal properties of phosphorous-containing compounds it was natural that these compounds were also screened for fungicidal properties. Many compounds with activity, especially against the powdery mildew fungus, *Erysiphe graminis*, were found. The basic structure for these compounds is:

The fungitoxicity of this molecule depends upon the presence of a bis-(dimethylamido) phosphoryl group in the 2-position.

Dialkylphosphorothioates and related compounds
As alternatives to organomercury compounds for the control of the rice blast pathogen, *Piricularia oryzae*, several compounds have been developed in Japan which have given good control of this cereal disease. One of these, *Kitazin*, has the structural formula:

It can be absorbed by the plant leaf and is readily translocated in the transpiration stream. Thus it is suitable for foliar application and as granules which are applied directly into the paddy fields.

2 Benzimidazoles This group includes *benomyl* and *thiabendazole* and they owe their activity to methyl benzimidazol-2-yl carbamate (MBC) to which they decompose within the plant or in water *in vitro*. They are particularly effective against Ascomycetes but the Basidiomycetes and Phycomycetes are quite insensitive.

The benzimidazoles are designated 'broad-spectrum fungicides' but this is rather misleading in that, in general practice, their use is rather restricted and many important pathogens are not controlled by them. *Benomyl* is particularly effective against eyespot of wheat and barley (*Pseudocercosporella herpotrichoides*), seed-borne bunts and covered smuts (*Tilletia caries* and *Ustilago hordei* for example) and, when applied with a dithiocarbamate such as *mancozeb*, against the glume blotch of wheat pathogen (*Septoria nodorum*).

Another newly introduced benzimidazole is 2-(2-furyl) benzimidazole. This is known as *fuberidazole* and shows promise against *Fusarium nivale* of rye and *Calonectria nivalis* on wheat and barley when used as a seed treatment.

3 Carbendazim   This is the MBC compound itself. It has been widely developed and is a recommended product against leaf blotch of barley (*Rhynchosporium secalis*) and eyespot of wheat and barley (*Pseudocercosporella herpotrichoides*). It can also be used as a broad spectrum fungicide as a tank mix with maneb or another dithiocarbamate for the control of glume blotch (*Septoria nodorum*), powdery mildew (*Erysiphe graminis*), yellow rust (*Puccinia striiformis*) and brown rust (*P. hordei*).

4 Thiophanates   The antifungal effect of thiophanate-methyl again depends upon the formation of MBC and it must be concluded that both benomyl and thiophanate methyl have the same mode of action which is by inhibiting mycelial growth but not affecting spore germination. It appears that DNA synthesis is the process most rapidly inhibited by MBC. Their performance against plant diseases is also very similar to benomyl.

5 Pyrimidine derivatives   These are highly selective against the powdery mildews. *Dimethirimol* has been shown to be systemically active against powdery mildews of cucurbits, chrysanthemums and sugar beet. It is less active against cereal powdery mildew. Its near relative, *ethirimol*, is formulated as a seed dressing to control powdery mildew (*E. graminis hordei*) on spring barley but is now also formulated as a foliar spray against the same pathogen on winter wheat, oats and barley. It can also be drilled into soil with spring barley.

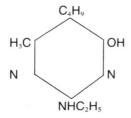

Ethirimol

6 Fluotrimazole   This compound has been shown to give good control of powdery mildew of cereals, in particular spring barley. It has both curative and protective properties but is not claimed to be truly systemic. Its chemical name is bisphenyl-(3-trifluoromethyl-phenyl)-1-(1,2,4-triazolyl)-methan. It has been developed as an emulsifiable concentrate containing 12·5% w/v active ingredient for use as a spray. It is usually applied at a rate of 1·5 litres/hectare (21 fl. oz/acre) per season either as a single spray or split application. Fluotrimazole also has some activity against brown rust in spring barley and winter wheat.

7 Triadimefon   A compound belonging to the imidazole group. It is particularly active against powdery mildews and rusts. Its chemical name is 1-(4-chloro-phenoxy)-3, 3-dimethyl-1-(1,2,4 triazol-l-yl) butane-2-one. It has been formulated both as a wettable powder (25% a.i.) and as an emulsifiable concentrate, the latter mainly for use on ornamentals. It also gives good control of brown and yellow rust of barley and powdery mildew and yellow rust of wheat. It only has a weak inhibition of spore germination and mycelial growth *in vitro* but both acropetal and basipetal translocation have been demonstrated.

8 Tridemorph   This chemical has been developed primarily as a foliage systemic for the control of powdery mildew of barley (*Erysiphe graminis hordei*). It is also widely used against wheat yellow rust (*P. striiformis*) and, in combination with carbendazim, to control *Rynchosporium secalis* on barley. It is a heterocyclic compound based on dimethyl-morpholine. Its mode of action is to inhibit haustorial formation. There is a tendency to be phytotoxic in some of the substituent compounds and even tridemorph can sometimes be phytotoxic on some varieties of winter wheat.

9 Triforine   This is yet another heterocyclic compound which is active against powdery mildews of cereals, apples, cucurbits and ornamentals when used as a foliage fungicide. It is also active against cereal rusts and apple scab. Haustorial formation by barley powdery mildew is impaired and reductions in conidial germination of several Ascomycetes and Fungi Imperfecti can be demonstrated *in vitro*.

10 Carboxylic acid anilides   Closely related to the early fungicide salicylanilide are the *oxathiins*. There are two closely related compounds in this group, carboxin and oxycarboxin. Both are used in the control of rust and smut fungi. *Carboxin* has been particularly widely used as a seed dressing for barley loose smut (*Ustilago nuda*). However, it should not be used on seed with a moisture content more than 16%. *Oxycarboxin*, the sulphone derivative, has also shown some promise against cereal rusts, especially yellow rust of wheat (*Puccinia striiformis*), and can be applied either to the seed or the soil. The latest formulations are mixtures of carboxin and thiram as protectant seed dressings against bunt of wheat (*Tilletia caries*), covered smut of barley (*Ustilago hordei*), leaf stripe of barley (*Pyrenophora graminea*) and covered smut of oats (*Ustilago hordei*).

A third member of this group, being a substituted benzanilide, is *benodanil* (2-iodobenzanilide). This compound has shown good activity against Basidiomycetes and is especially recommended against yellow rust and brown rust of cereals. It is very persistent and has a good margin of crop safety.

Methods of application of systemic fungicides
The inherent biological activity of the fungicide apart, the effectiveness of systemic fungicides, as with all fungicides, will depend upon: **a** the correct timing of application, **b** the correct placement of the chemical.

Systemics can be and are applied to the seed, the soil and to the aerial plant parts.

1 Seed treatment Systemics may be applied to seed as dusts, slurries or in solution. Traditionally, seed dressings were applied to destroy pathogens which were present on the seedcoat or to protect young seedlings from attack by soil-borne pathogens immediately after germination. The success of systemics as seed dressings is now an accepted fact as, for example, the treatment of cereal seed grain with carboxin (*oxathiin*) to control loose smut (*Ustilago nuda*) and with ethirimol for the control of spring barley powdery mildew. The treating of seed in this way will have limitations depending upon the nature of the pathogen against which control is aimed, as the effectiveness of the fungicide is likely to diminish by dilution and other factors as the plant grows. For this reason, there has been a greater use of foliar-applied systemics, such as tridemorph and triadimefon, for the control of barley powdery mildew as the activity of the seed-applied systemic reduces to neglible proportions by the time the plant is in the extension phase leaving it completely unprotected at the later vegetative and heading stages when the processes of grain filling will be very much affected by any reduction in photosynthetic capacity. It should also be emphasized that the practice of seed-dressing winter barley with ethirimol is not now recommended in the U.K., not because of any deficiency of the treatment but because it extends the time that the fungicide is present in the environment and this increases the likelihood of mutant strains being selected out of the fungus population which are insensitive to the fungicide.

2 Leaf and stem treatments   Foliar application of systemics is a very convenient treatment for the control of many cereal diseases.

Even though the main attribute of systemics is their activity after absorption by the plant, the distribution of the chemical over the plant surface is still of the utmost importance as some chemicals may not be translocated as well as others. With conventional protectant fungicides, application technology has received considerable attention and it is widely accepted that the efficiency of any treatment is related to the persistence of the active ingredient between one application and the next and its distribution during these intervals.

Quite obviously, if readily absorbed, systemics will not have to withstand the weathering of conventional protectants and their period of activity should, in consequence, be longer. Additives can also be included with systemic fungicides which will increase their uptake and biological efficiency. Surfactants and adhesive supplements have both been shown to improve systemics although their overall superiority is still mostly dependent upon their distribution and persistence.

3 Soil treatments   Systemic fungicides are now being used for the control of certain plant diseases which, in the past, could only be controlled by the application of soil sterilants such as methyl bromide, carbon disulphide or chloropicrin. In Japan, granules of the fungicide *kitazin*, an organophosphorous compound, are applied to the irrigation water to control rice blast (*Piricularia oryzae*) and there are many references in the literature to the use of benomyl and thiabendazole for the control of soil-borne pathogens of other crops.

Timing of application   With systemic fungicides, the timing of application is not as important as it is for non-systemic protectants although, with accurate forecasting of disease onset, the timing can be made more efficient. In many cases, the decision as to when to spray will involve a consideration of epidemiology, geographical location and possible yield loss. With barley powdery mildew (*Erysiphe graminis hordei*) the main aim is to protect the top leaves and ears. With winter barley varieties, an application with, for example, tridemorph, is mostly made in the spring when the mildew is developing but not before mid-April. A second application may be necessary where infection becomes severe. With spring barley, the high mildew risk varieties should be treated at the time the herbicide is applied, or, with varieties of lower mildew risk, at the first sign of mildew developing after G.S. 4 but not before mid-May. With the glume blotch pathogen of wheat (*Septoria nodorum*) early infections are often ignored and an application of benomyl or carbendazim plus a dithiocarbamate such as maneb, zineb or polyethylenethiuram disulphide made between G.S. 8–10 which is prior to the 'in boot' stage, and is timed to protect the latter stages of plant development.

Fungicide insensitivity

The arrival of systemic fungicides on to the agricultural scene was loudly heralded. The short-term usefulness of crop varieties which incorporated race-specific or vertical resistance had become only too apparent and it was hoped that systemic fungicides would provide high levels of control without the same disadvantages. Unfortunately, the action of systemics can be considered to be parallel to that of host resistance where selection pressure is put on the pathogen population for mutant races to develop. Mutants occur regularly and some of these may have the capacity to overcome the resistance conferred by specific host plant genes.

Similar events have already been reported after the use of systemic fungicides and even by 1969 a strain of *Sphaerotheca fuliginea*, the causal organism of powdery mildew of cucurbits, had been found which was insensitive to the pyrimidine derivative dimethirimol. A benomyl insensitive strain has also been reported in *Botrytis cinerea* and there are several examples of insensitivity to systemics in cereal pathogens reported in the literature. Wolfe (Proc. 6th Insectic. Fungic. Conf. Brighton, 1971) has found resistance in *Erysiphe graminis* to ethirimol and Miura *et al.* (Ann. Phytopath. Soc. Japan, **39**; 239, 1973) in *Piricularia oryzae* to Kasugamycin.

Systemic fungicides are quite certainly here to stay but their use will have to be carefully planned to overcome the problems of the emergence of fungicide insensitive strains in the field. The withdrawal of the recommendation for treating seed of winter barley with ethirimol has already been discussed in this context. The answer probably lies in an integrated approach to the control of plant disease where the systemic fungicide is used on varieties which have at least a moderate degree of resistance. The pathogen would then be confronted with two major obstacles.

Seed treatments for the control of plant diseases

The widespread acceptance of the principle of treating seed with chemicals arose from the empirical practice of steeping cereal seed in salt-brine in the 17th century. The disease most obviously controlled by 'brining' was bunt of wheat (*Tilletia caries*) and it soon became apparent that there was an important difference between the method of 'carry-over' of the bunt pathogen to that of the causal organism of the loose smut disease (*Ustilago nuda*).

Copper soon replaced brine but not without producing problems for it was noticed that copper sulphate produced a certain amount of injury to seed and seedlings. Following copper there has been a succession of chemicals starting with formaldehyde and progressing through the controversial mercury compounds to the less potent but more acceptable organic fungicides such as captan and more recently benomyl. Seed treatments have two functions:

a the destruction of any pathogens carried externally on the seed coat and, to a very limited extent, those carried internally within the seed (*Disinfestation*).

b to provide a protective chemical barrier on the seed and developing seedling roots to attack by soil-borne pathogens during germination (*Protection*).

Seed-borne cereal diseases are many and varied and include many which are economically important such as *Pyrenophora avenae*, *Septoria nodorum*, *Tilletia caries*, *Ustilago nuda* and *Piricularia oryzae*. The distinction has to be made between those pathogens whose propagules *contaminate* the seed and those which penetrate or *infect* the seed. Many diseases such as bunt of wheat (*Tilletia caries*) have been largely eliminated by the use of seed dressings especially mercury compounds, whereas the same chemicals are of little use against the deep seated loose smut pathogen (*Ustilago nuda*).

The protection of the young seedling immediately after germination is also of considerable importance. The young plant is particularly vulnerable at this time and appears to present a most desirable substrate for a large number of soil fungi. Many of the organisms concerned are facultative parasites which only affect plants during this critical juvenile phase. Such soil-inhabiting parasites as *Helminthosporium* spp. *Fusarium* spp. and *Rhizoctonia* spp. can be particularly damaging if the seedling is unprotected. The results from seed protection can often be most striking and are due to the dual disinfectant and protectant activity of most of the organic chemicals in use.

In the seed disinfectant category, copper sulphate can be used but there is a considerable risk from phytotoxicity. Formaldehyde is used to a limited extent on oats but by far the most widely used chemicals are the organo-mercury compounds which have the advantage of being sufficiently volatile to kill such propagules as smut spores trapped beneath the hulls of seeds. There is also an increasing usage of the carboxin and thiram mixtures as seed disinfectants. The disinfectants can be used as dusts, slurries or concentrated liquids. The slurry and liquid formulations were introduced because of the considerable toxic hazard to machine operators applying mercurial dusts. The liquids can be applied by machines which discharge a fine spray over the continuously moving seed. Examples of mercurial seed dressings now in use are Panogen 15 [cyano (methyl mercury) guanidine], Ortho LM (methyl mercury 8-hydroxyquinolate) and Ceresan L (methyl mercury 2,3-dihydroxy propyl mercaptide methyl mercury acetate).

In the seed protectant category the most important non-mercurial preparations are the dithiocarbamates, particularly Thiram which is used extensively against a variety of damping-off diseases. The heterocyclic nitrogen compound Captan is also widely used as a protectant for maize particularly against seed rotting organisms.

Disease forecasting

The incidence of plant diseases varies considerably from season to season for a variety of reasons. The amount of inoculum, environmental conditions, numbers and activity of vectors and the availability of susceptible hosts all contribute to oscillations in the incidence, severity and the timing of the onset of epidemics. The ability to forecast the arrival of inoculum or the initiation of an epidemic is both of value in the study of plant diseases and in providing the farmer with a more efficient basis for organizing control measures. It will also enable him to avoid wasting time and money on unnecessary control measures.

The commercial use of fungicides against cereal foliar diseases is a very recent event, beginning in the late 1960s and early 1970s and being mainly concerned with the use of the new systemic fungicides against powdery mildew of barley (*Erysiphe graminis hordei*). In order to optimize the use of these and later introduced fungicides for the control of other cereal diseases it has been necessary to evolve criteria for determining the necessity for and correct timing of their application. Disease forecasting became fully justified as a science and, although very much in its infancy, there can be no doubt about the potential value of predictive systems in disease control programmes. Most pathologists would agree that the present forecasting methods are merely prototypes of what will, hopefully, become definitive and efficient systems. At this stage, the authors can only describe what methods are available and to point out their limitations.

The forecasting of barley powdery mildew for England and Wales is reasonably well advanced. It is partly based on the effects of temperature and humidity on conidial germination and germ tube growth and partly on rainfall and wind speed. Meteorological data have been described which, it is suggested, are related to periods when there is a high risk of an increase in the numbers of mildew conidia above spring barley crops (Polley & King, Plant Pathology, **22**; 11, 1973).

a Day maximum temperature > 15°C.
b Day sunshine > 5 hours.
c Day rainfall < 1 mm.
d Day run-of-wind > 246 km (this may be replaced by the highest wind speed taken at 0000h, 0600h, 1300h and 1800h GMT; the critical value being >15 knots.

From these data, *high risk days* can be computed and predicted and these are circulated to the Advisory Service Centres from the Meteorological Office. A *high risk day* is one in which all four factors have been satisfied and denotes the start of a *high risk period*. This period terminates on a day when none or only one of the factors have been satisfied or the third consecutive day when only two factors have been satisfied. The information on *high risk periods* is used in conjunction with reports gathered over the country of mildew levels in crops. Spore trapping data over the years has confirmed the reliability of this predictive system and, in conjunction with information on the age of the crop, has assisted in the more efficient timing of spray applications.

The current recommendation for the timing of fungicide application to control *Septoria nodorum* on wheat is at GS 8–10 if environmental conditions are favourable for the development of this disease. King (unpublished) has suggested certain criteria for spring and summer infection of the foliage:

a Rain on 2 out of 3 days totalling at least 10 mm with rain on the first day.
b Rain on 3 consecutive days totalling at least 5 mm.
c Rain on 4 consecutive days.

In addition, a relative humidity of at least 90% must be recorded on at least one day in each period. These criteria have been shown to be useful in certain coastal areas in the South of England but were derived in seasons when *Septoria* was not as devastating as it can be. Another set of criteria have been devised by Jeger, Griffiths

& Jones (unpublished) who suggest that the following conditions are necessary for infection by *S. nodorum*:

a R.H. at time of infection $>$ 65%.
b Minimum temperature in succeeding 24 hours $<$ 6°C.
c Less than 4 hours in succeeding 24 hours with R.H. $<$ 60%.
d Less than 4 hours in succeeding 24 hours with R.H. $<$ 90%.

Quite obviously, there is still much work to be done to devise a more precise and practical forecasting method for this disease.

With eyespot of wheat (*Pseudocercosporella herpotrichoides*), it has been shown that a temperature range of 4–13°C. and R.H. $<$ 80% are favourable for infection (Ferhmann & Schrodter, Phytopath. Z. **74**; 161, 1972). When such conditions are satisfied it should be possible to predict infection and, in conjunction with assessment of the amount of the disease present in crops, advise on the necessity to apply fungicides. In the United Kingdom, recommendations to spray at present are made on the basis of the incidence of disease in the crop, 25% at GS 5–6 being deemed to be the critical amount. Work is now in progress to confirm or modify the German meteorological criteria to best fit United Kingdom conditions and varieties.

Attempts to devise forecasting systems for other diseases are already well advanced. Polley & Clarkson have already reviewed possible methods for predicting barley leaf blotch (*Rhynchosporium secalis*) and barley brown rust (*Puccinia hordei*) (Plant Disease Epidemiology and Dispersal of Plant Pathogens, Acad. Press, 1978). With *R. secalis*, infection has been shown to be correlated with critical periods of at least 14 hours commencing with rain and continuing as long as there is precipitation or RH $>$ 90%. The mean temperature must never fall below 10°C. For *P. hordei*, King & Polley (Plant Pathology, **25**; 63, 1976) found that days when at least 5 hours of dew were recorded following a day on which the maximum temperature exceeded 15°C. were conducive to infection. With both these diseases, as with many other cereal diseases of economic importance, there is much fundamental laboratory and field work still to be done. Forecasting methods are certainly necessary, their benefits being mostly in terms of the better timing of control measures and the reduction in wasteful, possibly unnecessary applications of fungicides.

Integrated control

It is becoming increasingly clear that the expectation of a simple solution to the problem of disease control in cereals is not likely to be realized. The hope that simply inherited host resistance to the major pathogens would provide a permanent solution and thus release breeders to tackle the problems of improving basic yield potential has certainly not been fulfilled and there is a growing fear that the new generation of pathogen specific fungicides may be subject to similar variation in pathogen populations resulting in the widespread occurrence of fungicide insensitive strains which would render the fungicides ineffective. It would appear more likely that a stable solution to the cereal disease problem will come through the continuing balanced application of a range of disease control measures. This integration of various controls and their balance will depend on the particular host : pathogen system in question, the controls available, their ease of application and the economic importance of the disease in question. The control of one disease must also take account of side effects on the control of another and so the totally integrated system must encompass all the important pathogens, both existing and potential, of the crop in question.

Although control measures may be pathologically complex they must be simple for the farmer to apply either by being delivered 'in the bag' to the farm, i.e. resistant varieties with seed dressings, or by being easily incorporated into farming practice, e.g. time of ploughing, stubble burning, avoidance of winter varieties, etc. There are three basic components to a control system, host resistance, fungicides and cultural procedures and it is these that have to be combined to give the correct balance in an integrated programme. There follow some propositions for potential systems but there are few examples of measures that have been applied in practice. It is, therefore, this area of research that offers one of the most exciting challenges in cereal pathology.

Combining different types of host resistance may be considered as a simple integrated system and is discussed in Chapter 5. Two points should be made here. Firstly, the use of complex resistances in homogeneous or heterogeneous host populations must take into account the overall heterogeneity of the population with regard to other pathogens, i.e. the population must not be genetically polarized for susceptibility to other diseases and secondly, different types of resistance, from a genetic and mechanistic point of view, should be combined where practicable. It can be argued that the effects of the host resistance component in an integrated system should be considered in terms of decreasing host susceptibility rather than producing a high level of resistance; high resistance being recognized as the main causal factor resulting in change to increased virulence in the pathogen population. In an integrated system it is the sum total of the components that gives the control required but no single component should subject the pathogen to undue selection pressure.

The **epidemic potential** of the pathogen is of importance in determining the level of resistance that is necessary. For example, in the United Kingdom, the official variety testing authority, the National Institute of Agricultural Botany, has imposed minimum standards of susceptibility for the major pathogens of wheat, oats and barley and, if a submitted variety falls below that minimum, it is rejected. These minimum standards are determined by the potential threat to British agriculture of the specific disease. Wheat brown rust (*P. recondita*) may be used as a lesson-teaching example. In recent years, the introduction of a range of high yielding, but highly susceptible, varieties has resulted in an increase in prevalence and severity of the disease. A return to the level of 'normal susceptibility' of pre-1970 varieties would redress the situation. With this level of resistance, it is only in exceptionally favourable years that brown rust is a problem and then fungicides would be brought into play.

Regional and local diversification of varieties is becoming more common thus allowing the farmer to spread the risk of disease but such an on-farm system should also be integrated with rotation and crop hygiene practices. This is particularly important for diseases with high local carry-over on stubble and crop debris, e.g. barley scald, wheat leaf and glume blotch, etc., but if sequential cropping is desirable it may be necessary to include lower yielding but resistant varieties later in the sequence. Fungicides, chemical stubble cleaning and deep cultivations should also be integrated into such a system.

Current thinking on the use of varietal mixtures suggests that genetically diverse components will give a much greater degree of buffering of the population against a range of diseases and other environmental stresses. The inclusion of fungicides, either as seed dressings to particular components of the mixture, or as foliar sprays in response to a particular disease threat will further buffer the population. For example, barley mildew (*E. graminis hordei*) is a constant threat in north west Europe and schemes are being devised to develop varietal mixtures with diverse resistances to the pathogen. The varieties currently available for such schemes also carry different resistances to *P. hordei*, another major pathogen and so, mixtures can be compounded which are heterogeneous for resistance to both pathogens. Two other diseases, scald (*R. secalis*) and yellow rust (*P. striiformis*) can be important in some years but although most of the potential mixture varieties are fairly resistant, some are not. Therefore, the highly susceptible varieties would be protected by buffering within a mixture but, if this were not adequate, fungicides are available to be used in a 'fire brigade' operation.

The current increased use of developmental and partially expressed types of host resistance, which it is hoped are more stable and effective in themselves, offers a further possibility of integration with chemical control measures, thus increasing the effectiveness of both the chemical and the host resistance. Take, for example, the case of barley mildew in north west Europe where seedling resistance, based on

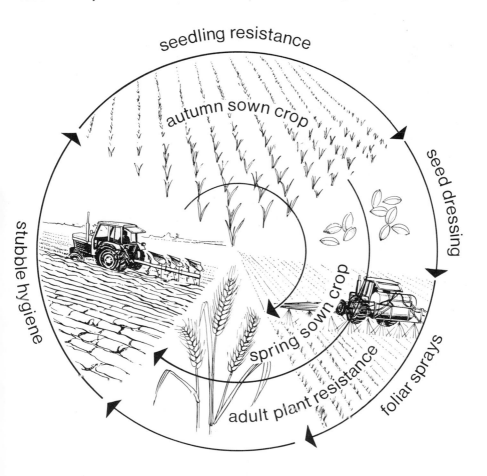

Fig. 6.1 *A scheme for the integrated control of barley powdery mildew.*

major resistance genes, has been so disappointing. Adult plant resistances appear to be more effective against oat and wheat mildew and so this may also be the case with barley mildew. However, barley mildew is endemic in the European barley growing areas, surviving on the autumn sown crop and infecting the spring crop when it is in the seedling and juvenile stages. Adult plant resistance types will, therefore, be exposed to infection during the early stages of growth. Fungicides, applied as seed dressings, would give protection during these early phases until the host's inherent resistance mechanisms take over. In addition to this, the problem of mildew on the winter crop could be tackled by using seedling resistances. This also reduces the amount of inoculum available for spring infection. Development of mildew in spring and summer on winter varieties could be countered by fungicide spray applications. Cultural control would also be practised by efficient stubble cleaning to remove volunteer plants and regrowth during the inter-crop period. This scheme (Fig. 6.1) has the advantage of minimizing the exposure time of each control measure to the pathogen population thus minimizing selection for virulence or fungicide insensitivity. Also, the fungus is confronted with at least three different types of barrier (seedling resistance, adult plant resistance and chemicals) throughout the year in sequence, thus the process of overcoming the control measures is made more difficult for the pathogen. The scheme is further strengthened by diversifying within each control measure, i.e. use of different seedling resistances, different adult plant resistances and different types of chemicals.

Further reading
Biological Control of Plant Pathogens *by K. F. Baker and R. J. Cook, Freeman, San Francisco, 1974*
Plant Diseases and their Chemical Control *by E. Evans, Blackwell, Oxford, 1968.*
Systemic Fungicides *Editor R. W. Marsh, 2nd edition, Longman, England, 1977.*
The Control of Plant Diseases *by B. E. J. Wheeler, Oxford Biology Readers No. 74, 1975*
Plant Disease, *Volume 1.* How disease is managed *Editors J. G. Horsfall and E. B. Cowling, Academic Press, New York and London, 1977.*

List of plates

Plate 1.1   **Stem rust** *(Puccinia graminis tritici)* of wheat. Uredial infection on stems. (Photo Purdue University)

Plate 1.2   **Stem rust** *(Puccinia graminis tritici)* of wheat. Teleutospore stage on stems. (Photo Crown copyright)

Plate 1.3   **Yellow rust** *(Puccinia striiformis)* of wheat. Uredial infection on mature leaf. (Photo BASF United Kingdom Limited)

Plate 1.4   **Leaf rust** *(Puccinia recondita tritici)* of wheat. Uredial infection on mature plants. (Photo Welsh Plant Breeding Station)

Plate 2.1   **Loose smut** *(Ustilago nuda)* of wheat. (Photo Welsh Plant Breeding Station)

Plate 2.2   **Flag smut** *(Urocystis tritici)* of wheat. (Photo Dr. R. F. Line)

Plate 2.3   **Leaf spot** *(Mycosphaerella graminicola = Septoria tritici)* of wheat. Head symptoms, rows of pycnidia on glumes. (Photo U.C.W. Aberystwyth)

Plate 2.4   **Glume blotch** *(Leptosphaeria nodorum = Septoria nodorum)* of wheat. (Photo BASF United Kingdom Limited)

Plate 3.1   **Leaf spot** *(Mycosphaerella graminicola = Septoria tritici)* of wheat. (Photo Crown copyright)

Plate 3.2   **Powdery mildew** *(Erysiphe graminis)* of wheat. Conidial stage. (Photo BASF United Kingdom Limited)

Plate 3.3   **Soil-borne mosaic** *(Virus)* of wheat. Resistant and susceptible rows. (Photo Purdue University)

Plate 3.4   **Common bunt** *(Tilletia caries)* of wheat. Healthy and infected heads. (Photo Crown copyright)

Plate 4.1   **Take-all – whiteheads** *(Gaeumannomyces graminis)* of wheat (Photo Crown copyright)

Plate 4.2   **Scab** *(Gibberella zeae)* of wheat. (Photo Purdue University)

Plate 4.3   **Sooty mould** *(Cladosporium* spp.) of wheat. (Photo BASF United Kingdom Limited)

Plate 4.4   **Yellow rust** *(Puccinia striiformis)* of wheat. Glume infection. (Photo Crown copyright)

Plate 5.1   **Eyespot** *(Pseudocercosporella herpotrichoides)* of wheat. (Photo BASF United Kingdom Limited)

Plate 5.2   **Sharp eyespot** *(Pellicularia filamentosa = Rhizoctonia solani)* of wheat. (Photo BASF United Kingdom Limited)

Plate 5.3   **Foot rot** *(Fusarium* spp.*)* of wheat. (Photo National Institute of Agricultural Botany)

Plate 5.4   **Take-all** *(Gaeumannomyces graminis)* of wheat. Foot and root rot symptoms. (Photo Crown copyright)

Plate 6.1   **Powdery mildew** *(Erysiphe graminis)* of barley. Conidial pustules. (Photo BASF United Kingdom Limited)

Plate 6.2   **Powdery mildew** *(Erysiphe graminis)* of barley. Cleistothecial stage. (Photo BASF United Kingdom Limited)

Plate 6.3   **Brown rust** *(Puccinia hordei)* of barley. Uredial stage. (Photo BASF United Kingdom Limited)

Plate 6.4   **Yellow rust** *(Puccinia striiformis)* of barley. Uredial stage. (Photo Welsh Plant Breeding Station)

Plate 7.1   **Genetic leaf spot** of barley. (Photo Welsh Plant Breeding Station)

Plate 7.2   **Septoria nodorum** of barley. (Photo Welsh Plant Breeding Station)

Plate 7.3   **Spot blotch** *(Cochliobolus sativus)* of barley. (Photo Crown copyright)

Plate 7.4   **Halo spot** *(Selenophoma donacis)* of barley. (Photo Welsh Plant Breeding Station)

Plate 8.1   **Net blotch** *(Pyrenophora teres)* of barley. (Photo Welsh Plant Breeding Station)

Plate 8.2   **Leaf blotch** or **scald** *(Rhynchosporium secalis)* of barley. (Photo BASF United Kingdom Limited)

Plate 8.3   **Herbicide scorch** on barley. (Photo BASF United Kingdom Limited)

Plate 8.4   **Manganese deficiency** on barley. (Photo Crown copyright)

Plate 9.1   **Covered smut** *(Ustilago hordei)* of barley. (Photo Washington State University, Plant Pathology Dept.)

Plate 9.2   **Leaf stripe** *(Pyrenophora graminea)* of barley. (Photo Welsh Plant Breeding Station)

Plate 9.3   **Barley yellow dwarf** *(Virus)* of barley. (Photo Welsh Plant Breeding Station)

Plate 9.4   **Resistant reaction** of barley to powdery mildew *(Erysiphe graminis)* (Photo Welsh Plant Breeding Station)

Plate 10.1   **Halo blight** *(Pseudomonas coronafaciens)* of oats. (Photo Welsh Plant Breeding Station)

Plate 10.2   **Seedling blotch** *(Pyrenophora avenae)* of oats. (Photo Crown copyright)

Plate 10.3   **Crown rust** *(Puccinia coronata)* of oats. Uredial stage. (Photo Welsh Plant Breeding Station)

Plate 10.4   **Powdery mildew** *(Erysiphe graminis)* of oats. (Photo Welsh Plant Breeding Station)

Plate 11.1   **Red leaf** *(Barley yellow dwarf virus)* of oats. (Photo Welsh Plant Breeding Station)

Plate 11.2   **Grey speck** *(Manganese deficiency)* of oats. Susceptible variety in foreground. (Photo Welsh Plant Breeding Station)

Plate 11.3   **Loose smut** *(Ustilago avenae)* of oats. (Photo Welsh Plant Breeding Station)

Plate 11.4   **Speckled blotch** *(Leptosphaeria avenaria = Septoria avenae)* of oats. (Photo Crown copyright)

Plate 12.1   **Ergot** *(Claviceps purpurea)* of rye. Sclerotia replacing grains. (Photo National Institute of Agricultural Botany)

Plate 12.2   **Brown rust** *(Puccinia recondita)* of rye. Uredial stage. (Photo National Institute of Agricultural Botany)

Plate 12.3   **Ergot** *(Claviceps purpurea)* Stromatal heads produced by sclerotium. (Photo Welsh Plant Breeding Station)

Plate 12.4   **Eyespot** *(Pseudocercosporella herpotrichoides)* of rye. Straggling symptoms. (Photo BASF United Kingdom Limited)

Plate 13.1   **Southern leaf blight** *(Cochliobolus heterostrophus)* of maize. Race T resistant and susceptible reactions. (Photo Dr. A. J. Ullstrup)

Plate 13.2 . **Northern leaf blight** *(Trichometasphaeria turcica)* of maize (Photo Dr. A. J. Ullstrup)

Plate 13.3   **Bacterial wilt** *(Xanthomonas stewartii)* of maize. Early systemic infection. (Photo Dr. A. J. Ullstrup)

Plate 13.4   **Common smut** *(Ustilago maydis)* of maize. (Photo National Institute of Agricultural Botany)

Plate 14.1   **Stalk rot** *(Diplodia maydis)* of maize. (Photo Dr. A. J. Ullstrup)

Plate 14.2   **Stalk rot** *(Gibberella zeae)* of maize. (Photo Dr. A. J. Ullstrup)

Plate 14.3   **Ear rot** *(Diplodia maydis)* of maize. (Photo Dr. A. J. Ullstrup)

Plate 14.4   **Ear rot** *(Gibberella zeae)* of maize. (Photo Dr. A. J. Ullstrup)

Plate 15.1   **Sharp eyespot** *(Pellicularia filamentosa = Rhizoctonia solani)* of maize. (Photo Crown copyright)

Plate 15.2   **Corn stunt** *(Spiroplasma)* of maize. (Photo Dr. A. J. Ullstrup)

Plate 15.3   **Cob rot** *(Nigrospora oryzae)* of maize. (Photo Dr. A. J. Ullstrup)

Plate 15.4   **Kernel rot** *(Gibberolla moniliforme)* of maize. (Photo Dr. A. J. Ullstrup)

Plate 16.1   **Partial resistance** of barley to brown rust *(Puccinia hordei)*. Resistant cv. Vada (left) compared with cv. Midas (right). (Photo Welsh Plant Breeding Station)

Plate 16.2   **Hypersensitive resistance** of barley to mildew *(Erysiphe graminis)*. Resistant and susceptible seedlings. (Photo Welsh Plant Breeding Station)

Plate 16.3   **Spreader bed nursery** to assess plants for resistance to foliar disease. (Photo Welsh Plant Breeding Station)

Plate 16.4   **Fungicide trial** showing control of eyespot lodging *(Pseudocercosporella herpotrichoides)* in winter wheat. (Photo BASF United Kingdom Limited)

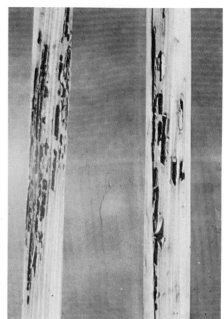

Plate 1.1 **Stem rust** *(Puccinia graminis tritici)* of wheat. Uredial infection on stems.

Plate 1.2 **Stem rust** *(Puccinia graminis tritici)* of wheat. Teleutospore stage on stems.

Plate 1.3 **Yellow rust** *(Puccinia striiformis)* of wheat. Uredial infection on mature leaf.

BASF

Plate 1.4 **Leaf rust** *(Puccinia recondita tritici)* of wheat. Uredial infection on mature plants.

Plate 2.1 **Loose smut** *(Ustilago nuda)* of wheat.

Plate 2.2 **Flag smut** *(Urocystis tritici)* of wheat.

Plate 2.3 **Leaf spot** *(Mycosphaerella graminicola = Septoria tritici)* of wheat. Head symptoms, rows of pycnidia on glumes.

Plate 2.4 **Glume blotch** *(Leptosphaeria nodorum = Septoria nodorum)* of wheat.

BASF

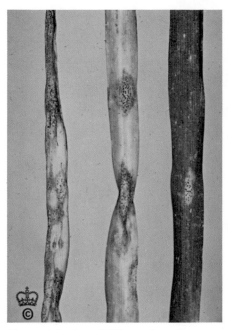

Plate 3.1 **Leaf spot** *(Mycosphaerella graminicola = Septoria tritici)* of wheat.

Plate 3.2 **Powdery mildew** *(Erysiphe graminis)* of wheat. Conidial stage.

Plate 3.3 **Soil-borne mosaic** (Virus) of wheat. Resistant and susceptible rows.

Plate 3.4 **Common bunt** *(Tilletia caries)* of wheat. Healthy and infected heads.

Plate 4.1 **Take-all – whiteheads**
(Gaeumannomyces graminis) of wheat.

Plate 4.2 **Scab** *(Gibberella zeae)* of wheat.

Plate 4.3 **Sooty mould** *(Cladosporium* spp.*)*
of wheat.

BASF

Plate 4.4 **Yellow rust** *(Puccinia striiformis)*
of wheat. Glume infection.

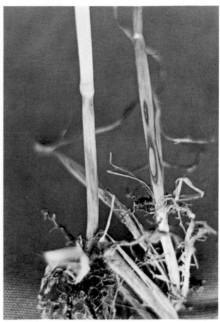

Plate 5.1 **Eyespot** *(Pseudocercosporella herpotrichoides) of wheat.* BASF

Plate 5.2 **Sharp eyespot** *(Pellicularia filamentosa = Rhizoctonia solani) of wheat.* BASF

Plate 5.3 **Foot rot** *(Fusarium spp.) of wheat.*

Plate 5.4 **Take-all** *(Gaeumannomyces graminis) of wheat. Foot and root rot symptoms.*

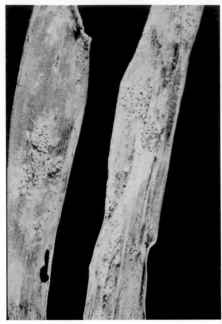

Plate 6.1 **Powdery mildew** *(Erysiphe graminis)* of barley. Conidial pustules. `BASF`

Plate 6.2 **Powdery mildew** *(Erysiphe graminis)* of barley. Cleistothecial stage. `BASF`

Plate 6.3 **Brown rust** *(Puccinia hordei)* of barley. Uredial stage. `BASF`

Plate 6.4 **Yellow rust** *(Puccinia striiformis)* of barley. Uredial stage.

Plate 7.1 **Genetic leaf spot** of barley.

Plate 7.2 **Septoria nodorum** on barley.

Plate 7.3 **Spot blotch** *(Cochliobolus sativus)* of barley.

Plate 7.4 **Halo spot** *(Selenophoma donacis)* of barley.

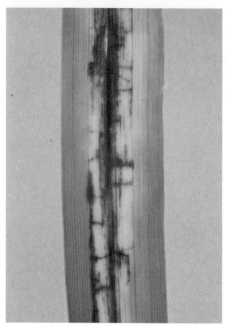

Plate 8.1 **Net blotch** *(Pyrenophora teres)* of barley.

Plate 8.2 **Leaf blotch** or **scald** *(Rhynchosporium secalis)* of barley. BASF

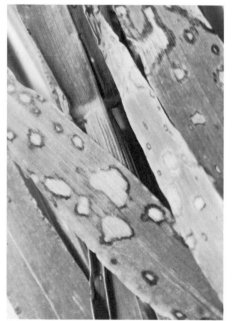

Plate 8.3 **Herbicide scorch** on barley. BASF

Plate 8.4 **Manganese deficiency** on barley.

Plate 9.1 **Covered smut** *(Ustilago hordei)* of barley.

Plate 9.2 **Leaf stripe** *(Pyrenophora graminea)* of barley.

Plate 9.3 **Barley yellow dwarf** *(Virus)* on barley.

Plate 9.4 **Resistant reaction** of barley to powdery mildew *(Erysiphe graminis)*.

Plate 10.1 **Halo blight** *(Pseudomonas coronafaciens)* of oats.

Plate 10.2 **Seedling blotch** *(Pyrenophora avenae)* of oats.

Plate 10.3 **Crown rust** *(Puccinia coronata)* of oats. Uredial stage.

Plate 10.4 **Powdery mildew** *(Erysiphe graminis)* of oats.

Plate 11.1 **Red leaf** *(Barley yellow dwarf virus)* of oats.

Plate 11.2 **Grey speck** *(Manganese deficiency)* of oats. Susceptible variety in foreground.

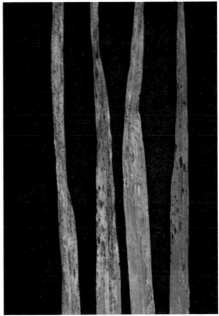

Plate 11.3 **Loose smut** *(Ustilago avenae)* of oats.

Plate 11.4 **Speckled blotch** *(Leptosphaeria avenaria = Septoria avenae)* of oats.

Plate 12.1 **Ergot** *(Claviceps purpurea)* of rye. Sclerotia replacing grains.

Plate 12.2 **Brown rust** *(Puccinia recondita)* of rye. Uredial stage.

Plate 12.3 **Ergot** *(Claviceps purpurea)* Stromatal heads produced by sclerotium.

Plate 12.4 **Eyespot** *(Pseudocercosporella herpotrichoides)* of rye. Straggling symptoms.

BASF

Plate 13.1 **Southern leaf blight**
(Cochliobolus heterostrophus) of maize.
Race T resistant and susceptible reactions.

Plate 13.2 **Northern leaf blight**
(Trichometasphaeria turcica) of maize.

Plate 13.3 **Bacterial wilt** *(Xanthomonas stewartii)* of maize. Early systemic infection.

Plate 13.4 **Common smut** *(Ustilago maydis)* of maize.

Plate 14.1 **Stalk rot** *(Diplodia maydis)* of maize.

Plate 14.2 **Stalk rot** *(Gibberella zeae)* of maize.

Plate 14.3 **Ear rot** *(Diplodia maydis)* of maize.

Plate 14.4 **Ear rot** *(Gibberella zeae)* of maize.

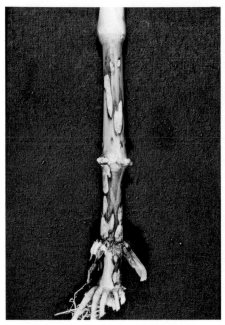

Plate 15.1 **Sharp eyespot** *(Pellicularia filamentosa = Rhizoctonia solani)* of maize.

Plate 15.2 **Corn stunt** *(Spiroplasma)* of maize.

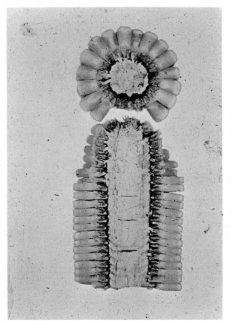

Plate 15.3 **Cob rot** *(Nigrospora oryzae)* of maize.

Plate 15.4 **Kernel rot** *(Gibberella moniliforme)* of maize.

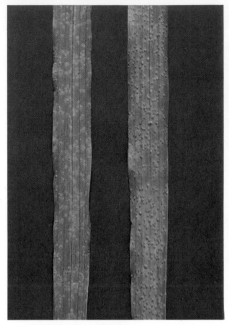

Plate 16.1 **Partial resistance** of barley to brown rust *(Puccinia hordei)*. Resistant cv. Vada (left) compared with cv. Midas (right).

Plate 16.2 **Hypersensitive resistance** of barley to mildew *(Erysiphe graminis)*. Resistant and susceptible seedlings.

Plate 16.3 **Spreader bed nursery** to assess plants for resistance to foliar disease.

Plate 16.4 **Fungicide trial** showing control of eyespot lodging *(Pseudocercosporella herpotrichoides)* in winter wheat. BASF

Compendium of cereal diseases

The diseases described in this Compendium have been arranged in alphabetical order according to the name of the sexual stage, if present, or asexual stage in the imperfect fungi. In the Compendium index both the sexual and asexual names are included as well as other synonyms. Bacterial diseases, virus diseases and diseases due to mineral deficiencies are included after the fungal diseases. The mycological details of the fungal and bacterial pathogens are based on the Description of Pathogenic Fungi and Bacteria published by the Commonwealth Agricultural Bureaux whom the authors acknowledge for permission to use this information.

List of Diseases

Diseases caused by fungi

Claviceps purpurea (Fr.) Tul – Ergot of cereals and grasses
Cochliobolus carbonum Nelson – Leaf spot of maize
Cochliobolus heterostrophus (Drechsler) Drechsler – Southern leaf blight of maize
Cochliobolus sativus Ito and Kuribay – Spot blotch or foot and root rot of cereals
Cochliobolus victoriae Nelson – Victoria blight of oats
Colletotrichum graminicola (Ces.) Wils. – Anthracnose of cereals and grasses
Diplodia spp. – Stalk and ear rot of maize
Erysiphe graminis DC. ex Merat – Cereal powdery mildew
Fusarium culmorum (W.G. Sm) Sacc. – Seedling blight, foot and root rot and head blight of cereals
Gibberella avenaceae Cook. – Seedling blight, spring yellows, foot and root rot and head blight of cereals
Gibberella moniliforme (Sheld.) Snyd. & Hans. – Kernel and stalk rot of maize
Gibberella zeae (Schw.) Petch – Seedling blight, foot and root rot of small grain cereals. Stalk and ear rot of maize.
Gaeumannomyces graminis (Sacc.) Arx & Oliver – Take-all or Whiteheads of cereals and grasses
Leptosphaeria avenaria f. sp. *avenaria* Weber – Speckled blotch of oats

Leptosphaeria nodorum Muller – Glume blotch of wheat and barley

Micronectriella nivalis (Schaffn.) Booth – Pre-emergence blight, root rot and head blight of cereals. Snow mould.

Mycosphaerella graminicola (Fckl.) Sanderson – Leaf spot of wheat

Nigrospora oryzae (Berk. & Br.) Petch – Cob rot of maize

Pseudocercosporella herpotrichoides (Fron.) Deighton – Eyespot of wheat and barley

Puccinia coronata Corda. f. sp. *avenae* Erikss – Crown rust of oats

Puccinia hordei Otth. – Brown or leaf rust of barley

Puccinia graminis Pers. – Black stem rust of wheat and other cereals

Puccinia polysora Underw. – Southern corn rust

Puccinia recondita Rob & Desm. – Brown (leaf) rust of wheat and rye

Puccinia sorghi Schw. – Common corn rust

Puccinia striiformis West – Stripe or yellow rust of wheat and barley

Pythium spp. – Root rot and seedling blight of cereals and grasses

Pyrenophora avenae Ito & Kuribayashi apud Ito – Leaf stripe and seedling blotch of oats

Pyrenophora graminea Ito & Kuribayashi apud Ito – Leaf stripe of barley

Pyrenophora teres Drechsler – Net blotch of barley

Pellicularia filamentosa (Pat.) Rogers – Sharp eyespot of cereals

Rhynchosporium secalis (Oud.) J. J. Davis – Leaf blotch or scald of barley

Sclerophthora macrospora (Sacc.) Thirum, Shaw & Naras – Downy mildew of small grain cereals and grasses

Sclerophthora macrospora (Sacc.) Thirum., Shaw & Naras – Crazy top of maize

Sclerophthora rayssiae var *zeae* Payak & Renfro – Brown stripe downy mildew of maize

Sclerospora sorghi (Kulk) Weston & Uppah – Sorghum downy mildew on maize

Selenophoma donacis (Pass) Sprague & A. G. Johnson – Halo spot of barley

Septoria passerinii Sacc. – Speckled leaf blotch of barley

Tilletia caries (DC.) Tul. – Bunt or stinking smut of wheat

Trichometasphaeria turcica (Luttrell) – Northern leaf blight of maize and sorghums

Urocystis tritici Koern – Flag smut of wheat

Ustilago avenae (Pers.) Rostrup – Loose smut of oats

Ustilago hordei (Pers.) Lagerh. – Covered smut of oats and barley

Ustilago maydis (DC.) Corda – Common smut of maize

Ustilago nuda (Jensen) Rostrup – Loose smut of wheat and barley

Diseases caused by bacteria and Spiroplasma

Corynebacterium tritici (Hutchinson) Burkholder – Yellow slime or 'tundu' disease of
  wheat
Erwinia stewartii (Smith) Dye – Bacterial wilt of maize
Pseudomonas coronafaciens (Elliott) Stapp. – Halo blight of oats
Pseudomonas striafaciens (Elliott) Starr & Burkholder – Bacterial stripe blight of oats
Corn Stunt *(Spiroplasma* Davis & Worley)

Diseases caused by viruses

Barley Yellow Dwarf Virus (BYDF)
Maize Dwarf Mosaic Virus (MDMV)
Soil-borne Oat Mosaic Virus (OMV)
Soil-borne Wheat Mosaic Virus (WMV)
Wheat Streak Mosaic Virus (WSMV)

Miscellaneous

Oat Blast

Deficiency Diseases

Diseases caused by fungi

Claviceps purpurea (Fr.) Tul – Ergot of cereals and grasses.

*Ergots (sclerotia) purplish-black, 2–20 mm long according to host species,
completely replacing the seed; stalked stromatal heads 5–25 mm, developing from
ergots, stalks white with spherical, pink, papillate heads; perithecia sunken over
surface of stromatal heads, ostiolate; asci clavate, slightly curved, interspersed with
paraphyses; ascospores eight, hyaline, filiform, septate when mature, 50–76 × 0·6–
0·7 um; Conidia (sphacelia stage) extruded from ovary in sugary slime (honeydew),
hyaline, ellipsoid, unicellular, 4–6 × 2–3 um.*

The ergot fungus can parasitize a wide range of cereals and grasses with rye being very susceptible and, in descending order of susceptibility, wheat, barley and oats being more resistant. It causes a disease which affects only the flowering parts of the host plant. Affected plants produce ergots or sclerotia which completely replace the grain in the ears. These hard, almost black sclerotia often fall to the ground before harvest or, in some cases, they may be harvested and either sown again with the seed or, possibly, eaten directly by animals. They might also be ground up along with the grain and contaminate the flour or corn-meal. Unfortunately, ergots contain noxious substances, mainly alkaloid materials, which are injurious to livestock and to humans if contaminated flour is eaten. There appears to have been only one occurrence of typical human gangrenous ergotism in the U.K. and that was as far back as 1762 in Bury St. Edmunds but other similar tragedies have been reported in Europe and other countries in recent times. The toxins can also produce severe convulsions in man and animals. Ergots also have a medicinal value and the drugs prepared from the ergot extracts are used extensively in surgical operations of the brain.

When ergots fall to the soil they remain in this resting state until the following year when they germinate, if they are on or near the soil surface, at about the time the cereal crops come into flower. Ergot germination is influenced greatly by temperature and it has been shown that ergots exposed to temperatures below freezing for one month will produce stromatal heads most rapidly at 9–15°C. and are inhibited at 18°C. and above (Krebs and Freisen, Plant Dis. Reptr. **43**; 1266, 1959). As many as sixty stromatal heads may arise from each ergot, the perithecia being completely sunken in the head. The ascospores are extruded from the perithecial ostiole in a viscous fluid under conditions of high air humidity (76–78% relative humidity). Spread of the ascospores to neighbouring flowers is by insects and, to some extent, rain-splash. It has also been demonstrated that when rain showers are followed by sunny periods, the ascospores may be forcibly ejected from the perithecia and then dispersed by wind. The co-ordination of ascospore development and discharge and the flowering period of the host is essential to epidemic development as the host flower tissues are only susceptible for a short period after anthesis. The susceptibility of various hosts may be related to the length of time the flowers remain open. This feature is of prime concern to the plant breeders who are at present engaged, in several cereal crops, in the breeding of hybrid varieties. The florets of the male-sterile lines of self-pollinated cereals are open for a long time and are thus susceptible for an extended period. Disease incidence of over 76% of the heads and 36% of the florets has been reported in male-sterile barley in the U.S.A. (Puranik and Mathre, Phytopathology, **61**; 1075, 1971).

The ascospores germinate on the stigmas and soon infect the developing ovaries. The conidial stage is produced as numerous short conidiophores closely packed over the convoluted surface of the remains of the ovary. The small, unicellular, hyaline conidia are produced at the tips of the conidiophores, being abstricted in succession and being embedded in a sticky fluid known as 'honeydew' which attracts insects which passively carry the spores to other healthy florets. Rain-splash can also account for the dispersal of these spores. This asexual stage was originally thought to be a separate fungus and is often referred to by its old name of *Sphacelia segetum* Lév. The generally accepted view is that these conidia germinate to produce mycelium which penetrates the ovary near its base. The mycelium gradually ramifies in the enlarging ovary and, instead of grain, a sclerotium is eventually produced which projects out of the floret to a length often three times that of a normal grain but the size varies according to the host.

Cool, wet weather during the flowering period increases the severity of this disease due both to the conditions being favourable for dispersal and to the prolongation of flowering. Much of the initial inoculum comes from the stromatal perithecia but there is now much evidence to implicate various grass species as alternative sources of inoculum. Cross-infection studies have shown that wheat, barley and rye could be infected with fungal isolates from 38 different graminaceous host species (Campbell, Canadian Journal of Botany, **35**; 315, 1957) and Mantle and Shaw (Plant Pathology, **26**; 121, 1977), have recently published a case study of the aetiology of the disease confirming, by use of thin layer chromatography to identify strains of ergot on the basis of the characteristic range of alkaloids found in sclerotia, that in Oxfordshire, England, *Alopecurus myosuroides* and *A. pratensis* have important roles in the epidemiology of the ergot disease of cereals.

The disease rarely achieves economic importance in most countries and it is not usually necessary to resort to control measures. Varietal resistance has been shown to differ and pathogenic races are known to exist. The use of ergot-free seed is most important and this can be achieved by a flotation method using solutions of sodium chloride or potassium chloride. Deep ploughing and rotation of crops are effective remedies because ergots buried about 25 cm deep do not germinate and appear to rot away after a year. It has also been demonstrated that reasonable control of ergot on male-sterile barley can be achieved by the application of 2,400 ug/ml benomyl applied three times prior to and during anthesis.

Notes

The fungus can be artificially cultured from either ascospores or conidia on ammonium citrate agar medium (Puranik and Mathre, *loc. cit.*) and incubated for 10–12 days at 24–26°C. Conidial suspensions can be prepared by shaking the cultures with water and filtering the suspension through six layers of cheesecloth. Infection can be achieved with a 10 conidia/ml suspension on barley but about 1000 conidia/ml is required for wheat. Maximum infection is produced with a suspension of about 10^5 conidia/ml. Artificial inoculation techniques involve the selection of open florets, the glumes of which are cut and the aqueous conidial suspension either dropped into each individual floret with a capillary tube or sprayed on by means of an atomizer.

Cochliobolus carbonum Nelson – Leaf spot of maize.

Conidial stage = Drechslera zeicola *(Stout) Subram and Jain.*
   syn. Helminthosporium carbonum *Ullstrup.*
Conidiophores single or in small groups, straight or flexuous, mid to dark brown or olivaceous brown, up to 250 um *long, 5·8* um *thick. Conidia straight to slightly curved, widest at centre tapering to rounded ends, 25–100* um × *7–18* um, *2–12 pseudosepta, hilum inconspicuous, germination polar, very dark or olivaceous brown. Perithecia black, ellipsoidal to globose, 355–550* um *high* × *320–430* um *in diameter, ostiolar beak well defined, 60–200* um *long with mass of hyaline cells frequently covering apex. Asci cylindrical or clavate, straight to slightly curved, 160–257* × *18·2–27·4* um *containing 1–8 ascospores. Ascospores coiled, filiform, hyaline, 5–9 septate, 182·0–306·4* × *6·4–9·6* um, *germination terminal or lateral.*

Leaf spot of maize is of minor economic importance and is only encountered on a few susceptible inbred lines. It is widely distributed in the Americas, south-east Asia, south-east Europe, south and central Africa and India. It occurs only on maize and exists as two physiologically specialized races which differ somewhat in the symptoms they produce. Race 1 is highly virulent and limited in parasitism to a few inbred lines of maize. It produces tan, oval to circular lesions which vary in size from very small to 2–3 cm and which often show a concentric pattern. Abundant lesions are formed under favourable conditions and sporulation is profuse on leaf sheaths. Ears are readily attacked resulting in a black felty weft over the kernels which gives them a charred appearance. The other form, race 2, gives identical ear rotting symptoms but the leaf symptoms, which are rarely found, are oblong, chocolate coloured spots ranging in size up to 2 cm. Race 2 is the less aggressive and shows no distinct host specialization. A host specific toxin is produced. Primary inoculum comes mainly from crop residues although carry-over can occur by deep-seated infections of seed. Secondary spread is by air-borne conidia and humid weather favours spread of the disease. Control is through the use of host resistance and a single recessive gene for resistance is widely used. It would, however, seem desirable to find additional forms of resistance to spread the risk.

Notes
The two races are similar in culture. Growth *in vitro* on corn meal agar is best at 26°C. The fungus is heterothallic and both races occur in the two compatibility groups *A* and *a*, although, in nature, race 1 is commonly in group *A* and race 2 in group *a*. *In vitro* production of ascocarps is achieved by pairing compatible isolates on opposite sides of a sterilized maize leaf (as with *C. heterostrophus*) on agar and functional asci are produced in 22 days at 24°C. if the corn meal agar is at pH 4. (Nelson, Phytopath, **49**; 807, 1959).

Cochliobolus heterostrophus (Drechsler) Drechsler – Southern leaf blight of maize.

Conidial stage = Drechslera maydis *(Nisikado) Subramanian and Jain.*
      syn.   Helminthosporium maydis *Nisikado.*
Conidiophores in groups of 2 to 3 arising from dark brown to black stromata, straight or flexuous, sometimes geniculate, mid to dark brown, pale near apex, smooth, up to 700 um long, 5 to 10 um thick. Conidia curved, fusiform, pale to mid dark golden brown, smooth, 5 to 11 pseudoseptate, 70 to 160 um long, 15 to 20 um wide, hilum dark, 3 to 4·5 um wide, germination polar. Perithecia numerous, ellipsoidal, 0·4 mm diameter, black, well-defined ostiolar beak. Asci numerous, short stipitate, rounded ends, 160–180 um long containing typically 4 ascospores. Ascospores filamentous, in parallel multiple (usually 4) coils.

Southern leaf blight occurs widely on maize in the warmer regions of the world and is common in the south-eastern and mid-western states of the U.S.A. It has also been reported on teosinte and sorghum in the field. Until recently it was a disease of fairly minor importance but in 1970 a severe epidemic leading to considerable yield losses occurred in the U.S.A. This was caused by a variant of the pathogen (race T) which was specifically virulent on lines carrying the Texas (T) cytoplasmic factor for male sterility (ms) and this cytoplasm was widely distributed in commercial hybrids. Race T was first reported from the Philippines in 1961 and was known to occur in the U.S.A. prior to 1970.

Symptoms of the common race O are parallel-sided greyish tan leaf lesions which vary from minute spots to 3 cm lesions. Young lesions are elliptical but gradually elongate and become rectangular due to restriction by leaf veins. The lesions may be zonate and older lesions may be grey with conidia. With race T the lesions are more diffuse and there may be marginal chlorosis and leaf tissue collapse. Race T is less restricted to the leaves, attacking ears more readily and also sporulating more freely than race O. Race T appears to have a lower temperature optimum than race O which may have contributed to its widespread occurrence in the U.S. corn belt in 1970. Environmental conditions of persistent high humidities and moisture were also particularly favourable for disease development in 1970. Primary inoculum is mainly from crop residues and secondary conidial infection and spread of the disease through the season is normal. Conidiospore dispersal is by air but there are no detailed studies. Penetration of leaves is normally direct but may be through stomata. A host-specific toxin is produced and relatively more is produced by race T. Control of the disease is normally through the use of host resistance and the toxin has been used to screen against genotypes with the T *ms* cytoplasm, as race T is only mildly virulent on genotypes with 'normal' or other *ms* cytoplasm. Genetic resistance to race O exists based on several additive genes and also two linked recessive genes for resistance have been described. Crop rotation, burying or burning crop debris are useful control measures and fungicides have been used to good effect particularly on sweet corn where the practice is more cost effective. (Reference to the southern corn leaf blight epidemic of 1970 in the U.S.A. Plant Dis. Reptr. **54**; Part II, 1099, 1970.)

Notes
The fungus grows well on P.D.A. and other standard media. *In vitro* growth of mycelium and conidial germination is best at 25–30°C. but conidia develop optimally at 23°C. The pathotoxin is produced in Fries modified medium plus 2% yeast extract (Smedegard-Peterson and Nelson. Can. J. Bot. **47**; 951, 1969) and is assayed by a maize seedling root inhibition test by symptoms on detached leaves floated on culture filtrates. *C. heterostrophus* is heterothallic (Nelson. Phytopath. **47**; 191, 1957) and mature perithecia are best produced by pairing isolates on opposite sides of a section

of sterile maize leaf placed in a petri dish containing corn meal agar or Sach's agar at 24°C.

Cochliobolus sativus Ito and Kuribay – Spot blotch or foot and root rot of cereals.

Conidial stage = Helminthosporium sativum.
Mycelium olivaceous, black at maturity, abundant on agar media. Conidiophores protrude in groups of 2–3 through stomates or from between epidermal cells of host, basal cell swollen. On agar, conidiophores are short modified branches of hyphae. Conidia curved or somewhat cylindrical, thick walled 3–10 septate, ends abruptly rounded, dark olive brown, 60–120 × 15–20 um. Perithecia erumpent from dead host tissue, black to brown, flask-shaped with ostiolar beaks, 370–530 × 340–470 um. Asci numerous, mainly cylindrical, straight or slightly curved, 4–8 spored. Ascospores flagelliform or filiform, 6–13 septate, 160–360 × 6–9 um, spirally coiled within the ascus.

This disease, which affects barley, wheat, rye and a number of weed and cultivated grasses, is widespread in occurrence in the warmer cereal growing regions, particularly in North America and parts of Australia. It is relatively unimportant in Europe especially where crops are grown with little moisture stress. On barley, the disease is most apparent on the leaves although it also causes a foot or root rot. On wheat, the foot and root rot phases are probably of more economic significance. Precise diagnosis is difficult and consequently the importance of the disease, especially the seedling blight and root rot stages, may have been underestimated.

The seedling blight is typically a dry rot and is particularly obvious in warm soil conditions. On barley, the first symptoms are dark, chocolate brown spots on young leaf sheaths. As infection progresses inwards it may be severe enough to kill the seedling, usually after emergence. Surviving infected plants tend to be dwarfed, dark green, erect and tiller excessively. The sheath lesions may extend into the leaf blade. Roots may exhibit a brown rotting. The characteristic leaf spots are variable in size but are mostly oblong or lens-shaped and may coalesce to form irregular blotches. The centres of the blotches are dark brown, gradually merging at the edges into the green colour of the leaf. On the older lesions there may be abundant conidial production which gives the lesion an olivaceous hue. The disease progresses up the plant by the spread of conidia. The glumes may also develop dark brown spots, especially at their base and also the grains at the embryo end may exhibit the characteristic 'black point' symptom. The fungus may attack the stem nodes (node canker or rot) producing brownish black spots that may coalesce and become velvety as conidia are produced abundantly. In the foot rot phase, especially in wheat, leaf sheaths, cortical tissues and crown roots are affected. The stem bases may have rust brown streaks and blotches. Affected roots may be covered with small irregular brown spots or may show more general browning. Root development is reduced and roots may become brittle and tear off at the crown if the plant is pulled. Rotting may cause the death of tillers, the stunting of surviving tillers and the partial emergence of the spike, sterility and shrivelled grain.

Infection of roots, crowns and basal stem portions can be dramatic and shows as scattered patches of stunted, reddish-brown plants in the field. There is often a gradation in severity from the centre of the patch to the edge.

The fungus may be either seed- or soil-borne or it may pass to the next crop from infected weeds or volunteer cereal plants. Seed- and soil-borne inoculum is responsible for seedling blight and the foot rot symptoms. Secondary spread is by means of conidia produced either in the primary lesions or, in the spring, from volunteer plants, weed grasses or stubble debris. Conidia may be abundant on the stubble and in the surface soil where they can survive the winter and are a most important source of primary infection of wheat seedlings. The perfect (ascospore) stage is uncommon in nature and of little epidemiological importance. Seedling blight and root rot of barley occur within the range 8–28°C. with the maximum rate of development at about 20°C. Leaf symptoms and ear infection are more pronounced at higher temperatures, within the range 24–28°C.

Control of seed-borne infection can be affected by seed dressing with organo-mercurial compounds. Proper stubble cleaning, ploughing in of stubble debris, grass weeds and volunteer cereals all help to reduce the overwintering inoculum. Crop rotations may also decrease the risk of crop losses. The fungus is adapted to higher temperatures (above 15°C.) so late autumn or early spring sowing is advisable. Genetic host resistance to the root rot and seedling blight phases of disease has been identified in barley and could provide the most practical control method. However, many physiologic races of the pathogen have been recognized.

Notes

Conidia can be produced abundantly on a sucrose: asparagine: yeast extract agar and mature perithecia can be obtained on seeds of maize surface-sterilized, boiled for one minute and partly immersed in Sachs' agar. Inoculum for root and seedling blight investigations can be produced by growing the fungus on a sand: corn meal: nutrient salt medium in culture flasks for 10 days at 24°C. The inoculum is then sieved and mixed 1:9 with white silica sand. The test seeds are planted direct in this medium. Storage is by standard methods of mineral oil immersion on agar slants.

Cochliobolus victoriae Nelson – Victoria blight of oats.

Conidial stage = Drechslera victoriae *(Meehan & Murphy) Subramanian & Jain.*
syn.   Helminthosporium victoriae *Meehan & Murphy.*
Conidiophores black to dark olivaceous, rounded at the base, slightly curved, conidia widest near the centre, tapering to a rounded tip, 40–130 × 11–25 um, 4- to 11-septate, moderately thin walls.

Perithecia black, ellipsoid to globose, 225–430 um in height × 210–370 um in diameter. Long brown setae are produced over the upper third of the perithecium. Asci, cylindrical or clavate, straight or slightly curved with a short stipe, 98–207 × 20–38. Ascospores, 1–8, coiled in a close helix, hyaline, filiform, 5–9 septate, 147–302 × 6–13 um.

Victoria blight of oats was only first described in 1946 when it was found in the mid-west of the United States of America. It has not been reported in the United Kingdom on oats but it has been found in some parts of Scotland on grasses. The limited distribution is probably due to the high degree of specificity of the pathogen to the cultivar Victoria and its relatives. A large number of new cultivars had been introduced into America based on Victoria in which resistance to crown rust had been found.

The symptoms of the disease are a necrosis and reddening of seedling leaves which is later accompanied by a rotting of the stem bases. The reddening often gives a striping effect to the young leaves and, in severe infections, leaves and seedlings can be killed. Some brown lesions do develop on leaves and root rotting can occur. There is also a weakening of the straw leading to strawbreaking and lodging. Conidia are produced as dark olivaceous or velvety spore masses around the nodes which become blackened. *C. victoriae* is a heterothallic species, each mating type being cross-fertile with two corresponding mating types of *C. carbonum* Nelson (*H. carbonum* Ullstrup). Mature perithecia have only been produced in culture when two isolates of opposite mating type are placed side by side. There have been no reports of the discovery of mature perithecia in nature.

Victoria blight provides a clear-cut illustration of toxin-regulated host specificity. It has been demonstrated that the production of toxin in culture is correlated with the relative virulence of the isolates. Non-pathogenic isolates produced no detectable toxin, the ability to produce toxin being apparently necessary for pathogenicity of *C. victoria* to blight-susceptible oat cultivars. Toxin production is qualitatively determined by a single gene whereas the amount of toxin produced appears to be controlled by several genes. The toxin has been shown to increase the permeability of the plasma membrane and tonoplast of susceptible oat plants but not of resistant plants.

The pathogen is both seed- and soil-borne. If the soil is uncontaminated, seed treatment with organo-mercurial compounds will give control as will a hot water treatment where the seed is steeped at 26°C. for 56 hours. However, with such a host-specific pathogen the use of resistant varieties must be the most sensible and efficient control measure.

Notes

The fungus can be isolated from infected seed, from the leaf lesions, directly from the sporing areas around the nodes. It has no special requirement for growth and can be cultured successfully on a range of fungal media incubated between 20–25°C. It produces a dark grey or grey-black cottony growth, not very distinguishable from *C. sativus*. For studies involving the toxins, cultures can be prepared in flasks on modified Fries medium. The flasks are inoculated with small agar blocks from a sporing culture and incubated at 21–23°C. The culture broth is then filtered for assay. The bioassay is conducted on hulled seeds which are germinated for 24 hours at 24°C. between moist filter paper. A dilution series of the culture filtrate is then added to petri-dishes containing the germinating seeds and the assay end-point determined after 48 hours as the maximum dilution which prevents the roots becoming more than 1 cm long. This method can also be used to screen segregating populations of oat seedlings for resistance. Isolates of *C. victoria* can be stored in soil at 5°C. where they have been shown to remain viable and pathogenic after twelve years.

Colletotrichum graminicola (Ces.) Wils. – Anthracnose of cereals and grasses.

Acervuli dark brown or black, elongate; setae few or many, dark brown or black, 1–2 septate, 60–120 × 6–8 um; conidiophores very short, 6–12 × 1–2 um; conidia falcate, spindle – or boat-shaped, 2 – to several – guttulate, 18–26 × 3–4 um.

Anthracnose is widely distributed on wheat and rye although barley, oats, maize and a very wide range of grasses are also attacked but to a lesser extent. It has been reported in North and South America, Asia, Africa, Australia and Europe but is absent from the United Kingdom. The symptoms are not easy to diagnose as, in the main, there is simply a reduction in vigour of infected plants. There may also be some premature ripening and plant death in some instances. There may be what appears to be a light covering of mould on the basal leaves but the fungus attacks the roots as well. The effect of the fungal presence is to cause a browning of the culm bases and the crown tissues. The dark-coloured acervuli then appear over these affected areas, especially if moisture is plentiful. The fungus is particularly sensitive to desiccation. There can be a considerable loss of photosynthetic tissue resulting in a reduction in grain size and quality.

As a saprophyte on infected plant debris, the fungus is in a good position to recommence the disease cycle infection of the young plants occurring from either mycelium or from conidia splashed by rain from the acervuli. Superficial grain infection can occur and this is a possible source of the seedling root and crown infection.

Anthracnose is very much associated with poor, infertile, coarse soils and its incidence and severity is closely linked with continuous cereal growing or rotations which include a high proportion of cereals and grasses. The disease can be ameliorated by good crop hygiene with adequate burial of crop residues. The decomposition of such debris can be aided by the improvement of soil fertility and by the incorporation of legumes and other dicotylodenous crops whose inclusion in the rotation will also reduce the level of inoculum.

Diplodia spp. – Stalk and ear rot of maize.

Diplodia maydis *(Berk) Sacc.*
Pycnidia immersed, globose, dark brown-black, 150–300 um diameter, ostiolar beak, 40 um diameter protruding through epidermis. Conidiophores simple, short and pointed. Conidia straight or slightly curved, smooth walled, pale brown, apex rounded, base truncate, 15–34 × 5–8 um, normally 2-celled occasionally 1–3-celled. Scolecospores, slender hyaline, reported in culture.

D. macrospora *Earle.*
As for D. maydis *except conidia 44–82 × 7·5–11·5 um, occasionally 4-celled (normally 2).*

The disease is widespread where maize is grown in Africa, the Far East, Europe and North, Central and South America. Two species are involved, *Diplodia maydis* being the more common and widespread whereas *D. macrospora* is more common in the warmer humid regions of maize culture. The fungus causes a seedling blight and may infect roots but the most common and severe effects are stalk and ear rotting. It is the most common stalk rot in the United States Corn Belt and can cause appreciable damage as an ear rot in localized areas. Grain losses up to 18% have been reported in the mid-west U.S.A. but it is less important in the cooler, drier regions. Symptoms are the same for both species. A seedling blight may develop on plants grown from infected seed and is characterized by cortical lesions which give a brown dry rot especially below the soil surface. Symptoms on growing plants are not usually obvious until after pollination when dark purple-brown blotches are apparent on leaf sheaths extending into the nodes and basal portions of the internodes. A weft of mycelium develops between the sheaths and stalk and penetration of the stalk occurs although this frequently develops from the buttress roots. When the lower stalk is split open the pith is seen to have disintegrated and often only the threads of vascular tissue remain intact. Leaves turn greyish or bleached and the rotted stalks break over in wind and rain. Ears may senesce prematurely resulting in light, shrivelled grain.

The ears themselves may become infected, the severity depending on the timing of infection and the environmental conditions. Infection typically progresses from the base of the ear upwards and the entire ear may become greyish-brown and shrunken. The husks appear bleached and the light ears tend to remain upright and the husks are held tight by the mycelial growth. Later infection may result in only a whitish mould growing between the kernels. Black minute pycnidia may be seen at maturity just beneath the surface of the lower internodes of the stalk, at the base of the husks and on the sides of badly infected kernels.

The fungus is seed- and soil-borne and overwinters on crop debris which normally provides the source of primary inoculum. When spores are mature, they are exuded from the pycnidia in warm, moist weather and dispersed by wind to the growing crop. It is reported that the fungus develops most aggressively in corn tissues approaching physiological maturity. *D. maydis* exists as physiologically specialized forms which differ in their overall aggressiveness. Isolates appear to be adapted to specific climatic regions and this relates to temperature sensitivity. Later maturing varieties are generally more resistant than early varieties in a particular climatic zone and 'flint' types tend to be more resistant than 'dent' types. Seed treatment, crop rotation and sanitation measures to remove infected crop debris are all advocated to reduce primary inoculum. Fertilizer balance is important and plants are less prone to attack when nitrogen and potassium are applied optimally.

Notes
D. maydis can be cultured on most common synthetic media but *D. macrospora* has a requirement for biotin. This nutritional difference is used as a distinguishing characteristic between the species. Plants can be artificially inoculated with wooden toothpicks which are previously sterilized and infested with a mycelial culture of *D. maydis* before insertion into the stems.

Erysiphe graminis D.C. ex Merat – Cereal powdery mildew.

Mycelium white to grey, becoming brown, superficial with large oval digitate haustoria in epidermal cells, short bulbous conidiophores abstricting chains of unicellular, hyaline, ellipsoid conidia, the most mature being distal on the chain, 25–33 × 14–17 um; cleistothecia dark, spherical 135–200 um, produced in clusters in the mycelial mat, simple myceloid appendages, 9–30 asci with usually 8 ascospores, 20–23 × 10–13 um hyaline, ellipsoid which usually form after detachment of the cleistothecia from the host tissue.

The symptoms are very similar on all cereals with yellowing, curling and dwarfing always associated with the disease which attacks leaves, sheaths, stems and inflorescences. Culms are often so weakened that lodging occurs. The first symptom on leaves is a small chlorotic spotting upon which a white to grey mycelial mat rapidly forms. Masses of conidia are produced from this superficial mat and it is these spores that give the powdery appearance. Later the mycelium darkens and dark brown cleistothecia appear embedded in the mycelium. The dirty grey flattened mycelial mat is similar in appearance on barley and oats but on wheat, colonies are often more discrete, raised and brighter in appearance. Infection of glumes is more common on wheat.

Infection by conidia or ascospores is by direct penetration of the cuticle. The spores germinate best at a relative humidity of 95% and within the temperature range 10 15°C. A short-germ tube is produced at the end of which an appressorium forms. From this a slender penetration peg pierces the host cuticle and epidermal cell. The peg enlarges to form an elliptical haustorium with finger-like appendages at opposite ends. Conidia are produced in great abundance from the mycelial mat and are able to cause new infections directly and thus serve to spread the disease during the growing season. Warm, relatively dry conditions favour development although mildew can develop and cause yield losses under less favourable conditions. Heavily fertilized crops are very susceptible to attack. In the United Kingdom, ascospores generally infect volunteer plants after harvest and the autumn-sown wheat and barley crops are infected by conidia produced on such late tillers. The discharge of ascospores requires the inbibition of water by the cleistothecium and this can take place in the autumn, in which case the ascospores can infect any autumn sown host species or perennial grass, or, it may survive the winter, as in North America, and discharge its spores in the spring.

Conidia, although generally classified as being short-lived, may travel considerable distances in wind currents and be responsible for epidemics in countries neighbouring the inoculum source.

Within *Erysiphe graminis* there exist *formae speciales* distinguishable by the hosts attacked. Wheat is attacked by *E. graminis* f. sp. *tritici*, barley by f. sp. *hordei* and oats by f. sp. *avenae*. Mostly, these *formae speciales* are specific to the type host or closely related species but it has been shown that a certain promiscuity does exist in cases of mixed inocula or when the leaves are pre-disposed to infection by the non-specific *formae speciales* by being previously infected by the specific *formae speciales*.

Physiologic races occur within each *formae speciales* and these can be recognized by testing on differential host varieties. The presence of such races is continually monitored in Great Britain and information of race changes made available to the plant breeders.

Cultural methods of control are aimed at reducing the carry-over of inoculum on stubble or on volunteer plants. Fields should be cultivated or sprayed with herbicide to eliminate these sources of inoculum before the emergence of the autumn-sown crops. Similarly, with the knowledge that the pathogen overwinters on the winter cereals, attempts have been made to control the disease by either banning this bridging crop, as in the case of winter barley in Denmark, or by applying systemic fungicides as seed dressings. Such measures have been shown to delay the development of the epidemic but have not succeeded in eliminating the disease because of the long distance transport of spores from neighbouring countries or from volunteer plants in the same country.

Resistant varieties have been the main form of control but new races of the fungus have frequently overcome such resistance. There are several ways in which *race specific resistances* are being used to give more stable control. For example in the United Kingdom varieties of barley with the same resistance factors are grouped together and farmers are advised to choose varieties from different groups to spread the disease risk. Theoretically, *mixtures* of varieties with different resistances may be blended to give even better disease control. Breeding programmes are also in progress to incorporate different resistances into **isogenic lines** of a single desirable variety to produce *multiline varieties*. Plant breeders are also searching for new sources of resistance of the *partial* and *adult plant* types in barley and oats in the hope that this will be *race non-specific*. Collections of the wild *Hordeum spontaneum* from the Middle East are very promising in this respect. Varieties with partial resistance form part of an *integrated control* programme incorporating good husbandry and chemicals.

The chemical control of cereal mildew has become more practical with the advent of effective, translocatable compounds applied either as seed dressings or foliar sprays.

Such chemical usage is standard practice in the high cost, high return farming systems in north-west Europe. Ethirimol is widely used as a seed dressing to control early infections in spring barley. It is also used as a foliar spray as is tridemorph, fluotrimazol and triadimefon. There is some laboratory evidence for the existence of strains of *E. graminis hordei* which are relatively insensitive to ethirimol but there is no field evidence to support this at present. Tridemorph is also effective against the wheat and oat strains of *E. graminis*, ethirimol is less so.

Notes

Erysiphe graminis is an obligate pathogen and must be maintained on living plants. Conidiospores are ephemeral and should be used to infect fresh plants as soon after collection as possible. Optimum conditions for infection and spore production are at a 16 hour photoperiod at 17°C. but mildew is tolerant of a wide range of conditions. Cultures are best maintained on leaf segments floated on 50 ppm benzimidazole or laid on 0·5% agar containing 150 ppm benzimidazole at 5°C. with a 16 hour photoperiod of a fairly low light intensity. A similar method is used for race testing but at 17°C. Ascospore production is rather more capricious. Cleistothecia are produced most abundantly on senescing tissues with a heavy conidial infection. Successful infection of susceptible barley has been obtained by placing cleistothecia on moist filter paper above plants kept in glass or clear plastic chimneys. The filter paper must be kept moist and eventually cleistothecia erupt and the discharged ascospores fall on and infect the seedlings. A similar technique may be employed using detached leaves floated on benzimidazole in clear polystyrene boxes. At 18–20°C. cleistothecia from barley open in 5–7 days producing sporulating pustules on leaf segments after a further 3–5 days. Wheat cleistothecia take a few days longer to open and to produce pustules.

Fusarium culmorum (W.G. Sm) Sacc. – Seedling blight, foot and root rot and head blight of cereals.

No perithecial state is known. Microconidia absent, macroconidia produced occasionally from conidiophores formed laterally on aerial mycelium but more frequently formed from loose sporodochia. Macroconidia 3–5 septate, slightly curved, strongly dorsiventral, fusoid with apical cell suddenly constricted, 3-septate 26–36 × 4–6 um; 5-septate 34–40 × 5–6 um. Chlamydospores oval to globose, generally intercalary but occasionally terminal, smooth to rough walled, single, in chains, or in clumps.

In pure culture F. culmorum *produces floccose, aerial hyphae, yellow in colour. On the surface of the medium a red pigmentation develops which diffuses into the agar. This pigment eventually develops in the mycelium and the spores, the colony becoming a deep reddish-brown after 7–10 days.*

F. culmorum is one of four species of *Fusarium* which attack cereals. It is the only species in which the perithecial state is unknown. It causes a variety of disease symptoms on a wide range of cereals and grasses and is widespread in occurrence in the main cereal growing countries of the world. It can cause serious reductions in yield, especially wheat, and is associated both with seedlings and the adult crop. Extensive losses have been reported from many countries often resulting in over 50% reductions in grain yield.

The pathogen is mainly soil-borne being a true 'soil inhabitant' possessing a highly competitive saprophytic ability. It has been shown to remain viable on buried stubble trash for two years and is very resistant to cold temperatures. It may initially attack germinating seedlings, often causing a pre-emergence death. Surviving seedlings may show brownish lesions at the base of the coleoptile or on the roots. From a visual examination of diseased seedlings it is almost impossible to distinguish between *F. culmorum*, *F. avenaceum* and *F. nivale* at this stage and it may be necessary to resort to isolation techniques to obtain the correct diagnosis. However, the scraping of coleoptile lesions sometimes yields conidia which may be detected micro-scopically.

Infection at the seedling stage may be in the regions of the hypocotyl and coleoptile, or the pathogen may enter the crown of plants. Entry may be through stomata or between epidermal cells or through wounds made by crown root emergence. Dry conditions as well as poor drainage, wet, acid, heavy soils or deep sowing favour infections in the seedling stages. This is probably due to the longer time taken for the seedling to emerge under such conditions. Once infection has occurred, then a humid microclimate within the crop is favourable for serious attacks of foot rot.

Plants which survive these early attacks may later succumb to foot and root rots. Here, the symptoms may either be a brown discolouration of the basal leaf sheaths or a more pronounced rotting of the tiller bases at about soil level. This is the 'brown foot rot' stage. Plants severely affected by foot rot often produce bleached, poorly filled ears. Some tillers may fail to produce ears completely. Sporodochia may be produced on the ears, those of *F. culmorum* being coral in colour and those of *F. avenaceum* apricot in colour. The effect on the ears depends upon the time of infection, an early infection producing the most shrivelled grains or the most empty heads.

There may also be a brown spotting on the glumes of infected plants and the whole ear may become tinted a red/pink colour. From the head infection, the grains are sometimes infected but this is not the main inoculum source. Conidia can also be produced on infected ears especially under wet conditions.

Fusarium diseases of cereals have not been ranked sufficiently high in the league of economic importance to warrant much attention in terms of control and, in the long term, control will probably be best achieved by the development of resistant cultivars. Partial control can be achieved by seed treatment using organo-mercurial prepara-tions and also by spray application of MBC generating compounds. However, since the inoculum is soil-borne the proper sanitary measures and rotations will also help. The deep burial of crop residues and the late sowing of winter wheat are treatments which have given some success but often environmental conditions favourable to the pathogen will nullify the effects of such attempts to control the disease.

Notes

F. culmorum is one of the most stable and uniform *Fusarium* spp. although mutants do occasionally occur. It can be cultured on a wide range of fungal media and has a wide temperature range for growth with a high optimum (25°C.). It can be easily distinguished in pure culture from *F. avenaceum* by the distinctive sickle-shaped, pedicillate macroconidia and by its abundant production of chlamydospores. It also produces cinnamon-brown sporodochia in culture whereas these are either absent in *F. avenaceum* or orange in colour. Long-term storage can be facilitated under mineral oil.

Gibberella avenaceae Cook – Seedling blight, spring yellows, foot and root rot and head blight of cereals.

Conidial stage Fusarium avenaceum *(Corda ex. Fr.) Sacc.*
Mycelium floccose, generally tinted peach. Sporodochia absent or, where present, orange in colour. Macroconidia fusiform to falcate, 3–7 septate, orange in mass, ranging from 10–70 × 3·5–5 um. Microconidia mostly absent, oval, 0–3 septate; perithecia globose, 125–265 um, ascospores 13–17 × 3·5–6·5 um, hyaline, ellipsoid, mostly one septate. Chlamydospores absent in mycelium, rarely present in conidia.

In general, *F. avenaceum* is not as virulent as the other *Fusarium* species pathogenic on cereals but it is widespread in its distribution in most temperate regions and is also found in the tropics. It is considered mostly as an asexual pathogen although the perfect state, *G. avenaceae*, has been reported in the Pacific, north-west of the United States. It does not normally kill seedlings but does produce shorter and less well-developed plants. Infected seedlings may develop a browning of the basal leaf sheaths although severe foot rotting rarely occurs.

It is both seed- and soil-borne and the disease may be transmitted by mycelium or conidia blown in the wind from crop residues remaining on the soil surface. Although not as important as the other *Fusarium* pathogens it can cause serious losses both as a pre-emergence and seedling blight especially in the colder areas such as the U.S.S.R. in spring wheat and in oats in Scotland. There can also be losses associated with the premature ripening of the infected plants but the disease is most important at the seedling and early vegetative stages. The head blight stage is very similar to that caused by *F. culmorum* but *F. avenaceum* can be distinguished by producing apricot coloured sporodochia on the diseased ears.

As with all the *Fusarium* diseases of cereals, control is mainly concerned with sanitary measures and crop rotation. Crop residues should be deep ploughed and, mostly as a precautionary measure, the seed should be treated with organo-mercurial compounds. Resistant varieties of barley and wheat have been reported and future control would appear to centre around their use in an integrated approach utilizing all methods.

Notes
The fungus can be readily isolated from infected seed which are plated on to potato dextrose agar after surface sterilization in a solution of ethyl alcohol and mercuric chloride followed by several washes in sterile water. The plates are then incubated at 25°C. The cultures can be maintained over long periods on agar slants in screw-capped tubes by consecutive mono-conidial or hyphal tip transfers. They can also be stored under mineral oil on agar slants.

Gibberella moniliforme (Sheld.) Snyd. & Hans. – Kernel and stalk rot of maize.

Conidial stage = Fusarium moniliforme *Sheld.*

       syn.   G. fujikuroi *(Saw) Wr.*

Macronidia sparse, hyaline 15–60 × 2·5–5 um, curved towards tips, 3–5 septate. Microconidia borne in chains or false heads on hyphal branches, abundant, 5–12 × 2–3 um, single celled. Sexual stage rare. Perithecia superficial, globose, smooth, blue-black. Asci elongate, sac-like, 75–100 × 10–16 um containing 8 ascospores arranged in two irregular rows. Ascospores straight, tapering to tips, 1–3 septate (usually 1 septate), 12–17 × 4·5–7 um.

Also Gibberella fujikuroi *(Saw.) Wr. var.* subglutinans *Ed.*
Conidial stage = Fusarium moniliforme *(Sheld.) var.* subglutinans *Wr. & Rg.*
Macroconidia similar to the species, less curved, usually 3 septate. Microconidia borne singly or in false heads, never in chains. Sexual stage rare, similar to the species. Asci usually contain 8 spores, sometimes 4 or 6, arranged in one oblique row.

This disease has a worldwide distribution and is most prevalent in the warmer, drier areas of maize culture, for example in the drier areas of the United States corn belt, California and the south-eastern States. The causal organisms, *Fusarium monili-forme* and the variety *subglutinans* are widely adapted and attack all types of cultivated maize although the sweet corn types are relatively more susceptible to kernel rotting. This is possibly because of the more suitable sugary substrate although the thinner seed coat of these types has been implicated. Some lines which have a relatively high fraction of lysine in the endosperm amino acids are reported as being susceptible to kernel rotting. The pathogenicity of *F. moniliforme* is open to question. Some consider it to be only weakly parasitic, occurring mainly on injured, senescent or decaying tissues, but others ascribe to it a more active role. The fungus, the sexual stage of which is rare in nature, causes a kernel and a stalk rot. On the ear, randomly scattered groups of kernels are seen to be covered with a whitish-pink, lavender or reddish-brown mycelial mat, the colour varying with the environment and host genotype. The symptoms, which are readily seen when the husks are peeled back, occur more frequently towards the tip of the ear. Infection is often associated with damage caused by ear-boring worms. In the stalk rot stage, the interior of the lower internodes are discoloured, the pith is disintegrated and pale pink to white mycelium is often present both in these tissues and at the lower nodes. Kernel infection may result in seedling death before or after emergence although infected seed often produces normally developing plants. Seedling blight is more common with *Gibberella zeae.*

The fungus survives on crop residues and is also commonly carried over to the next crop by infected seed. Stalk rotting becomes apparent after pollination and ear infections occur, apparently, from wind-blown conidiospores. These spores may enter through the silk channel and infect immature kernels and it has recently been suggested that, because the fungus has been observed to be associated with nodal and internodal stalk tissue, that kernel infection may result from systemic vascular infections. This has not been proved conclusively.

There are no specific control measures. Standard practices of chemical seed dressings, destruction of, or ploughing in of, crop debris and crop rotation will all reduce inoculum potential. It has been suggested that host resistance, which is quantitatively inherited, could be increased by practising reciprocal recurrent selection in breeding programmes.

Gibberella zeae. (Schw.) Petch – Seedling blight, foot and root rot of small grain cereals. Stalk and ear rot of maize.

Conidial stage = Fusarium graminearum *(Schw.).*
Macroconidia produced very sparsely on dead tissues near soil level from doliiform phialides 10–14 × 3·5–4·5 um formed laterally or on short multi-branched conidiophores. Conidia sickle-shaped, mostly 4–5 septate, with a well-developed, often

pedicellate foot cell, 40–80 × 4·0–6·5 um. Perithecia black, ovoid with a rough tuberculate outer wall, 140–250 um diameter. Asci clavate with a short stipe, usually 8-spored. Ascospores, hyaline to light brown, straight or curved, mostly 3 septate, 19–24 × 3–4 um. Chlamydospores, when present, intercalary, single in chains or clumps, globose, 10–12 um diameter.

This disease, often described as scab, is of worldwide distribution infecting wheat, oats, barley and rye in temperate regions and maize and rice in the tropics. Although accurate estimation of crop losses due to this pathogen are very sparse in the literature, there are reports of small grain yield reductions reaching as high as 50% and it is almost certain that, in general, estimates are a little conservative due to poor diagnosis of the disease symptoms. On maize, the disease is prevalent in the cooler moist regions of cultivation and in cool seasons. Economically important losses due to stalk rot and ear rot occurred in the United States corn belt in 1965 and again in 1972.

On small grain cereals, the pathogen can kill seedlings before they emerge through the soil or shortly after. Infected seedlings which survive will most likely develop a pronounced foot rot at about soil level and just above. Perithecia of *Gibberella zeae* may often be found at the base of infected plants on both stems and adjacent roots. The fungus also can attack the ears, causing a shrivelling of the grains, the ears often being covered with a pinkish mat of mycelium. The ears may be infected at any time but the peak time is around the flowering stage when the stigma surface is available and receptive to spores which may arrive by wind, rain-splash or by plants rubbing together. The spores will penetrate the ovary wall and inhibit its development. An infected ear will appear ripe in contrast to the green healthy ears near by. At first, only conidia are produced from the mycelium coating the ear but perithecia may occur later giving the typical 'scabby' symptoms. The development of the grain may be totally suppressed or, depending upon the time of attack, they may be infected but show no outward signs of disease. Such seed, if sown, represent a potential hazard to the next crop as they may produce seedling blight or foot rot. Moisture is very much associated with the build-up of the head phase of this disease, severe attacks being correlated with wet cloudy weather.

On maize ears, the disease is sometimes called red ear rot and is characterized by a pinkish-red mould on the tip which usually does not progress further than half way down the ear. All kernels are affected thus distinguishing it from fusarium kernel rot with its scattered infections. The pink colour separates it from diplodia ear rot which is greyish and which progresses from the base of the ear to the tip. The husks are often pink to reddish and lightly adherent and late in the season black masses of perithecia are evident on the distal parts of the husks. Stalk rot symptoms are similar to those caused by *Diplodia* spp. The first signs are a sudden wilting and the leaves become dull green and eventually turn straw coloured and senesce prematurely. Cutting the lower stems reveals a disintegrated pith and exposed threads of vascular tissue. There is often a pinkish-red colour which distinguishes it from diplodia stalk rot although both are diseases of senescence and commonly occur together. Later on, masses of black perithecia are seen on the surfaces of stalks around the lower nodes.

Apart from the direct losses due to the disease in maize, infected grain is toxic to pigs. Ingestion of affected grain results in vomiting, refusal to eat and consequent deterioration in the health of the animals. Another toxin, which is produced in grain following storage, causes more severe physiological disturbances of the hormonal system in pigs. This results in precocious sexual receptivity in young females, uterine prolapse in adult females and abortion. Entire males show abnormal mammary development. No toxin antidotes have been developed although dilution of infected grain with normal to less than 3% is recommended.

Primary infection of cereals may result from infected seed, from stubble, or from the soil. The fungus can survive the intercrop period as mycelium in crop debris but, unlike *F. culmorum*, chlamydospores do not represent the overwintering inoculum. Perithecia require an overwintering period to mature and spring infection can then occur from ascospore inoculum. There is an interesting host/temperature interaction between maize and wheat. *F. graminearum* can produce a severe attack of seedling blight on maize at fairly low temperatures (8°C.) whereas the optimum for infection on wheat seedlings is much higher (24°C.). In addition, these effects are more pronounced in soils with a low moisture content.

Crop rotation and ploughing reduce the soil or debris inoculum and seed treatment with organo-mercurial compounds can result in partial control. Sprays of benzimidazole type compounds applied just after G.S.10 to control glume blotch in wheat (*Septoria nodorum*) have also reduced the earblight stage and probably also reduce the seed-borne inoculum. There is no evidence of physiologic specialization on wheat although there is a distinction between the strain for wheat, barley and oats and another which is restricted to maize. This situation would suggest that future control may be achieved by developing resistant cultivars. Resistance in maize is correlated with resistance to the diplodia disease and is quantitatively inherited. It is probably associated with the time and rate of host maturation as full season hybrids are more resistant.

Notes

The fungus can readily be isolated from infected ears or straws. Where the pinkish mycelial mat is evident, mycelial transfers can be made directly on to malt agar (acidified to pH 4·5) and incubated at 25°C. If necessary, sub-cultures can be made, again on to acid malt agar, before the final transfer on to potato dextrose agar (PDA) where they can be maintained. *Fusarium* species can be differentiated on PDA by the pigmentation on the reverse side of the culture plate, *F. graminearum* showing a range of colour from carmine to eosine pink. Isolation from perithecia can be made by first crushing the perithecium in a drop of sterile water between two sterile slides, the ascospores coming out into suspension. A drop of this suspension is then smeared over the surface of water agar and, without incubation, single ascospores can be picked off and sub-cultured to produce pure cultures. The cultures can be maintained by continuous sub-culture or immersed under mineral oil.

Gaeumannomyces graminis (Sacc.) Arx & Olivier – Take-all or Whiteheads of cereals and grasses.

G. graminis *var* tritici *– runner hyphae brown, septate, 4–7 um wide, branched to form paler hyphae bearing hyphopodia. Hyphopodia simple and unlobed, either terminal or intercalary with a minute pore where host penetration occurs. Black perithecia formed in basal leaf sheaths, bodies embedded and necks protruding. Perithecial body 200–400 um diam., neck 100–400 um long × 70–100 um wide. Asci unitunicate, elongated clavate, 80–130 × 10–15 um when mature. Ascospores light yellow, slightly curved 80–100 × 2·5–3 um. Phialospores often formed in culture, hyaline, unicellular, slightly to strongly curved, 4–7 × 1–1·5 um. Phialides aerial or submerged, slightly curved 9–18 × 2–3 um.*

G. graminis *var. avenae – runner hyphae, phialides, phialospores and simple lobed hyphopodia as in var.* tritici. *Perithecia similar to var.* tritici *but sometimes larger, 300–500 × 250 × 400 um. Asci 115–145 × 12–16 um. Ascospores 100–125 × 2·5–3·5 um.*

The intensive cultivation of cereals, especially continuous cereal growing, has resulted in the take-all disease becoming of considerable importance. Perhaps better known as *Ophiobolus graminis*, this pathogen has been renamed. There are two distinct forms of this fungus important on temperate cereals, *G. graminis* var. *tritici* which attacks wheat, barley and rye, the latter less seriously, whilst oats are mostly immune. Several grasses can also be attacked by this form. *G. graminis* var. *avenae* attacks oats very readily and also wheat, barley and rye.

The first indication of the presence of this disease is often the appearance of patches in the crop where many young seedlings have been killed outright. As the crop develops, these patches will become infested with weeds giving another indication of the presence of this pathogen. Infected seedlings may survive with little obvious damage except that they may be stunted and produce fewer tillers. Eventually, such plants may die at a fairly mature stage and the emerged heads have empty spikelets and appear bleached. This symptom has given rise to the name 'whiteheads'.

Below ground the root system of infected plants is much reduced and blackened and the whole plant can easily be removed from the soil by gently pulling. The blackening of the roots often spreads upwards to the lower leaf bases at ground level on the culms. In wet weather, perithecia may be readily observed in this region as small black raised spots. These are the necks of the perithecia which protrude through the leaf bases with the main body being sunken in the stem tissue. Microscopically, a good diagnostic feature is the presence on the surface of the roots of thick, brown runner hyphae.

There is only the one reproductive stage, the production of perithecia, asci and ascospores. The ascospores are forcibly ejected from the asci after a period of rain but are not thought to be of great importance in the infection process as the normal soil microflora exerts an almost complete biological control of ascospore infection although ascospores have been shown to be able to infect any seminal roots exposed above the soil surface. Infection takes place by means of slender hyphae which emerge from the hyphopodia formed on the runner hyphae. The endodermis and vascular system can be invaded but the fungus does not grow systemically within the developing plant, death resulting from the restriction or cessation of the flow of nutrients and water.

The fungus survives the intercrop period on the roots or stubble debris of previously infected crops and this constitutes the main source of inoculum. The roots of autumn-sown crops may become infected during the winter but, mostly, infection occurs after May with the fungus spreading through the soil over the roots of susceptible cereal or grass plants. The soil inoculum can rapidly build up and even as few as 1% infected plants in a crop can result in sufficient residual inoculum to produce severe take-all infection in the next cereal crop.

Take-all is most serious on light, loose alkaline soils of poor nutrient status where moisture is abundant. The fungus is also very sensitive to competition from other microorganisms in the saprophytic phase and to the presence of nitrogen in the soils. The pathogen will disappear more quickly in soils deficient in nitrogen for, without a nitrogen source, cellulose breakdown will cease and the pathogen is thus deprived of its carbohydrate source. An abundance of nitrogen will enable the plants to grow more strongly and to replace roots damaged by take-all even though it does not reduce the level of disease in the field in absolute terms. However, nitrogen applied the year before the cereal is sown will increase the survival time of the inoculum in the soil and thus increase the disease potential in the cereal crop.

An interesting feature of continuous cereal cultivation has been the decline of take-all after about the fourth year of cropping. Many explanations have been put forward to explain 'take-all decline', none have been positively confirmed but the phenomenon is unquestionable.

The control of take-all presents serious problems as there is very little prospect at present of controlling the disease by chemicals. Rotation appears to be the most rewarding in terms of reducing the inoculum and even one year free of a susceptible crop will almost eliminate the potential for disease in the next cereal crop. Otherwise, control can be achieved by a combination of a balanced fertilizer programme, the control of susceptible grass weeds and the early ploughing under of diseased stubble to encourage decomposition of the plant debris and the eventual starvation of the fungus. Seedbeds should be firm and well drained. The firmer the seedbed the slower will be the subsequent spread of the fungus along the roots. Sowing rate should also be carefully calculated for too dense a stand encourages the development and spread of this disease. Bare fallowing is still one of the best control methods although the loss of a crop presents economic difficulties. Conditions under grassland are relatively unfavourable to the take-all fungus compared with conditions under a cereal crop. One of the reasons for this is the presence of highly competitive *Phialophora* species. It has been demonstrated that the *Phialophora* – like fungus from grass roots decreases the spread of *G. graminis* along wheat roots, the degree of restriction depending upon the amount of root surface colonized by the *Phialophora*. For this reason, direct drilling of wheat into a pasture after treatment with a herbicide like paraquat produces less take-all than in wheat drilled into cultivated land.

Some cereal varieties show a degree of take-all resistance and the possibility of obtaining an increase in resistance in commercial varieties should not be overlooked. This may be especially useful when used jointly with cultural and other methods aimed at minimizing take-all.

Notes

Direct isolation of G. graminis from soil is very difficult and rarely obtained. The usual procedure is to bait the soil with susceptible seedlings and plate out the resulting root lesions. Washed pieces of infected root are placed on water agar with 50 ppm each of streptomycin and aureomycin. Surface sterilization techniques can very much influence the result, mercuric chloride generally being much less satisfactory than silver nitrate. Sterile extraction and plating of infected root stele tissues also gives good results and ascospore cultures can be readily obtained. The fungus will grow on a variety of fungal media and grows well on P.D.A. at 25°C. Viability and patho-genicity are easily lost in agar cultures but can be prolonged by plant inoculation and re-isolation. Vacuum-drying of macerated mycelium in skim milk has been suggested as a conservation medium to overcome this problem. Perithecia of G. graminis can be obtained with some difficulty in culture although there is much variation between isolates. There is a light requirement for perithecial production, wavelengths between 390 and 450 um and an intensity of 200 ft c. being most successful. Perithecia will also form on cultures growing in sterilized soil in flasks, the perithecia being formed between the glass and the soil when exposed to light. Inoculation of plants can be carried out using cultures on agar, wheat straw, cereal grains, or mixtures of maize meal, sand and soil.

Leptosphaeria nodorum Muller – Glume blotch of wheat and barley.

Conidial stage = Septoria nodorum Berk.
Pycnidia 140–220 um in diameter, honey-brown in colour but darkening later.
Pycnidiospores cylindrical, mostly 3-septate, hyaline, 22–30 × 2·5–3·0 um.

This is the most important disease of winter wheat in the United Kingdom. It occurs less frequently and causes little damage on barley. On wheat, in wet seasons, the disease can be particularly serious reducing yields by as much as 50% mostly by causing a shrivelling of the grain. The disease affects all aerial parts of the plant, the leaves showing symptoms about 10 days after infection. The leaf lesions are up to 1 cm long, yellow at first but becoming golden-brown later. Badly infected plants often appear to be ginger in colour. The shape of the lesion varies considerably but is approximately elliptical and is surrounded by a darker, somewhat purplish margin. The leaf spots often coalesce resulting in the death of leaves. Pycnidia occur abundantly in the dead tissue. On barley, the symptoms are very similar but never as extensive.

The nodes of the culm and rachis are also often attacked and become purplish-black and also bear pycnidia. Although leaf infections have been shown to cause reductions in yield, infection of the heads causes even greater losses and is mainly responsible for the drastic reductions in grain size. Infected heads are very conspicuous due to the discolouration of the glumes on which the lesions can be very extensive, mostly spreading from the tip of the glume downwards and being a dark, purplish-brown colour. Pycnidia are produced in the glume lesions which may be found on almost all the glumes in a severe infection or on a few glumes only in a light infection. Compared with a healthy crop, infected heads give the crop a much darker colour at ripening time.

Recently, perithecia of *Leptosphaeria nodorum*, the sexual stage of this pathogen, have been found on wheat stubble in the United Kingdom. Inoculation of healthy plants with ascospores from these perithecia has proved successful but their importance in the epidemiology of the disease has not been elucidated.

The pathogen can be seed-borne and, under suitable environmental conditions, diseased seed is undoubtedly an important source of inoculum. Very little work has been published on the conditions necessary for infection by pycnidiospores but it appears that high humidity is a prime requirement. Laboratory studies on germination and infection have demonstrated that pycnidiospores will germinate and infect between 5 and 30°C. in the presence of free moisture on the leaf surface with the optimum being approximately 22°C.

The pycnidia sporulate over long periods extruding the pycnidiospores in a gelatinous, worm-like tendril called a cirrhus. The spores may be disseminated by rain drops and accompanying air turbulence or winds. Spore trapping experiments have detected spores at 2 m above the crop canopy although other studies show that the initial spread from a point-source of inoculum is only about 1 m, normally in the direction of the prevailing wind. The fungus is also able to overwinter on stubble and leaf trash and it has also been shown to be able to infect several common grasses although pycnidia are rarely produced on these alternative hosts until the infected leaves senesce.

Seed treatment with hot water, organo-mercurials or systemic chemicals only give partial control on a field scale, presumably because of other inoculum sources. Cultural methods, such as the early ploughing to bury infected trash, should also be practised. There is considerable variation in the resistance of present-day commercial varieties although none exhibit the character to a very high degree. However, there is much potential for improving varietal resistance and breeders are engaged on such programmes. The increased value of the cereal crop and the latest technology of culture which leaves 'tram-lines' for the tractor to traverse the mature crop, have resulted in a greater use of fungicides.

Foliar sprays with 'tank-mix zineb' have been shown to give good control but the method requires repeated application and is uneconomical. More recently, spray applications of the benzimidazole type applied about G.S. 10 have been shown to give a beneficial effect, especially in reducing the shrivelling of the grain. Mixtures of carbendazim and either maneb or mancozeb are also very effective if applied between G.S. 9–10.1.

Notes

The fungus can easily be cultured artificially on many agar media with potato dextrose or Czapek Dox with added vegetable juice being the most efficient. The fungus is photosporogenic, being especially stimulated to sporulate by Near Ultra Violet light. To produce spores *en masse* for field trials the cultures should be first incubated in the dark for two days and then transferred to an N.U.V. cabinet at around 22°C. for around 16 days. Spore suspensions are then prepared by removing the cirrhi by scraping and placing them in water. This is then homogenized in a mixer, filtered through muslin and adjusted to the required spore concentration. The suspension can then be sprayed on to plants for artificial inoculation studies. The addition of a surfactant to the suspension, e.g. 'Tween 20' at 2 drops per 100 ml, and the enclosure of the plants under a polythene bag for 48–72 hours will ensure successful infection.

Micronectriella nivalis (Schaffn.) Booth – Pre-emergence blight, root rot and head blight of cereals. Snow mould.

Conidial state of Fusarium nivale (Fr.) *Ces.*
In pure culture, mycelium white to apricot in colour with little discolouration of the agar. Conidia sparse on aerial mycelium, abundant in salmon pink sporodochia, curved or sickle-shaped, 1–3 septate, 10–30 × 2·5 × 5 um. *Chlamydospores not*

produced. Perithecia develop on agar but more readily on steam-sterilized straw at 18°C., globose, pink then grey-black 80–300 um; asci clavate, occasionally cylindrical, 60–70 × 6–9 um with 6–8 ascospores; ascospores hyaline, straight or curved, 1–3 septate, 10–17 × 3·5–4·5 um.

F. nivale is a serious pathogen of cereals, especially in temperate regions where the complete loss of winter sown wheat or rye may occur. It is the most common of the *Fusarium* pathogens of cereals in the United Kingdom. Germinating seedlings may be killed outright before emerging or, if less infected, they may exhibit brown lesions at the base of the developing coleoptile. Surviving seedlings may then develop the typical *Fusarium* root rot symptoms which can vary from a brown discolouration of the basal leaf sheaths to a more pronounced rotting of the plant base at about soil level.

It is particularly damaging on winter wheat and rye in areas where the snow cover is heavy and the soil temperatures mild. As the snow melts the fungus becomes conspicuous on the leaf and crown tissues. It is the only *Fusarium* pathogen to regularly produce symptoms on the foliage where the first and second leaves may exhibit ginger, oval spots bordered by a darker brown margin. Penetration and killing of the leaf tissues result in a bleaching and drying out of these parts which are easily recognizable by the pink-white mycelium covering the dead tissues. Conidia are produced abundantly throughout the mat of mycelium.

There is a requirement for light for the production of the perithecial stage. Perithecia are, at first, confined to the exposed basal leaf sheaths and are completely immersed in the tissues below the epidermis where they appear as numerous black dots but higher leaf sheaths can be infected later from ascospores spread by the wind. Infection by the sexual stage of the fungus can also result in a dark brown discolouration of the basal nodes.

Head infection by F. nivale does occur but with a low frequency. The symptoms are very similar to the head blights produced by F. culmorum with occasional empty, bleached ears or a brown spotting of the glumes. The affected heads will also display a light covering of mycelium of the characteristic delicate pink shade. F. nivale can survive on crop debris for up to 12 months where it is a potential hazard to subsequent crops. It is considered to be a soil-borne organism, although it is rarely isolated directly from soil, and it can also be seed-borne although this method of transmission has not been reported in North America. The pathogen can also be dispersed by water and by the aerial dissemination of ascospores during the summer. Unlike the other *Fusarium* species infecting cereals, F. nivale infection is favoured by low temperatures and thrives under a covering of snow. Infection is also favoured under dry soil conditions.

The seed-borne phase can be controlled by seed treatments such as a mixture of the systemic oxathiin, carboxin and copper oxyquinolate. Seed treatment with various organo-mercurial preparations also give partial control through protection against soil-borne propagules. There is very little evidence for the existence of pathogenic strains, i.e. physiologic specialization, and, in the long term, the control of *F. nivale* may best be achieved by the development of resistant cultivars.

Notes
The fungus can be isolated from seed after normal surface sterilization methods and can be cultured on a range of media including potato dextrose agar on which it is recognizable by the apricot colour of the colony. Cultures can be maintained by mono-conidial or hyphal tip transfers or, for longer periods of storage, under mineral oil.

Mycosphaerella graminicola (Fckl.) Sanderson – Leaf spot of wheat.

Conidial state = Septoria tritici *Rob. and Desm.*
Perithecia, globose, becoming laterally compressed, 76–80 um, *dark brown. Perithecial wall two-layered. Asci bitunicate, obpyriform, 34–41* × *11–13* um; *ascospores eight, biseriate or irregularly arranged, two-celled, hyaline, elliptical, with one cell tending to be slightly larger, 10–15* × *2·5–3* um. *Pycnidia globose to elliptical, 80–150* um *in diameter, honey-brown turning black with maturity. Conidia hyaline, filiform, 2–3 septate, slightly curved and tapering to an acute apex, 43–70* × *1·5–2·0* um.

Leaf spot of wheat is very common and causes significant reductions in yield in seasons favourable to the spread of the conidia. The symptoms are usually most conspicuous in the early leaf stages and often disappear as heading approaches. On the leaves, light green or yellow spots are produced in which prominent black pycnidia develop. There is often considerable defoliation due to the merging of individual spots. Pycnidia can sometimes be found in rows between the veins on the glumes but attempts to isolate the pathogen from the seed have failed and there is no evidence of the disease being seed-transmitted although the seed may be contaminated with infected chaff and plant debris. Wheat and rye are attacked but oats and barley are resistant. The disease is favoured by cool weather with prolonged precipitation and heavy applications of nitrogenous fertilizer are also conducive to infection.

It is likely that infected host debris and infected volunteer plants are sources of inoculum although spores which are produced on infected plant debris lose their viability after burial for one month in soil. Several grass species have also been shown to be susceptible to *S. tritici* and isolates from wheat, rye and *Poa pratensis* were cross-inoculable on these hosts but not on 20 other cereals and grasses.

The disease can be controlled by a programme of protectant sprays such as Zineb but this method is not an economical practice. Although no varieties have shown outstanding resistance, field resistance has been reported for several spring and winter varieties. Cultural methods of control include the removal of volunteer plants and the destruction of straw and stubble of infected crops by deep ploughing or burning.

Notes

Methods for isolation and culturing *S. tritici* are essentially the same as for *S. nodorum* although the former is very much slower in its growth on artificial medium.

Nigrospora oryzae (Berk & Br.) Petch — Cob rot of maize.

syn. Basiporium gallarum *Moll.*
Conidia oval to spherical, black, 10–20 um *diameter, borne on short lateral branches.*

Cob rot of maize, caused by *Nigrospora oryzae*, is widely distributed in maize growing areas but rarely causes damage of economic significance. The pathogen has been associated with a seed rot and seedling blight although its main effects are on the maize ear where the distinguishing symptom is a shredding of the cob. This disintegration of the cob tissue occurs mainly at the basal end and may extend into the stalk tissue resulting in stalk breakage below the ear and consequent harvest losses. Symptoms are rarely obvious on whole ears, although surface mycelium may be seen when the husks are peeled back. Kernels appear poorly filled and have a soft starchy appearance. The kernels are easily pressed into the disintegrated cob and this latter condition is obvious on shelling when the infected cobs shatter. The ear appears chaffy and the glumes are chocolate brown rather than reddish and dark masses of spores are also seen when infection is severe.

N. oryzae is a weak parasite and tends only to attack plants that have been subjected to stress conditions. Such stressed plants can result from inclement weather such as early frosts, drought, poor or imbalanced nutrition or attack by other diseases.

No specific control measure is recommended. Good husbandry and the use of full season, adapted hybrids will result in crops more likely to resist attack.

Pseudocercosporella herpotrichoides (Fron.) Deighton – Eyespot of wheat and barley.

An asexual fungus producing colourless, straight or slightly curved conidia, 26–47 × 1–2 um, normally 3–7 septate. The conidia are produced from almost colourless sympodial conidiophores up to 20 um long and 3–3·5 um wide arising from pale, olivaceous hyphae.

This pathogen is present in most temperate countries where it can cause considerable damage to cereals, mostly wheat and barley with oats and rye being quite resistant. The symptoms are a characteristic pale oval spot with a brown margin on the basal leaf sheaths and culm of the cereal tillers at or just above ground level. These elliptical, eye-shaped lesions have a rather diffuse margin and a dark 'pupil'. These symptoms develop in the spring and the disease may be confirmed by the presence of grey mycelium in the internal cavity of the straws when cut open. The presence of this mycelium distinguishes this disease from that of 'sharp eyespot' caused by *Rhizoctonia solani* which produces no mycelium in the cavity and, in which, the lesion is sharply defined at its margin.

The fungus usually invades through the stomata of the outer leaf sheath and progressively penetrates inwards to reach the hollow stem centre. It produces a true foot rot rather than a root rot and severely attacked stems, where there may be one or several lesions, may break at the site of the lesions and may topple over ('lodge') creating a network of untidy criss-crossed stems, a symptom known as 'straggling'. The eyespot pathogen can also result in post emergence death of young seedlings or tillers; shrivelled grain and partially empty ears ('whiteheads') can also occur on maturing crops.

The pathogen survives the inter-crop period on infected stubble and it has been shown to be infective even after burial for three years. Conidia can be produced at any time during the winter but develop most abundantly during periods of wet autumn or spring weather, spore dispersal being effected mainly by rain-splash. In culture, conidial production only occurs under fluctuating temperatures between 0–13°C. The incidence and development of the disease is much influenced by the environment with infection being severe at soil temperatures of 6–10°C. and becoming negligible at temperatures above 15°C. There is also a relationship between the severity of disease and soil moisture. Infection occurs at the very young seedling stage or on young tillers, the most susceptible parts being the coleoptile and the leaf sheaths. During moist, cool springs secondary infection within a crop can occur from conidia dispersed from diseased plants.

Whilst debris constitutes the main source of inoculum, volunteer wheat plants have also been shown to act as secondary hosts but they are not as important as stubble debris in this context. The disease builds up under continuous cereal growing systems and is most common on heavy wet soils. Heavy applications of nitrogen will also accentuate the disease by producing an abundance of tillers with an accompanying dense crop with high humidity beneath the canopy. The weakening of the straw by the eyespot lesions is also aggravated by too liberal a manuring regime which also increases the tendency to lodge. Some differences in pathogenicity between wheat, rye and barley isolates have been reported but no *formae speciales* are recognized.

The control of eyespot mainly involves the use of resistant varieties although there is an increasing usage of 'systemic' chemicals. Much can be done to reduce the risk of disease by appropriate cultural practices especially in terms of stubble burning, rotation and correct manurial practice. There are many varieties which exhibit a high degree of resistance, the resistance mechanism acting through a reduction in the degree of penetration of the leaf sheaths and not necessarily in the number of eyespot lesions.

The short-strawed and stiffer strawed varieties are more resistant to lodging and should be used in high-risk situations. Partial control by the use of straw shortening and stiffening chemicals such as CCC (chloride-choline-chloride) can also be beneficial.

Systemic chemicals can be effective either as seed-treatments or as early foliar sprays, the increased value of the cereal crop now making such practices economical. Winter wheat can be sprayed with benomyl 0·25 kg a.i./ha or carbendazim 0·25 kg a.i./ha or thiophanate-methyl 0·7 kg a.i./ha The treatment of barley is the same as for wheat and, whereas the disease is frequent on oats, it is rarely serious enough to warrant control in the United Kingdom.

Notes

The fungus can be readily isolated either from the eyespot lesion after surface sterilization or from hyphae taken from the lumen, or cavity, of infected straws. It grows well on nutrient agar at about 15°C. although much of the literature reports cultures being maintained at 23°C. on Potato Dextrose Agar often containing 100 units/ml streptomycin and 50 units/ml penicillin. To obtain good sporulation in pure culture a fluctuating programme of 12 hours dark at 5°C. and 12 hours light at 12°C. is most often adopted.

Puccinia coronata Corda f. sp. **avenae** Erikss. – Crown rust of oats.

Uredosori amphigenous, oblong, pulvurlent, orange, paraphyses few, clavate, thin-walled; uredospores globoid to ovoid, yellow, 14–39 × 10–35 um, wall finely echinulate, germ pores 3–5 scattered. Teleutosori scattered, long covered by epidermis, black; teleutospores clavate, tapering to base, wall smooth, brown, pedicels short, thick, pale, apex crowned with 5–8 digitate, sometimes branched projections. Spermogonia, or pycnia, amphigenous, with projecting paraphyses. Aecidia amphigenous, in groups or scattered, cylindrical or cup-shaped, whitish, laciniate, revolute margin; aecidiospores angular-globoid, finely verruculose, orange, 16–25 × 12–20 um.

Crown rust, caused by *Puccinia coronata avenae*, is probably the most important disease of oats on a world-wide basis. A number of forms of *P. coronata* Corda exist which are specialized on various genera of the Gramineae but *P. c.* f. sp. *avenae* is the form that parasitises cultivated and wild *Avena* spp. The disease, also known as leaf rust, is particularly important in the more temperate and humid regions of oat culture. It is widespread in North America from the southern, central and mid-western states of the U.S.A. up into Canada making a broad band known as the Puccinia Path. It is also important in Australia and parts of north-west Europe, particularly in cool, moist coastal regions. Losses in grain yield of up to 20% are reported for some mid-western states of the U.S.A. and grain quality is also affected.

The typical and distinctive symptoms on oats are bright orange uredial pustules which occur as oblong spots varying in size from about 1 mm to 1 × 5 mm. Secondary pustules are produced around the primary one and these and others may run together under favourable conditions on susceptible varieties. Powdery orange spores are produced profusely and shed easily onto the leaf, into the air and on the ground around the plants when infection is severe. This, and the confluent nature of pustules, may give a rather patchy irregular and 'untidy' appearance to the infections especially later in the season. Uredial pustules also occur on sheaths and floral parts and occasionally on culms. Teleutosori may be produced in rings around uredial pustules but they occur more commonly as lines of black sori, long covered by the epidermis, on leaf sheaths later in the season. The effects on the host are rather general, including loss of vigour, premature ripening, reduction in tillering, poor seed set and shrivelled grain of poor quality. *P. coronata* is a long-cycle heteroecious rust, the alternate host of which is the buckthorn (*Rhamnus catharticus* L.) The two-celled teleutospores survive the winter on host plant debris and germinate in the early spring to produce basidiospores which infect the buckthorn to produce the pycnial stage and, later, the conspicuous orange-yellow aecidia which liberate aecidiospores to infect oats in late spring when the oats are in the juvenile stages of growth. Aecidiospore infection is important in regions where buckthorn is grown in hedgerows and as an ornamental plant, but the other major source of primary inoculum is uredospores. In regions with mild winters and where autumn-sown oats are common, the fungus survives as mycelium or uredial infections which are able to tolerate quite low temperatures. The limiting factor is probably the survival of host tissue, in that oats are the least winter hardy of the cereals. In North America, uredospore inoculum emanates from the southern regions of Mexico and Texas and moves northwards to Canada on successively planted crops. Although long-distance spread can occur, it is relatively unimportant compared with local spread of uredospores from neighbouring crops or of aecidiospores from nearby buckthorn bushes. Repeated cycles of infection by the summer uredospores can occur in as little as 7 days under favourable conditions of temperature and free moisture, the latter condition being required for spore germination and penetration. The fungus is adapted to a fairly wide temperature range but the generation time becomes correspondingly longer as temperatures decrease below the optimum of about 25°C.

Physiological specialization is highly developed in *P. coronata* and a large number of virulence genes and virulence gene combinations have been detected in relation to corresponding genes for specific response in the host. Hypersensitive seedling resistance has been widely used in North America, Australia and Europe to control the disease but the familiar pattern of emergence of virulence in the pathogen has resulted in other approaches to disease control. The deployment of major genes for resistance in multiline varieties of spring oats was pioneered by workers in the state of Iowa in the U.S.A. and is now an accepted agricultural practice. The regional deployment of major genes along the North American Puccinia Path has also been advocated. Other types of host resistance, for example that of the adult plant type and partially expressed resistance that results in *slow rusting*, have been identified and are being used. Additional sources of hypersensitive resistance (Pc genes) have been identified from Israeli collections of *Avena sterilis*. Cultural methods of control include the eradication of *Rhamnus* spp. and the use of early maturing varieties that escape infection. Recently developed systemic chemicals such as the oxathiins are effective in controlling crown rust but may only be economic on high-priced seed crops.

Puccinia hordei Otth. – Brown or leaf rust of barley.

Pycnia and aecidia occur as elevated, light orange-yellow areas on Ornithogallum *spp. Aecidiospores ellipsoid or globoid sub-hyaline and minutely verrucose. Uredosori scattered, minute and cinnamon brown on* Hordeum vulgare *and* H. murinum. *Uredospores sub-globoid or ellipsoid, yellow 22–27 × 15–20 um, wall echinulate with 8–10 scattered indistinct pores. Teleutosori minute, round to oblong, confluent and long covered by the epidermis. Teleutospores oblong to clavoid, slightly constricted brown 40–54 × 15–24 um, wall smooth, pedicels short. Mesospores usually more numerous than teleutospores.*

The disease occurs commonly in the barley growing areas of the world but it is of only local importance. The first signs of the disease are small, round, light yellowish-brown uredial pustules on the leaves which darken somewhat with age. A chlorotic halo is normally associated with the pustules and a more general yellowing of the leaf is common. Infection is normally confined to the leaves and leaf sheaths although head infection can occur late in the season. At this time slate grey teleutosori may be formed. These may run together to form patches, especially on sheaths as the leaf blades senesce.

The uredial stage will survive fairly low temperatures and penetration by uredo-spores can occur at 5°C. The winter barley crop is therefore a potential source of spring inoculum. Infection by uredospores requires free moisture and this is normally satisfied by night-time dew or light rain. Infection occurs over a wide temperature range (5–25°C.) and the optimum is 17°C. Dispersal is favoured by warm, windy, dry weather. The infection conditions are best satisfied by summer anticyclonic conditions. Field infection is therefore not normally noticeable until after heading in spring varieties. This may be somewhat earlier on winter varieties. The sexual stage is rare and insignificant epidemiologically.

Control measures have normally involved the use of resistant varieties. A number of hypersensitive resistance reactions are known and these are governed by major genes (Pa genes). To date, eight such genes have been described but others are also known. The fungus exists in physiologically specialized forms which render the majority of the Pa genes ineffective. International surveys of virulence in the pathogen population are carried out so that the available resistances may be used more effectively. Sources of partial resistance have been recently identified and are used in European varieties. These may prove to be more durable although evidence exists for specialization by the pathogen for one of these resistances derived from *Hordeum laevigatum*. Other sources of resistance have been found in wild barleys, particularly *Hordeum spontaneum* from Israel. Chemical control is now more practicable with the introduction of translocatable (systemic) compounds which both eradicate and protect. These are now commonly used in intensive farming situations in north-west Europe. For example, benodanil at 1·1 kg a.i. plus wetter in not less than 225 litres of water/hectare applied as soon as an early attack is noted can be beneficial. The combined use of such fungicides with partially resistant varieties may offer more stable control in the future.

Notes

A period of darkness and free moisture is necessary for the germination and infection by uredospores. Cardinal temperatures are 5, 17 and 25°C. A period of 16 hours at 17°C. is optimum. The usual techniques for handling rusts in the field and greenhouse are applicable (Chapter 4). Storage of uredospores is best in liquid nitrogen or by vacuum drying. Spores stored in this way will remain viable for up to 5 years. The viability of fresh spores can be maintained at a high level under refrigeration at approximately 2°C. for several weeks but declines to about 20% after 6 months or so.

Puccinia graminis Pers. – Black stem rust of wheat and other cereals.

Uredospores, ellipsoid or ovoid, golden-brown, 21–42 × 16–?? um, echinulate with four equatorial germ pores, teleutospores stalked, two celled, ellipsoid or clavoid, rounded and thickened at apex, smooth, chestnut brown but appearing black en masse, *35–60 × 12–22 um; pycnia produced on upper surface of secondary host, pycniospores minute, uninucleate; aecidia produced on the lower surface of secondary host, aecidiospores angular becoming globoid, smooth, orange, 14–26 um in diameter.*

Black stem rust is distributed generally throughout the wheat growing areas of the world. It causes serious losses in North America, India and Australia but is only of minor importance in the United Kingdom. The disease causes the grain to be shrivelled and weakens the stem which leads to lodging. It is heteroecious with the pathogen alternating between the cereal host, where it produces the uredo- and teleutospore stages and the secondary host, the common barberry (*Berberis vulgaris*) where it produces the pycnial and aecidial stages.

The first signs on the wheat plant are elongated, brown uredosori on the leaves and stems. As the season progresses the uredosori are replaced by black teleutosori which also erupt elsewhere on previously undamaged tissue. The teleutospores overwinter on straw debris and germinate in the spring to produce a germ-tube like protuberance, the basidium, which divides to give four cells upon which four laterally borne sporidia or basidiospores are produced. These basidiospores are the products of meiosis from the diploid nucleus formed after the fusion of the two nuclei in one of the bi-nucleate cells in the teleutospore. These are wind-borne and infect the *Berberis* by direct penetration through the epidermis. Flask-shaped pycnia are then formed on the upper leaf surface which produce masses of very small, uninucleate pycniospores which are exuded through the ostiole in a sugary tendril which attracts insects which then passively disperse the spores.

P. graminis is heterothallic producing basidiospores of two mating types. The pycniospores will thus be of the same mating type as the infecting basidiospore and plasmogamy occurs if the pycniospores, or spermatia, of one mating type fuse with the flexuous hyphae which protrude from the ostioles of pycnia of opposite mating type.

This fusion reconstitutes the dikaryotic state, i.e. the cells all contain two nuclei each of a different mating type, which is normal for most of the life-cycle. The dikaryotic state can also be achieved by the fusion of mycelium of opposite mating type within the barberry leaf. The aecidia are produced following such fusion and can be found embedded in the lower epidermis of the barberry leaf. These inverted cup-shaped structures produce masses of orange aecidiospores which are packed together at the base of the cup to give a uniform appearance of a compaction of polyhedral spores. As the pressure is released towards the mouth of the aecidia the spores assume a more global appearance. The aecidiospores are dispersed by wind and can only infect the wheat plant, entering through the stomates in the same way as the uredospores. The aecidiospores contain two nuclei, one of both mating type and hence the mycelium produced in the cereal host is also of the dikaryotic type.

In the United Kingdom, *P. graminis tritici*, the form attacking wheat, does not overwinter on the barberry but the inoculum originates from epidemics in the western Mediterranean and is blown northwards as uredospores where it occasionally arrives early enough to cause epidemics. In the southern states of North America the rust overwinters as uredospores on autumn-sown wheat and, from such sources, the inoculum travels progressively northwards during the summer. However, in the eastern U.S.A., overwintering does occur on the barberry.

P. graminis is divided into a number of specialized forms or *formae speciales* which have a range of hosts in the cereals and grasses. Each form can be further sub-divided into numerous physiologically specialized forms or physiological races which can originate by hybridization on the barberry, mutation or the parasexual cycle. In *P. graminis tritici* alone there are known to be at least 200 races.

The control of stem rust on wheat has been attempted mainly by the breeding and use of varieties incorporating major gene or race specific resistance. Unfortunately, such resistance has usually been eroded within a very few years by the appearance of new physiological races which possessed the ability to attack such varieties. Consequently, the emphasis in breeding programmes has altered to include the incorporation of race non-specific resistance although the continued use of race-specific resistance is still important even if the benefits are very much in the short term.

There has also been a considerable increase in the use of the new translocatable or systemic fungicides in particular, the oxathiins and a mixture of carbendazim and dithiocarbamates. However, their use is confined at present to areas of intensive wheat cultivation and this does not include the United Kingdom or north-western Europe where the disease rarely reaches the level of economic importance.

Notes

P. graminis can now be cultured on artificial media (Scott and McLean, Ann. rev. Phytopath. **7**; 123, 1969). For preservation and inoculation techniques, please refer to Chapter 4 and the notes on other rust fungi in this compendium.

Puccinia polysora Underw. – Southern corn rust.

Uredospores ellipsoidal often subangular 28–38 × 22–30 um, wall pale, minutely echinulate, 4–5 equatorial pores, in roughly circular uredosori, approx. 1·0 mm diameter. Teleutosori circular, dark, covered by epidermis. Teleutospores obvate or clavate, irregular, constricted at septum 35–50 × 16–26 um, mesospores numerous, wall smooth, pedicels up to 30 um. Pycnia and aecidia unknown.

Puccinia polysora occurs on *Zea mays* and also on *Tripsacum* spp., *Erianthus* spp. and *Euchlaena mexicana.* It is the incitant of southern corn rust, named for its common occurrence in the southern United States of America but which is now widespread in the warm (25°C.) humid regions of maize culture. It occurs in central and south America, Africa and India and the eastern regions. It is now one of the most important endemic diseases of maize in West Africa where severe epidemics have occurred. A total crop failure was experienced there in the early 1950s and yield losses of up to 40% are still common. More recently it has increased in severity in parts of the U.S.A., particularly North Carolina. The symptoms can be distinguished from *P. sorghi* in that uredosori are lighter in colour and somewhat smaller and rounder. Also the epidermis remains covering the pustule for a longer time. Teleutosori are chocolate brown to black and often occur in circles around the uredo pustules. They are smaller than those of *P. sorghi* and the epidermis is more persistent. Pustules occur on all plant parts but most commonly on both leaf surfaces. The alternate host is not known and it therefore appears that the disease cycle involves only the uredospore stage on maize. Primary inoculum therefore comes either from volunteer or weed maize plants locally or uredospores are blown in from growing crops elsewhere. It was presumably introduced to the Old World from the New by man. The fungus exists as a number of physiologically specialized forms which are separated on the basis of their interaction with maize lines carrying monogenically controlled 'hypersensitive' resistance. Control is therefore through the use of resistant varieties and breeding programmes have been developed for this purpose particularly in West Africa where the disease is severe. There has been a shift in the importance of *P. polysora* recently, for example in the U.S.A., with a consequent increase in breeding efforts. Selection of quantitatively resistant types, not based on monogenic hypersensitive resistance, would seem to offer the best long-term solution to the problem but major gene resistance has short-term advantages.

Notes

Successful inoculation methods include dusting with dry spore : talc mixtures, hyperdermic injection and dropping a water suspension into leaf whorls. Detached leaf culture on 20 ppm benzimidazole solution is used to maintain specific cultures in isolation.

Puccinia recondita Rob & Desm. – Brown (leaf) rust of wheat and rye.

syn. Puccinia triticina *(Eriks).*

P. rubigo-vera *(DC) Wint.*

Uredosori epiphyllous, scattered, round to oblong 1 × 1–2 mm, cinnamon-brown; uredospores globoid to broadly ellipsoid, 13–24 × 16–34 um, wall pale cinnamon-brown to yellowish, 1–2 um *thick, echinulate, pores 4–8 scattered, distinct. Teleutosori hypophyllous and on sheaths, small, oblong, long-covered by epidermis, black; paraphyses subepidermal, dark brown, in thin layers surrounding or dividing sori; teleutospores 2-celled (occasionally 1- or 3-celled), oblong, to clavoid, 13–24 × 36–65 um, rounded, truncate or obliquely pointed above, slightly constricted, wall brown; pedicel short, persistent; germ tube, basidium and basidiospores hyaline. Spermogonia chiefly epiphyllous, scattered in small groups. Aecidia hypophyllous, grouped, cupulate, rarely cylindrical, yellow; aecidiospores 13–26 × 19–29 um, wall colourless, finely verrucose.*

Within the complex species *Puccinia recondita*, which causes brown or leaf rust of cereals and grasses, there are *formae speciales.* One of these, *P. recondita* Rob & Desm. f.sp. *tritici* Eriks & Henn. is essentially confined to wheat and the other, *P.r.* f.sp. *recondita* Rob & Desm., occurs on rye. Although there is some cross infection between these forms and also between these and other forms which are specialized on other genera of grasses, there is a high degree of isolation between them.

The disease is relatively unimportant on rye but it is, arguably, the most important single disease of wheat on a world-wide basis. It is more common, prevalent and damaging than even stem rust (*P. graminis tritici*) in many of the major wheat producing areas. It is important on both winter and spring varieties of wheat especially in the warmer, humid and semi-humid regions including central and southern Europe, the U.S.S.R., Australia, the south, central and mid-western states of the U.S.A. and in Canada. It can also be damaging in north-west Europe, particularly in the Netherlands and France. Losses in yield of between 5 and 10% are common and may be much higher in epidemic years. In Illinois in the mid-west of the U.S.A., for example, losses averaged 11% during 1946–56. The fungus is macro-cyclic, heteroecious and heterothallic, the alternate host for *P.r.* f.sp. *tritici* being the meadow rue (*Thalictrum* spp.) and less commonly *Isopyrum fumarioides* and *Anchusa italica.* The sexual (aecidial) stage is uncommon in the major wheat areas where the fungus survives primarily as uredial infections.

The uredial pustules on wheat are discrete, round to oblong and usually 2 mm or less in length. They are orange-brown in colour, the colour deepening with age, and they occur primarily on the upper (adaxial) surfaces of leaf blades. Pustules occur less frequently on lower leaf surfaces and sheaths and rarely on culms – hence the common name of leaf rust. This pattern of distribution of pustules is affected to some extent by host variety. The pustules can be distinguished from those of *P. graminis* by being smaller, lighter in colour, confined more to the leaves and by the lack of a conspicuous turned back epidermis which gives the stem rust pustule a ragged appearance. Rings of uredosori may occur around primary infection sites and the black teleutosori may also appear in this way. This latter stage, however, develops more commonly on leaf sheaths in rows of small, black sori, long-covered by the epidermis (cf. stem rust). Teleutosori occur less commonly on culms and floral bracts. The main effects on the wheat host are a reduction in seed numbers, seed size and density. Grain shrivelling is not a common effect.

The aecidial stage is unimportant epidemiologically and the fungus persists mainly in the uredial stage, which can survive relatively low temperatures. Uredospore infections of autumn-sown wheat survive as mycelial colonies within the host tissues under quite extreme conditions; the limitation in survival appears to be in the survival of host tissue. In regions of mild winters, new uredospore infections may occur as spore germination and penetration occurs over a temperature range of 5–25°C. although the optimum is in the range 10–20°C. However, the incubation period (from penetration to sporulation) is greatly extended at low temperatures, and this limits disease development. The disease develops most rapidly under conditions of warm, moist weather with anticyclonic conditions being most favourable as dry, windy days favour spore dispersal and cool nights with dew favour spore germination and penetration. Under such favourable conditions, the generation time is only approx-imately 7–10 days. Uredospore dispersal can occur over long distances. More local spread accounts for dispersal between crops and this type of movement results in spread from early to later sown crops in the major wheat growing regions of North

America and Central Europe. The spread is eventually from winter- onto spring-sown crops in the more northern regions of wheat culture and this occurs in North America, for example, where movement is from Mexico, through the Great Plains and mid-western states of the U.S.A. and up into Canada.

Control of *P. recondita tritici* is principally through the use of host resistance and the importance of the disease has stimulated a great deal of research and development particularly in North America and more recently in Europe. Seedling hypersensitive resistance, which is governed by major genes, has been widely used by breeders but the emergence of physiologically specialized races of the pathogen has rendered much of this resistance ineffective. The pathogen is highly plastic from a virulence point of view and over 200 races have been identified. Adult plant resistances have been more widely used in recent years but pathogen variants capable of overcoming many of these have been detected. Resistance has been introduced into *Triticum aestivum* from related species and genera such as *Aegilops* spp. and *Agropyron* spp. (see Table 5.3) as the result of pioneer work on interspecific and intergeneric hybridizations. Other mechanisms and expressions of resistance such as *slow rusting* and *pattern rusting* have been identified in the search for stable, effective host resistance. More recently, systemic fungicides have been developed which are effective against *P. recondita* and these are economical to use in intensive farming systems. In extensive farming, fungicides are less economic but disease forecasting systems have been developed, e.g. in the U.S.A., to reduce the risk of applying chemicals unnecessarily.

Puccinia sorghi Schw. – Common corn rust.

Pycnia amphygonous, in small groups, honey yellow, globoid 90–110 um diameter. Aecidia in groups usually around pycnia, up to 400 um diameter. Aecidiospores globoid or ellipsoid 18–26 × 14–20 um, walls hyaline, verruculose. Uredospores ellipsoid to globoid 32–34 × 20–28 um, finely echinulate, cinnamon brown, 4 equatorial pores. Teleutospores oblong to ellipsoid, constricted at septum, wall dark chestnut-brown, 28–48 × 13–25 um, pedicel up to 80 um long, persistent, hyaline.

Common corn rust is almost universal where maize is grown but is generally unimportant and rarely causes damage although severe infections may cause yield reduction in sweet corn. It also infects teosinte. Symptoms of uredial infection on maize are scattered oval to elongate cinnamon-brown pustules on upper and lower leaf surfaces. The ruptured epidermis around the pustules is turned back around the margins. Later in the season the pustules become blackish brown as teleutospores are produced. Infection occurs on all above ground parts of the plant but mainly on leaves. Uredo- and teleutosori break through the epidermis early in their development (cf *P. polysora*). The uredospores are wind dispersed and infect maize under favourable conditions of free moisture on the leaf surface. Overwintering occurs through teleutospores which germinate after a ripening period to produce basidiospores which can infect several species of *Oxalis*. In North America *O. stricta*, *O. cymosa* and *O. corniculata* are chiefly concerned whereas in Europe, *O. europe* is reported as an aecidial host. Aecidia formed on the alternate host produce aecidiospores which infect maize or teosinte to initiate the uredal cycle. In mild climates, the fungus can survive the winter in the uredal state thus providing the primary inoculum for spring infection both locally and more distantly through the wind-dispersed uredospores. Physiologic specialization has been reported and monogenic host resistance is known in, for example, the variety Cuzco from Peru which carries a single dominant gene for resistance to all known races of *P. sorghi*. However, most maize varieties appear to carry a degree of *partial resistance*, or rather *hypo-susceptibility*, which is adequate to maintain the pathogen population at a low level.

Notes
The normal procedure for storage, inoculation, infection, etc. with rust fungi are applicable to *P. sorghi*.

Puccinia striiformis West – Stripe or yellow rust of wheat and barley.

syn. Puccinia glumarum *Eriks. & Henn.*
Uredosori amphigenous, oblong 0·5–1·0 × 0·3–4·0 mm wide, in lines up to 70 mm long; uredospores lemon-yellow, globoid to broadly ellipsoid 25–30 × 12–24 um, contents orange, wall hyaline with short blunt spines, germ pores 8–10, scattered, indistinct; teleutosori in lines or scattered, oblong, dark brown to black, long covered by epidermis, paraphyses numerous, brown, thick-walled, curved, elongate, sub-epidermal, separating groups of spores into a compound sorus; teleutospores clavoid, 30–70 um long, upper cell 16–24 um wide, basal cell 9–12 um wide, wall 4–6 um at apex, smooth, chocolate-brown, pedicel short, yellowish; mesospores sometimes present 26–32 × 12–16 um; basidium 4-celled; basidiospores broadly ellipsoid, contents orange-yellow. Spermogonia and aecidia unknown.

Stripe, glume or yellow rust, caused by *Puccinia striiformis* (= *P. glumarum*) is the most common rust disease of wheat in the cooler, humid regions of cultivation. It is particularly important in north-west Europe (United Kingdom, Netherlands, Denmark) and also in the Pacific coastal and inter-mountain regions of the north-western U.S.A. It also occurs in S. America, Kenya, China, the Mediterranean, the Middle East and India. It is most damaging on winter wheat, although winter and spring barley can also be severely affected and rye is also susceptible. It is reported on a number of grass species and, although these are unimportant epidemiologically in Europe, in the U.S.A. wheat races occur commonly on wild grasses. Forms on barley generally do not infect wheat and *vice verca*. Although potential crop losses in wheat are high and have been shown experimentally to be in the order of 20–30%, actual losses are very much less. Annual losses in England and Wales are in the order of 0–2% nationally, although individual farm losses may be much higher when highly susceptible varieties are grown.

The typical symptom, which gives the disease its common name, is a yellow striping of the leaves. This results from the linearly-arranged, lemon-yellow uredial pustules which run between the veins of the leaf. On seedling and juvenile leaves the pustules are scattered and resemble those of *P. recondita* on wheat or *P. hordei* on barley but their pale yellow colour distinguishes them from the orange-brown pustules of these other two rusts. Small linear lesions occur on the outside of wheat glumes and pustules also erupt on the inner surfaces of glumes, pales and leaf sheaths.

In barley, pustules appear on the awns when infection is severe. Under adverse conditions of high temperatures or cold, wet weather, the lesions cease sporulating and may become necrotic. The presence of black teleutosori in these lesions can give a symptom somewhat similar to *Septoria* spp. on wheat. Effects on the host vary with the duration and severity of infection. Early severe infection results in reduction in vigour, reduced tillering, lowered seed set and poor grain filling. The root system can be drastically affected which results in general loss of plant vigour and sensitivity to soil water stress. Later infections have their main effect on grain size and quality.

No sexual stage or alternate host is known for *P. striiformis* and so it is dependent for its survival on the primary cereal host. The uredial stage, which is responsible for repeated cycles of infection, is adapted to relatively low temperature conditions. The optimum for spore germination and penetration is 8–12°C. with a maximum of 25°C. Rate of colonization within host tissues increases with temperature and the latent period, or time from infection to sporulation, can be up to 5 months at low temperatures. Infection occurs on autumn-sown wheat or barley crops and the rust survives as mycelium or uredosori over winter in the host. Rapid disease increase can occur early in the spring and severe levels of disease are evident by May. As the summer progresses, further cycles of infection may occur but these are curtailed by hot, dry weather.

Free moisture, usually in the form of dew, is necessary for spore germination and penetration and this is greatest at relatively low temperatures. However, existing infections are less sensitive to environmental conditions and the systemic nature of the fungus allows colonization to proceed even under high temperature conditions. Extensive colonization can occur from a single penetration event and subsequent development from runner hyphae which grow within the tissues. Summer survival (oversummering) is often more critical than overwintering to the survival of the fungus and hot, dry summers result in severe depletion of uredospore inoculum for the autumn-sown crop. This factor is particularly critical at the fringes of the range of adaptation of *P. striiformis*, for example in India. Under such unfavourable environments the fungus will survive in cooler, moist localities such as coastal areas and at higher altitudes. Although there is evidence for long distance spread of uredospores, the majority of inoculum derives from local sources and so the restriction of oversummering inoculum to limited regions will curtail epidemic development the following season.

The fungus exists in a number of physiologically specialized forms and this diversity of virulence reflects the corresponding diversity of host resistance. *P. striiformis* has a place in history as the pathogen for which the Mendelian inheritance of resistance was first demonstrated by Biffen in 1907. The incorporation of resistance into west European winter wheat varieties has been of major concern to breeders for the last 20 years and, although this effort has resulted in a high degree of control of the disease, the type of seedling resistance used has not been stable and physiologic forms of the pathogen capable of overcoming the resistance have commonly developed. More recently, resistances of the adult plant type have been used but most of these have also proved to be race specific and inherited in a simple manner. Resistance governed by additive genes has been incorporated into winter wheats grown in north-western U.S.A. and some other partially-expressed resistances, which have remained effective in cultivation over a number of years in north-west Europe, are being more widely used in breeding programmes to develop varieties with stable, effective resistance.

In barley, the use of hypersensitive seedling resistance has resulted in a similar unstable situation with regard to physiologic specialization in the pathogen but a range of host resistances are available to breeders. Resistance to stripe rust has recently been extensively reviewed by Röbbelen and Sharp (Advances in Plant Breeding. Journal of Plant Breeding, Supp. 9. 88p. 1978). In intensive farming situations in north-west Europe, chemical control of stripe rust is now being more widely practised. These chemicals include the recently developed systemic fungicides such as tridemorph, benodanil, oxycarboxin and triadimefon.

Pythium spp. – Root rot and seedling blight of cereals and grasses.

Pythium graminicola *Subram.*
Hyphae up to 7 um diameter, aerial mycelium strong to profuse, no swelling on agar media. Sporangia formed in water as lobulate complexes aggregated or strung out along hyphae. Zoospores readily produced, 15–48 per sporangium, 8–11 um diameter when encysted, capable of repeated emergence. Oogonia terminal or intercalary, 16·5–36·2 um (mean 25 um) diameter, wall smooth, persistent. Antheridia 1–3 up to 6, monoclinous, occasionally diclinous, crook necked, persisting after fertilization. Oospores in all oogonia, usually plerotic occasionally aplerotic, 15·4–35·3 um (mean 23 um), wall 2 um thick.

P. arrhenomanes Drechs.
Similar to P. graminicola *but differs mainly in the following: Hyphae rarely greater than 5·5 um diameter, Lobulate hyphal complexities formed on some agar media. Zoospore production in most strains meagre. Oogonia terminal, more rarely intercalary, 24–36 um (mean 30 um) diameter. Antheridia numerous, usually 5–15 (up to 25) per oogonium, degenerate after fertilization.*

Pythium spp. are parasitic on roots and rootlets of many of the *Gramineae* throughout the world. A number of species are involved in the production of seedling blights and root rots of cereals but those principally concerned are P. arrhenomanes and P. graminicola. The former is most important on maize and is the most common cause of root rot of maize in the U.S.A., but it also attacks wheat and approximately 30 other genera of grasses. P. graminicola causes similar damage but principally on wheat although maize, sugar cane and other *Gramineae* are also affected. The two species occur commonly together and are particularly important under wet soil conditions and in monoculture systems of farming.

The fungi cause a seed rot or seedling blight and also a browning rot. Lesions on the mesocotyl are often brown and sunken and light brown water-soaked lesions develop on the finer rootlets. The rot may advance into the main roots and crown tissue under unfavourable conditions where plant growth is poor. These conditions are cold wet soils and poor fertilizer levels and balance. Attack by other root pathogens such as nematodes may also predispose the plant to invasion. The fungus is soil-borne and survives as oospores, the germination of which is stimulated by contact with host roots. Mycelium develops in association with crop residues and will invade plant tissues under favourable conditions. The fungus is distributed mainly in the top 20–30 cm of the soil. Strains of *P. arrhenomanes* specifically adapted to sugar cane have been identified and isolates of *P. graminicola* from maize and oats were found to be specialized on these hosts. Isolates from barley and rye were reported as being less virulent and less specialized. Seeds of low germination vigour are more prone to attack and so high quality seed should be sown. Attention to drainage and fertility balance are also of value in controlling the disease. Host resistance in maize to *P. arrhenomanes* and in barley to *P. graminicola* has been reported.

Notes

Zoospore production in *P. arrhenomanes* is best if infected root pieces are placed in water. Both species grow rapidly on agar. Cardinal temperatures are 4°, 28–30°, 41°C. for *P. arrhenomanes* and 5–7°, 28–30° and 38°C. for *P. graminicola*. Isolation of *Pythium* spp. from the soil is facilitated by using host roots as traps.

Pyrenophora avenae – Leaf stripe and seedling blotch of oats.

Conidial stage = Drechslera avenae.
        syn.   Helminthosporium avenae.
Conidiophores solitary or in groups of 2–4, up to 350 um *long, 8–11* um *thick. Conidia more or less cylindrical, solitary, brown, 1–10 septate, 30–175 × 15–22* um. *Perfect stage uncommon in field but can be produced on oat seed or straw in Sachs agar.*

A seed-borne pathogen with long-lived resting mycelium contaminating the seed coat. It is not a disease of major importance due to reasonable control being effected by the use of seed-dressings. It is most serious in the colder and wetter areas and sporadic heavy outbreaks do occur particularly if undressed seed is sown. The fungus may kill the seedlings outright, often before they emerge through the soil. If the infected plant survives, the first leaf may show brown spots or a stripe as in *P. teres*. It may also emerge at an angle between the vertical and the horizontal and be twisted and distorted. Plants often grow away from a light infection but conidia are produced on the dead leaves which later may cause secondary infections of the foliage, the symptoms being similar to those of the seedling stage but are more pronounced. Further cycles of conidial production can continue to spread the disease but later leaves are often free from attack. The ears can be infected by conidia and ultimately lead to seed contamination. The infection of the ear can result in the loss of spikelets, 'spikelet-drop', and infection of the culm to a 'stem-break' which occurs at about the third or fourth node.

Control has been mainly achieved by the use of organo-mercurial compounds but some control is effected by thiram and other dithiocarbamate fungicides. However, mercury-resistant strains have emerged which have reduced the efficiency of this type of chemical control and a frequent change of chemicals seem to offer the best control with either benomyl-thiram or carboxin-thiram seed treatments giving the best results. Resistance has, however, been reported in some lines of *Avena* spp.

Pyrenophora graminea Ito & Kuribayashi apud Ito – Leaf stripe of barley.

Conidial stage = Drechslera graminea.
       syn.   Helminthosporium gramineum.
Conidiophores in groups of 2–6, light brown, up to 250 um long, 6–9 um thick. Conidia straight, mostly cylindrical, 1–7 septate, brown, 40–105 × 14–22 um. Perithecia uncommon, but overwintering sclerotia have been found on crop debris.

This disease is widespread in barley growing areas but is rarely of economic importance except in north-east Europe and parts of Asia. The disease is almost exclusive to barley but it has been reported on wheat, oats, rye and maize.

The fungus is seed-borne and it is by this means that the host becomes infected. Infection from crop debris or soil inoculum does not appear to occur. Severe seedling infection can occur often leading to stunting or death. If plants survive seedling infection the mycelium becomes systemic in the culm. The early symptoms, which may be overlooked, are small yellow spots on the seedling leaves which result from infection of the coleoptile and the first leaf by mycelium growing from the seed coat.

The first clear symptoms are the appearance of long chlorotic stripes, longitudinal down the leaf blade. The fungus also penetrates and infects the sheathing bases of the young leaves. Several weeks before heading, the more characteristic symptoms appear. The stripes turn brown along the margins and become straw coloured along the centre and often cause the leaves to senesce and be shed prematurely. Conidia are readily produced on the stripe lesions but it is not thought that they contribute much to secondary infection cycles although they are the main sources of inocula which contaminate the grain. The spores land on the inflorescence, germinate and grow between the hulls and within the pericarp of the developing seed.

Severely infected plants will be stunted and there may be a partial or complete suppression of ear emergence. Ears that do emerge may be deformed and discoloured and they may also be 'blind', i.e. the grain may fail to develop.

There is some controversy as to the mode of spread of the pathogen up the plant after the initial infection of the inner surface of the coleoptile. It has been suggested that the mycelium grows up within the plant, always being slightly behind the growing point but contrary evidence indicates that spread is by the contact of a healthy leaf with the infected leaf below. Normally, most leaves of an infected plant exhibit stripe lesions but, under some environmental conditions, the upper leaves and ears may escape infection. This is a disease in which infection is more severe at fairly low soil temperatures (10–16°C.) which, by slowing down the growth of the plant extends the susceptible period. The critical stage for infection is before the seedlings emerge from the soil. A change to higher temperatures later accentuates the appearance of symptoms. Perithecia are very uncommon although plants have been infected by artificial inoculation with ascospores.

Traditionally, the disease has been kept very much under control by seed treatment with organo-mercurial fungicides. With their enforced withdrawal in some countries, alternatives have been utilized especially maneb, thiram and captan often in combination with carboxin which also controls the loose smut pathogen *Ustilago nuda*. The use of undressed seed is very often associated with sporadic outbreaks of leaf stripe and should be avoided. Farm crops which are harvested for seed should be inspected for freedom from stripe early in the season as, by harvest time, severely infected plants will have withered away and will not be seen. Stripe is also a problem in breeding nurseries where small seed lots cannot be easily dressed. However, effective control of head infection has been obtained by spraying at heading and one week later with a mixture of carbendazim and mancozeb. The more widespread use of tramlines may allow this treatment to be applied to farm crops required for seed.

Notes

Microscopically, the pathogen is readily identifiable by its large, multiseptate conidia. It can easily be cultured on a range of nutrient media especially P.D.A. although sporulation does not occur unless the culture is subjected to U.V. or N.U.V. light. Mycelial cultures have been recovered in a viable state after storage under mineral oil for 7 years. Mycelium infesting dry seed will remain viable for several years and provides another method of storing cultures. Plant inoculation may be effected by placing dry barley seed on a 4-day old mycelial culture growing on agar and allowing the seed to germinate. Alternatively, 125 ml flasks containing 15 g of wheat grains and 15 ml sterile water are inoculated with a culture of *P. graminea* and after 5 days 25–100 grains of barley, surface sterilized in ethanol, are added and incubated for 4 days at room temperatures. The entire contents are then planted. Considerable variation in pathogenicity between isolates exists and hyphal tip cultures from the same single conidium culture exhibit a wide range of variation but no formal physiologic races have been recognized.

Pyrenophora teres Drechsler – Net blotch of barley.

Conidial stage = Drechslera teres.

    syn.   Helminthosporium teres.

Mycelium white to olivaceous in tissues, sparse tufted growth in culture. Conidial development limited both on host and in culture. Conidiophores solitary or in groups of 2–3, straight or flexuous, often swollen at the base, pale brown or olivaceous brown, 120–200 × 7–11 um. Conidia large, cylindrical with rounded ends, commonly 4–6 septate frequently with constriction at septa, 70–160 × 16–23 um. Perithecia brownish-black, 0·5 mm diameter. Asci numerous, sub-cylindrical, 220–230 × 30–36 um, 8 spored; ascospores light brown, 3-septate, much constricted at septa, centre cell usually divided longitudinally at maturity, 50–60 × 18–22 um.

Net blotch is primarily a disease of barley although sporadic outbreaks do occur on wheat, oats and many other *Gramineae*. It is most common in cool climates such as north-west Europe and Canada but is usually of minor importance except in crops grown from undressed seed or where stubble clearance has not been carried out effectively where barley follows barley.

    The first symptoms may be seen on the first leaf as pale stripes which may later turn brown. These blotches are usually found near the tip of the lamina rather than at the base as in spot blotch (*Cochliobolus sativus*). The reticulate or net-like markings are not easily discernible at this early seedling stage but may be seen if the leaf is held up to the light. The lesions increase in size to form narrow streaks of irregular length which do not extend into the sheath (cf. *Pyrenophora graminea*).

Conidia are produced on these stripe lesions and are the causal agents of secondary infections which give rise to irregular, brown blotches with the characteristic net-like appearance. Around the brown tissue a narrow chlorotic zone normally appears. There may be some confusion in the later stages of infection between net blotch and leaf stripe (*P. graminea*) especially as there is a tendency for the lesions to coalesce to form more or less parallel stripes. Unlike *P. graminea*, this pathogen does not cause extensive damage to the ears although small brown streaks can occur on the glumes and pales and infected grains may have dark spots at their bases. The mycelium grows into the sheath and culm tissue as the plants mature.

The fungus survives between crops either in the vegetative state in the outer coats of infected seed and on straw or, as sexually produced perithecia on old straw or stubble. Infection of autumn sown crops or volunteers in the autumn can occur from ascospores or conidia, infection being abundant during cool humid weather, mild open winters being particularly conducive to the build-up of disease.

The seed-borne inoculum is controlled by organo-mercurial or carboxin-thiram seed treatments. Proper stubble cleaning and ploughing-in of debris and volunteer plants is also an effective measure especially in intensive barley growing systems. The fungus is heterothallic, producing perithecia when both mating types are present. The perithecia are produced in the spring on dead leaves and stubble which thus provide a potential major inoculum source. Physiologic races have also been reported in several countries, the U.S.A. and W. Australia for example. Sources of host resistance, effective against known races, are available in many wild barleys and have been introduced into some commercial varieties. The genes (designated Pt) are reported as being inherited as single dominant or partially dominant factors.

Notes

The fungus grows well on P.D.A. at 15–25°C. but sporulation is enhanced under N.U.V. light. It is best sub-cultured from single conidia, hyphal tips or proto-perithecia. A method to induce perithecial formation involves the use of surface-sterilized sorghum seed that is rinsed in sterile water and boiled for 2 minutes. The seed is placed in petri dishes and Sachs' nutrient agar poured to half cover the seed. Plates are inoculated with 2 ml of a spore suspension or mycelium suspension and incubated at 15°C. for 2 months in the light or the dark. Water agar plates are then inverted over the culture dishes and the forcibly ejected ascospores picked off and sub-cultured. For inoculation purposes, single spores are cultured for 7 days, harvested and conidia and mycelial fragments sprayed on to plants at 2–10,000/ml with 0·25 g/ml gelatin as a sticker. Isolation of the fungus from infected leaf tissue is by normal methods. A method for long-term preservation by freeze-drying involves the suspension of conidia in 10% sodium glutamate prior to drying. Sporulation and pathogenicity were maintained in cultures stored for 6 months at 5°C.

Pellicularia filamentosa (Pat.) Rogers – Sharp eyespot of cereals.

Mycelial state = Rhizoctania solani *Kuhn.*
Mycelium hyaline at first but darkens with age, branching at right-angles and slightly constricted at point of attachment, no clamp connections. Sclerotia dark brown, up to 5 mm in diameter, basidia borne on powdery white hymenium in clusters, 12–18 × 8–11 um, mostly four sterigmata, basidiospores 7–12 × 4–7 um.

Rhizoctonia solani is the mycelial state of the basidiomycete *Pellicularia filamentosa* which used to be called *Corticium solani* (Prill & Delacr.) Bourd. & Balz. It is widely distributed in the cereal growing regions of the world but heavily infected crops are rare and it is doubtful whether crop losses due to this disease are of economic importance. Certainly, a high incidence of infected plants may be observed with no apparent loss in yield. The pathogen exists as numerous different strains which can attack a very wide range of crop plants from cereals and grasses to potatoes and peas.

Although a pre-emergence damping-off stage has been reported in several countries, the most diagnostic symptom is the typical 'sharp eyespot' lesion which may be found on mature plants on the outer leaf sheaths from about ground level to about 30 cm up the stem. These lesions can be wrongly diagnosed as eyespot lesions (*Pseudocercosporella herpotrichoides*). The distinguishing features are that the margins of the lesions are more sharply defined in the *Rhizoctonia* disease and the centre portion is a pale or cream colour. Over this 'pupil' area, mycelial strands may criss-cross to form a loose network which can easily be scraped away, unlike the very dark centre of the true eyespot lesion. Sclerotia may sometimes form between the leaf sheaths and the stems and, if a section is cut longitudinally through the stem behind a lesion, no grey mycelium will be found in the stem cavity as would be expected with *P. herpotrichoides.*

Plants may be attacked at any stage of growth and early infections can result in considerable thinning out of stands. Late infections, in contrast, appear to have very little effect. Lodging is frequently associated with this disease, the straws often collapsing at the level of the lesion. The pathogen can also cause a disruption of the translocation of nutrients which results in the subsequent emergence of 'whiteheads' and any reduction in grain yield is a result of the production of smaller grains rather than a reduction in the number of grains per ear. *R. solani* is regarded as a typical soil inhabiting parasite but its persistence in the soil is aided by its host range and it has been suggested that its ability to parasitize cereals, being more severe on oats than on wheat and barley, potatoes and grasses, is very important and there may be considerable carry-over of inoculum from a potato crop to the following cereal crop. The disease is favoured by dry, cool (9°C.) conditions, a wet autumn and spring being unfavourable to disease development and the incidence of disease is often quite high on sandy soils which tend to dry out more rapidly.

With the disease not being included amongst those which regularly produce economic crop losses very little attention has been paid to its control. No varieties of any cereal are consistently resistant to infection and the emphasis has been on cultural methods.

Since the disease is favoured by cold dry conditions, winter crops should be sown as early in the autumn as possible before the soil temperature drops too much. For the same reasons, the spring-sown crops should not be sown too early. Rotation seems to have little effect on disease incidence but it is unwise to follow a heavily infected cereal crop with another cereal. Under such circumstances, ploughing should be carried out as early as possible in order to maximize the time available for the decomposition of the infected crop debris.

Notes

To isolate the fungus, pieces of stem bearing sharp eyespot lesions should be washed in running water for 30 minutes and then immersed in 1% sodium hypochlorite solution for 2 minutes. They are then washed six times in sterile distilled water and then soaked overnight at 3–4°C. in sterile distilled water containing 100 ppm each of aureomycin hydrochloride, neomycin sulphate and streptomycin sulphate. The stem pieces are then plated out on water agar containing 50 ppm each of the above antibiotics and incubated for two days at 20°C. The fungus will also grow on 2% malt agar but, for isolation, the antibiotic-containing medium should be used.

Rhynchosporium secalis (Oud.) J. J. Davis – Leaf blotch or scald of barley.

Mycelium hyaline to light grey, developing sparsely as a subcuticular compact stroma. Conidia borne sessilly, hyaline, aseptate, cylindrical to ovate with short oblique apical beak, nearly median septum, 12–20 × 2–4 um. Microconidia rare, hyaline, globose-oblong 2·5–7·5 × 1·5–2·5 um.

The disease is widely distributed in the cereal growing areas and is important in cooler maritime regions. It is particularly severe in the west and south-west of Great Britain where yield losses of 20 to 30% may occur on susceptible varieties. The pathogen, *Rhynchosporium secalis*, can attack barley, rye and several grasses including *Bromus* spp., *Dactylis glomerata*, *Phleum pratense* and *Agropyron repens*. It mainly attacks the leaves where it produces large (1 cm or more) creamy-buff, irregular or diamond-shaped blotches with dark brown or purple edges. This discolouration is usually more intense on the lower leaf surface. Stems and awns may also be attacked producing similar blotchy lesions. In the early stages of symptom development the leaf lesions have a dark bluish-grey colour and appear water-soaked. In severe epidemics, the lesions may coalesce and completely kill the infected leaf. Many infections often start at the auricles forming a lesion at the base of the leaf; one such lesion can kill the rest of the leaf. The optimum conditions for infection are free surface moisture on leaves and a temperature of 15–18°C., although infection can also occur between 12 and 24°C. Conidial production occurs only in the presence of free moisture and ceases above 20°C. Several crops of conidia are produced from the same lesion. This is stimulated by alternate wetting and drying of the leaves. The conidia are produced on the upper leaf surface only and arise directly from cells of the subcuticular stroma, the cuticle eventually being sloughed off. The conidia are produced abundantly and are dispersed mainly by rain-splash.

The fungus overwinters on volunteer barley plants and on autumn-sown barley crops. It can remain infective on barley debris for 8 months and is carried over in seed from infected ears. In spring barley, the disease develops during the tillering stages of growth where it may be damaging. The plant may grow away from the disease during stem extension. Infection on the upper leaves after flag leaf emergence is most damaging. *R. secalis* exists as physiologically specialized forms and these have been detected in North and South America, Japan, South Africa, north-west Europe and Australia. Classification into races is somewhat arbitrary. Major resistance genes numbered 1 to 11 have been identified. Five exist as alleles or pseudo alleles at one locus on chromosome 3. Partial host resistance is known and is effective in all but dwarf barley varieties with a prostrate juvenile growth habit. Cultural measures for control include crop rotation, destruction of volunteer plants and burning and burying barley crop debris and the use of clean seed. In situations known to be prone to leaf blotch, sprays of captafol at 900 g a.i./ ha or captafol at 720 g a.i. plus ethirimol at 140 g a.i./ha (which also controls powdery mildew) *or* thiophanate methyl at 700 g a.i./ha (which also controls eyespot) or tridemorph at 530 g a.i. plus carbendazim at 125 g a.i. in not less than 250 litres/ha (also controls powdery mildew and yellow rust) may be beneficial in epidemic years.

Notes
Spores can be produced from lesions cut from washed leaves and incubated at 10°C. for 48 hours on plain or lima bean agar. A spore suspension from such lesions may be used to directly inoculate plants. Single spore isolates can be made by transferring single germinating conidia from 2% water-agar, 48 hours after inoculation, on to lima bean agar slopes. After 5–8 weeks, spore suspensions may be made or the culture may be stored under mineral oil. A suspension of 200,000 spores/ml is atomized on to test plants which should then be kept in a moist chamber for 48 hours at 17°C. Spores mixed with soft agar may be spread on to leaves with a brush or scalpel. Inoculum may be stored on dried infected straw or seed or spores may be preserved by drying on porcelain beads. (See review by Shipton, Boyd and Ali. Rev. Pl. Path. **53**; 839, 1974).

Sclerophthora macrospora (Sacc.) Thirum., Shaw & Naras – Downy mildew of small grain cereals and grasses.

syn. Sclerospora macrospora *(Sacc.).*
(See S. macrospora *on maize).*

This pathogen occurs in occasionally restricted outbreaks on cereals, especially wheat and oats and grasses throughout the world although it has not yet been reported in the United Kingdom. It is not of great economic importance on either wheat or oats but it is a disease which ought not to be ignored as it causes serious losses in maize and sugar cane in tropical countries.

The infected plants are erect, somewhat chlorotic and are dwarfed. Some affected plants tiller excessively but these often turn brown and wither when only a few inches high. The leaves are thickened and erect often being twisted and curled into unnatural positions in a whorl around the culm. Slightly infected plants only show a partial yellowing and some leaf thickening and twisting but most diseased plants fail to produce ears and those that are produced are deformed and empty.

Large brown oospores are produced in the mesophyll tissue between the veins of the leaf blade and the sheath and a quick diagnostic test is to hold a leaf up to the light where the presence of the oospores will be seen as rows of numerous clear spots. The disease only becomes a problem under excessively wet conditions. It has been reported as being serious on oats in low, moist, flooded ground in Mississippi, U.S.A. and on wheat in flooded ground in Kentucky as well as in Australia and Japan. These conditions are conducive to the germination of the oospores and are necessary for the spread of the motile zoospores liberated from the macrosporangia which develop from the germinating oospores. Under laboratory conditions oospores failed to germinate under moist conditions if the temperature was more than 18°C. Sporangial production has been induced on plant debris in water under laboratory conditions and there have been isolated reports of a sporangial stage occurring in the field.

The control of this disease involves good surface drainage, soil preparation and a suitable rotation free of susceptible graminaceous crops.

Sclerospora spp. and **Sclerophthora** spp. – Downy mildews of maize.

Maize is attacked by at least eight species of *Sclerophthora* and *Sclerospora*. Three occur in the temperate and warm-temperate regions of the New World. In the United States of America *Sclerophthora macrospora*, *Sclerospora graminicola* and *S. sorghi* are found and may be locally damaging although the most severe effects of the downy mildews are found in the tropical and sub-tropical regions of south-east Asia, India and Africa. Brown stripe downy mildew, caused by *Sclerophthora rayssiae* var. *zeae*, is particularly damaging in India, Philippine downy mildew, caused by *Sclerospora philippinensis*, is the most serious disease of maize in the

Philippines, Javanese downy mildew (*S. maydis*) is severe in Indonesia and the sugar cane downy mildew (*S. sacchari*) is important throughout south-east Asia. The causal organisms are all obligate parasites which are systemic in their hosts. Most of the diseases they cause have certain symptoms in common including chlorotic streaking and mottling, stunting, phyllody and excessive tillering. Certain symptoms are specific to the particular organisms, which themselves show many morphological similarities making disease diagnosis difficult. These difficulties may be increased by host genotype or environmental modification of the more typical symptoms.

Sclerophthora macrospora (Sacc.) Thirum., Shaw & Naras – Crazy top of maize.

syn. Sclerospora macrospora *Sacc.*

Sporangia hyaline, lemon-shaped, 60–100 × 30–65 um. Sporangiophores short, simple, hyphoid. Spore germination by release of biciliate, subspherical to reniform, hyaline zoospores or occasionally by germ-tubes. Oospores hyaline to yellowish, multi-nucleate, globose, 45–75 um diameter, contents granular. Germination by thin-walled tube bearing a sporangium which produces zoospores. Mycelium coenocytic, thin walled, intercellular, abundant in meristems.

This disease occurs in the more temperate regions of maize culture. It is widespread in North America and occurs in Europe, Africa and Asia. It is of only local economic importance. The pathogen has a wide host range among wild and cultivated *Gramineae*. The most characteristic symptom, which gives the disease its name, is the replacement of the normal tassel organs with leafy structures. This phyllody may also occur in the ears. Normal leaves are often narrow, strap-like and leathery, tillering is often excessive and stunting and chlorotic striping of the leaves are also common. Mycelium may be detected in host tissues by staining with zinc chloriodide which results in deep blue-purple differential staining of the fungus tissue. The disease is associated with soils that have been flooded after planting and before the plants are in the 4 to 5 leaf stage. Saturation for 24 to 48 hours is sufficient to initiate germination of soil-borne oospores and gives a liquid medium for the motile zoospores to infect the host plants. Infection occurs over a wide range of soil temperatures. Control of the disease is through prevention of soil waterlogging by correct drainage and by avoiding planting in soils subject to flooding, e.g. river bottom land.

Sclerophthora rayssiae var. **zeae** Payak & Renfro – Brown stripe downy mildew of maize.

Sporangia produced sympodially in groups of 2–6, hyaline, ovate to cylindrical, peduncle prominant, smooth-walled, 29·0–66·5 × 18·5–26·0 um, germination to produce 4–8 zoospores. Encysted zoospores hyaline, spherical, 7·5–11·0 um diameter. Sporangiophores short, determinate, arising from substomatal hyphae. Oogonia subglobose, thin-walled, hyaline to pale straw, 33–44·5 um diameter. Oospores spherical to subspherical, 29·5–37·0 um diameter, walls smooth, glistening, 4 um thick, confluent with oogonial wall. Oospores and oogonia numerous, scattered in leaf mesophyll or under stomata.

This disease occurs commonly and widely in India where it is very destructive. The characteristic symptom, from which the disease derives its name, is a reddish or purple-brown striping of infected leaves. Initially, these lesions appear as narrow, chlorotic or yellowish stripes, 3–7 mm wide with well-defined margins which are delimited by the leaf veins. Further lateral development of the stripes results in severe striping and blotching. Severely infected plants do not set seed and the plants may die prematurely. A downy or woolly growth on both adaxial and abaxial surfaces of the lesions results from sporangial development. Malformation of plants does not occur neither do leaves shred. Primary inoculum derives either from infected debris, from which oospores germinate to produce sporangia which either liberate infective zoospores or which germinate directly if temperatures are high enough, or from mycelium which overseasons on grass hosts and which produces sporangia. Secondary spread is by sporangia produced from primary lesions. Temperature and moisture govern the epidemiology of the disease, sporangia being produced at relatively low temperatures (ca. 21°C.) whereas oospores are produced at higher temperatures. A film of moisture for 12–96 hours is required for sporangial production, germination and infection. Zoospore germination occurs in the range 15–30°C. with an optimum of 22–25°C. Spores are spread by wind, rain and by animals and soil temperatures of 28–32°C. favour disease development. It is reported that zinc deficiency can predispose plants to infection. Control is through the use of resistant varieties, planting before the rainy season begins and by the use of fungicides either as foliar sprays or soil drenches.

Sclerospora sorghi (Kulk.) Weston & Uppal – Sorghum downy mildew on maize.

syn. S. graminicola *var.* andropogonis-sorghi *Kulk.*
Sporangia hyaline, oval to spherical 15–26·9 × 15–28·9 um, borne on elongated tapering sterigmata. Sporangiophores erect, fragile, hyaline, 180–300 um long, dichotomously branched, emerging through abaxial leaf stomata. Spore germination by germ-tube. Oogonia spherical, 40–55 um diameter, embedded in mesophyll. Oospores 25–42·9 um, hyaline, spherical, walls pale yellow.

This disease, first recognized in India, occurs also in Africa and Asia where it causes serious losses. More recently, it has occurred in the southern United States on maize, sorghum, sudangrass and johnsongrass and appears to be spreading into the main areas of maize cultivation, having been identified in southern Indiana in 1973. Symptoms are variable and show initially on systemically infected seedlings as stunting and chlorotic striping. On some diseased first leaves there is a distinct transverse demarcation between healthy and chlorotic tissue giving a 'half-diseased leaf' appearance. Leaves of infected plants are narrower and more erect than those of healthy plants. Phyllody of tassels is common and stalks are often brittle with grey-brown marbling of the pith and prolification of brace roots at nodes above those of normal plants. Downy growth may appear on infected leaf surfaces and local infections appear as elongated chlorotic striping.

Most infected plants are barren but ears may set seed, which although they may become infected, will rarely transmit the disease as the fungus does not survive long in seed. Oospores will survive several years in the soil and germinate by germ-tubes to infect susceptible hosts. Sporangia on the leaves are wind-borne and provide inoculum for secondary spread of infection. Conidia require high humidity and low temperatures (below 20°C.) to germinate. They are delicate and ephemeral. Control of the disease on maize is through the use of resistant varieties, destruction of infected crop debris, roguing of diseased plants and avoidance of maize-sorghum rotations. Host resistance has been identified that appears to be governed by oligogenes which are dominant to intermediate in effect.

Selenophoma donacis (Pass) Sprague & A. G. Johnson – Halo spot of barley.

Pycnidia erumpent, brown, globose, 40–150 um; pycnidiospores arising from short conidiophores on inner pycnidial wall, stoutly falcate to boomerang-shaped, non-septate, 18–35 × 2·0–4·5 um.

S. donacis is known as halo spot in the United Kingdom and as eye spot in the United States of America. It attacks barley, wheat, rye and many grasses, especially timothy (*Phleum pratense*) and cocksfoot (*Dactylis glomerata*). Recent surveys in the U.K. indicate that the disease is of frequent occurrence but at low intensity levels although severe local epiphytotics have been reported in Eire, Norway, Scotland and Wales. The disease mainly affects the leaf blade but it can also occur on the leaf sheath and on the awns of the ear.

The symptoms can be seen towards the tips and edges of the leaves and are scattered oval lesions, pale fawn in colour with a purple-brown border. The pycnidia are produced in the lesions in rows between the veins. They are small and dark brown, erumpent and can be found on both upper and lower surfaces of the leaves. The lesions may eventually coalesce and destroy large areas of leaf surface.

Halo spot is favoured by cool, moist conditions and luxuriant growth and spread of infection probably occurs when spores of the fungus, which are extruded from the pycnidia, are dispersed in rain splashes. The disease is not generally associated with the seedling stage and symptoms tend to be more prevalent on the latest formed, or top leaves. Artificial inoculation studies have shown that the flag leaf is particularly susceptible although, under natural conditions, the disease is usually of little significance by the time the grain is starting to form. Its effect upon grain yield is, in consequence, slight and, although 20% reductions in 1000 grain weights have been reported in artificially induced epidemics, a natural survey in the United Kingdom estimated the loss in yield to be less than 1%. There may, however, be an additional loss in malting quality.

Large differences in the resistance of cultivars to *S. donacis* have been recorded and, in the long term, probably offer the best control. The fungus can be transmitted on the seed and seed treatment with systemic fungicides may reduce the inoculum from this source. No other control measures for this disease are advised at present although the disease can be controlled by spray applications of zineb, lime-sulphur and dichlofluanid.

Notes

The fungus can be isolated from barley leaves after surface sterilization of the leaf segments in a 1% sodium hypochlorite solution for 30 seconds, washing with sterile water and then plating on to Czapek Dox V-8 agar. The fungus is photosporogenic, responding to NUV irradiation by an increase in sporulation. The fungus can be cultured on numerous fungal media but conidial production occurs without the development of pycnidia. It is also necessary to sub-culture every 3 to 4 days to maintain spore viability. Using C.D. V-8 agar plus NUV, the viability and pathogenicity of *S. donacis* can be maintained as well as the production of large quantities of pycnidia and pycnidiospores. Dark incubation at 18°C. for 4 days produces white mycelial colonies which are subcultured on to fresh agar plates and then incubated for 2 days in the dark at 18°C. before being exposed to continuous NUV at 14°C. for 21 days. Cultures to be irradiated are placed on a cool plate through which coolant is pumped. Thick agar (40 ml/plate) is advised to counteract the drying out of the medium in the plastic petri-dishes which transmit NUV radiation. The cultures and cool plate assembly are placed in a cabinet illuminated by NUV and lined with aluminium foil to maintain uniform radiation.

Leptosphaeria avenaria f. sp. **avenaria** Weber – Speckled blotch of oats.

Conidial stage = Septoria avenae *f. sp.* avenae *Frank.*
Pycnidia sub-epidermal, scattered or in rows, globose to sub-globose, brown to black 90–150 um, ostiole slightly elevated. Macropycnidiospores produced from phialidic conidiophores on inner wall of pycnidium, cylindrical with rounded ends, straight or slightly curved, 3-septate, 25–45 × 3–4 um. Micropycnidiospores spermatial-like, 4–5 × 0·6–1 um, produced in smaller pycnidia, 50–150 um.

Ascocarps immersed, globose to sub-globose, black, ostiole not protruding, 60–130 um. Asci clavate, 8-spored, 30–100 × 10–18 um. Ascospores bi- or triseriate, fusoid, 3-septate, second cell from the top slightly swollen, light yellow, 23–28 × 4·5–6 um.

Although not of major importance, speckled blotch of oats occurs quite frequently and can cause reductions in yield. It has been reported to be of increasing importance in Canada. It is a seed-borne disease and heavily infected seedlings often fail to emerge. The most obvious symptoms are purple-brown coloured leaf spots with orange margins on the leaf blades of mature plants but, on careful examination, black necrotic streaks may be seen at the base of the coleoptile. The disease has no apparent symptoms from the seedling stage until the plants are almost full grown.

Macropycnidia are formed in the leaf lesions and the macro-pycnidiospores ooze out in a worm-like tendril where they are exposed to rain-splash dispersal or may be washed down to the base of the leaf and ultimately infect the culm. As the culm extends, internodal lesions may be seen which may cause the plant to lodge at the point of infection. The nodes themselves may also be infected and macropycnidia and later micropycnidia produced. The rachis and glumes may also become infected again producing the typically purplish-brown lesions. From the infected glumes the seeds can become infected and are a potential source of inoculum if sown.

Mycelium persists in oat stubble and can survive the winter. In fact, overwintering appears to be necessary for the production of perithecia. Ascospores have been shown to cause widespread disease in the subsequent oat crops and obviously play an important part in the epidemiology of this disease.

The conidial stage of *L. avenaria* f. sp. *avenaria* is distinct from *L. avenaria* f. sp. *triticea* in that it only infects oats whereas f. sp. *triticea* does not infect oats and does not produce micropycnidiospores.

Considerable variation between oat varieties exists for resistance to speckled blotch but this is of the field resistance type. Cultural methods of control include seed treatment especially with M.B.C. generating compounds, burning or ploughing of the stubble and crop rotation.

Notes

The fungus is easily isolated from seed or from infected leaf material by conventional means (see Chapter 4). The fungus grows well on Czapek-Dox V-8 agar and sporulation is stimulated if the cultures are kept at about 20°C. under N.U.V. light. For the rapid production of spores for field inoculation purposes 10 mm plugs of mycelium and spores from an established culture are transferred to C.D. V-8 plates and smeared as evenly as possible over the complete surface. After 7 days each plate should yield up to 300 × 10⁶ spores. The cultures may be stored for long periods under mineral oil.

Septoria passerinii Sacc. – Speckled leaf blotch of barley.

Pycnidia immersed, dark brown, globose, 100–140 um diameter; conidiophores hyaline, arising from inner pycnidial wall, simple, non-septate; conidia hyaline, straight or slightly curved, basal end blunt, apical end rounded, 26–42 × 1·5–2 um, 0–3 septate; microconidia hyaline, 3–7 × 1 um.

Although of very minor importance in Europe and the United Kingdom, speckled blotch of barley has been reported as a disease causing serious losses in malting barley in Canada. It has a deleterious effect both on grain yield and quality with reductions in yield as high as 20% with an additional reduction in the malting quality.

The disease symptoms are linear, straw-coloured lesions on the leaves. The lesions have indefinite margins as the chlorosis of the blotchy lesion gradually blends into the green of the leaf. Defoliation is not as common as with the other *Septoria* cereal diseases but the reduction in photosynthetic tissue can result in a variety of effects, depending upon the severity and timing of the infection, the most drastic being the reduction in grain size. Numerous, small dark-brown pycnidia can be found embedded in the infected tissue and these extrude masses of conidia in worm-like spore cirrhi under conditions of high humidity ($>$93% RH). The spores can be spread by rain-splash and wind and by insects.

There is no evidence of a seed-borne phase but the pathogen is known to overwinter as mycelium or as pycnidia in infected crop debris. Both macro- and microconidia can be produced in the following season. There are three types of control measure that have been attempted, cultural, chemical and biological. Obviously, crop rotation, good hygiene to bury crop debris and the ploughing in of volunteer plants should always be practised. Frequent applications of dithiocarbamates such as nabam and zineb have given good but uneconomical returns and it is likely that single applications of a systemic fungicide, especially the MBC generators, plus a dithiocarbamate such as maneb or mancozeb immediately after flag leaf emergence, would be better but the incidence of this disease is very unpredictable. There are cultivars with resistance to this disease and the resistance has been shown to be governed by dominant genes. There is an unfortunate linkage of genes in many barley cultivars in that, in all the cultivars in the U.S.D.A. collection, plants which have resistance to *Cochliobolus sativus* are susceptible to *S. passerinii*. However, the gene for resistance to *S. passerinii* has been shown to be linked to the gene for resistance to *Ustilago nuda.* In addition, pathogenic differences among isolates from barley have been reported which will complicate breeding programmes and it is not certain what role some of the grass hosts play in the epidemiology of speckled leaf blotch.

Notes
The fungus can be isolated by conventional techniques (Chapter 4) and will grow on various media. When grown on oat medium the colony has a sparse mycelium development and forms no pycnidia but produces copius conidia in a yeast-like growth habit. It grows particularly well on 2% cornmeal agar supplemented with 2% glucose and 2% peptone but it is necessary to sub-culture to fresh medium every 4 to 5 days to maintain viability and pathogenicity. *S. passerinii* can be successfully maintained as soil-spore preparations at 4°C. in the dark for at least two years. The

fungus also survives cryogenic storage when applied to the surface of wood segments sealed in ampoules. The cultures are grown on the glucose : peptone – supplemented cornmeal agar and a small amount of the yeast-like fungus material is transferred from a 4-days-old culture to a sterile microscope slide. Dry, sterilized 2 cm wood segments of the wooden shaft of cotton-tipped applicators are then rolled through the fungus material with a sterile forceps and placed in sterile glass ampoules. The ampoules are then sealed with an oxygen-natural gas flame, placed on semitubular aluminium canes, as in the storage of rust spores, and stored in liquid nitrogen. The cultures maintain their sporulating capacity and pathogenicity for at least a year.

Tilletia caries (DC) Tul. – Bunt or Stinking smut of wheat.

Internal tissue of grains replaced by black, powdery teleutospore mass. Teleuto-spores globose to sub-globose, pale brown, markedly reticulate, distinctive foetid smell on release, 14–20 um in diameter. Eight to sixteen filiform sporidia (40–55 um in length) produced terminally on promycelium from germinating teleutospore.

Bunt of wheat is a classical example of a disease which has been virtually eliminated by seed treatment. It is now only of importance in countries where seed treatment and seed inspection are not a regular routine. The disease can also cause severe outbreaks in areas such as the Pacific north-west of the U.S.A. where the pathogen is known to survive in the soil as well as being seed-borne. Bunt is also a classical disease in that it was the first case in which the pathogenic relation of a micro-organism as a causal factor in disease was established. In the United Kingdom, during and after the 1914–18 war, bunt was so common that often up to 50% of the ears in a wheat crop were bunted. In fact, the incidence of bunt as recorded from samples sent to the Official Seed Testing Station, Cambridge has declined from 33% in 1921 to 0·2% in 1957 (Marshall, Ann. appl. Biol. **48**; 34, 1960).

Plants infected with bunt cannot be recognized easily until the ears emerge and even then the symptoms are not pronounced. The stem of an infected plant is usually shorter than in healthy plants and the bunted ears are narrower, rather longer and have a bluish tinge. The whole ear has an open rather than compact habit due to the affected grains being more plump than normal resulting in the glumes being pushed apart. The diseased grains tend to be grey in colour, in distinct contrast to the golden-yellow or red of healthy grain. This discolouration is due to the interior of the grain being filled with a black mass of spores, the teleutospores. The pericarp is intact but is easily broken during threshing, the teleutospores being released at this time and contaminate the healthy grains. When freshly released, the spores give off a characteristic smell of rotten fish due to the production of trimethylamine, hence the old name Stinking Smut. Contaminated grain, if milled, produces off-white flour and thus is of little commercial value. If sown untreated, such grain provides the source of inoculum for the start of a new season of this disease.

When contaminated grain is sown, the teleutospores germinate on the seed surface to produce a short outgrowth, the promycelium. The optimum temperature for germination is between 14–16°C. The diploid teleutospore nucleus undergoes a meiotic division which is followed by further mitotic divisions to give between 8–16 haploid daughter nuclei. One nucleus passes to each of the same number of **hyaline**, **filiform**, slightly curved sporidia, or basidiospores, which are formed on projections at the distal tip of the promycelium, which is functionally a basidium, two sporidia per projection. The sporidia fuse in pairs by means of a lateral conjugation hypha to form the characteristic H-structures. This fusion reconstitutes the dikaryon which is the normal nuclear state for the smut fungi but in *T. caries*, being heterothallic, fusion only occurs between sporidia of opposite (+) or (−) mating type. The fused sporidia germinate to produce dikaryotic mycelium which can directly infect the new host or, sickle-shaped, hyaline, dikaryotic secondary sporidia are produced on the mycelium. The secondary sporidia can themselves germinate to produce hyphae which can infect the host. Low soil temperature and high soil moisture are also conducive to infection of the young wheat coleoptile with the optimum soil temperature between 9–12°C. and around 13% soil moisture.

The hyphae formed from primary or secondary sporidia form an appressorium on the developing host coleoptile and penetrate directly through the cuticle. Once the fungus is inside the young seedling it grows both inter- and intracellularly, keeping pace with the seedling's growth without materially affecting the health or outward appearance of the plant. The fungus eventually reaches the growing plant and continues to grow with the host until heads are produced. After the ear is formed and the grain is developing, the fungus then replaces the internal tissues of the grain with a mass of black teleutospores which will be liberated at threshing.

Physiologic race determination in *T. caries* is difficult as a result of recombination of heterozygous factors on the germination of the teleutospores. However, there seems to be good evidence for at least twenty races on a world basis and new races have been produced experimentally by hybridizing two existing races (Holton, Phytopath. **41**;

511, 1951). Differences in host resistance have also been reported, often the fungus being halted when it reached the epidermal cells in resistant varieties. However, these differences between host varieties have not produced the same dramatic control of bunt as has the use of seed treatments.

Bunt can easily be prevented by disinfecting the seed before sowing. In particular, organo-mercury dusts or liquid formulations have proved highly successful in countries where mercury is allowed and, in other countries, copper carbonate dusts or slurries and formaldehyde have all been successfully used. In the Pacific north-west of the U.S.A., both the seed-borne and soil-borne sources of inocula have to be countered. Here, hexachlorobenzene has found favour especially in soils where wireworms may also be a problem.

Notes

The smut fungi are readily cultured in the haploid state on artificial media. By culturing two monosporidial isolates of differing mating types it is possible to grow the dikaryotic mycelium and to produce teleutospores. The medium used is potato sucrose agar (Kendrick. Phytopath., **47**; 674, 1957).

Trichometasphaeria turcica (Luttrell) – Northern leaf blight of maize and sorghums.

Conidial stage = Drechslera turcica *(Pass) Subram. and Jain.*

    syn. Helminthosporium turcicum *Pass.*

Conidiophores straight or flexuous, olivaceous brown, 150–300 um *in length, 7–11* um *thick, emerging singly or in groups of 2–6 through stomata. Conidia variable in size and shape, 45–132 × 15–25* um, *straight or slightly curved, ellipsoidal to obclavate, pale olivaceous, 3–8 pseudoseptate, hilum conspicuously protruberant, germination characteristically polar. Ascocarps black, ellipsoidal to globose, 359–721* um *in height, 345–497* um *in diameter, short stiff hairs, brown, around upper third. Asci cylindrical to clavate 176–249 × 24–31* um, *bitunicate, stipe short, containing 1–6 (commonly 2–4) ascospores. Ascospores hyaline, fusiform, straight or slightly curved, septa 2–6 typically 3, constricted at septum, 42–78 × 13–17* um.

Northorn leaf blight is widespread in most humid areas where maize is grown. The fungus attacks maize, sorghum (*Sorghum vulgare*), sudangrass (*S. sudanense*) johnsongrass (*S. halepense*) and teosinte (*Euchlaena mexicana*). It may be locally severe under favourable conditions of warm humid weather and, if infection starts early before silking, losses in grain yield up to 30% may occur, together with lowering of the feed value and a predisposition of the infected plants to stalk rots. Leaf symptoms appear typically as long elliptical or lens-shaped lesions which are at first water-soaked and then turn greyish green or tan. They may be up to 15 cm or more in length and extend into the sheaths. They begin on the lower leaves and progress up the plant and coalesce under severe conditions leading to death of the leaves and a frost-injured appearance. Sporulation occurs on the undersides of leaves and often the spores appear in concentric target patterns in the lesions. Lesions occur on the husks and tassels but kernels are not affected. Seedling infection and crown rot occur where conditions favour the fungus as in southernmost Florida.

Overwintering of the fungus is on infected crop debris and volunteer plants in mild climates and sporulation occurs in these old lesions under favourable conditions. Conidia are apparently violently discharged and air dispersed to maize leaves where germination occurs in 6–18 hours if free moisture is present on the plant surface. Penetration is either direct or through stomata and occurs best at 25–30°C. and symptoms appear in 7–12 days. The sexual stage is rare in nature. The fungus exists in physiologically specialized forms but they are not clearly defined although cross inoculations indicate two groups of isolates, one which attacks maize, sudangrass and johnsongrass and another group which attacks these hosts and sorghum. Control is achieved through the use of host resistance. A qualitative mono-genically inherited resistance expressed as minute necrotic flecks surrounded by chlorotic halos has been described but a more valuable quantitatively expressed and polygenically inherited resistance is also available. Fungicides are used to control the disease on sweet corn.

Notes

Ascocarps are produced on pieces of barley straw (culm plus sheath) sterilized in propylene oxide, half immersed in Sachs agar and inoculated with small infested agar blocks and incubated at 25°C. Ascocarps form on the leaf sheaths in about 21 days (Luttrell, Phytopath. **48**; 281, 1958). Inoculum can be maintained in culture or stored on dry, infected leaves over winter. Field inoculation can be with an aqueous spore suspension sprayed into leaf whorls or by applying dried, ground up infected leaves. Field screening for resistance is described by Ullstrup (Phytopath. **60**; 1597, 1970).

Urocystis tritici Koern – Flag smut of wheat.

Sori black, linear, in leaves and culm tissue. Sporeballs globose to oblong, 18–35 × 35–40 um, comprising 1–4 chlamydospores; smaller, sterile cells around the fertile cells. Chlamydospores angular to globose, dark reddish-brown, smooth, 14–20 um diameter, germinating to produce short promycelium with or without septations; sporidia, or basidiospores, 3–4, hyaline, borne near apex of promycelium.

The disease is potentially destructive in areas with mild winters where wheat is grown, such as the Pacific north-west of the U.S.A. The fungus, *Urocystis tritici* is limited in its host range to wheat, although a related species, *U. occulta,* causes a stalk smut of rye (*Secale cerealc*). *U. tritici* is typically a leaf smut and the characteristic symptoms are long lead-coloured stripes on the upper leaf blades and sheaths. These stripes, which run parallel to the veins, are made up of sori of the smut fungus which contain masses of dark-brown powdery spores. The early symptoms are of chlorotic striping on the upper leaves of plants during stem elongation. These stripes turn leaden as the dark spore masses are produced under the epidermis. The epidermis soon ruptures exposing the spore masses, and the leaf tissues split along the length of the sori. Twisting and curling of leaves and sheaths accompanies infection and plants are dwarfed and often fail to head. The spore balls in the sori are liberated and fall to the ground when the stripes rupture and these provide one source of inoculum for infection of the autumn-sown wheat crop. The other main source is on seed which becomes contaminated by spore balls when infected crops are harvested. Under favourable conditions of warm, moist soil, the chlamydospores germinate to produce sporidia which infect the young cereal grain sprouts. The fungus develops in the host tissues where it overwinters. The following spring the fungus grows with the developing plant and produces the typical linear sori on leaves and sheaths. The chlamydospores can survive in dry soil for more than a year and the disease will increase if crops of wheat are grown in succession. Crop rotation is therefore one means of disease control although the main control measure is the use of resistant varieties. In addition to this, chemical seed treatments are effective in eliminating seed-borne inoculum.

Ustilago avenae (Pers.) Rostrup – Loose smut of oats.

Sori in the spikeloto often completely replacing the ovaries and very often the glumes. Spore mass firm at first, powdery, dark greenish-brown. Teleutospores spherical to subspherical, pale greenish-brown but lighter on one side, minutely echinulate, 5–8 um diameter.

This disease is of world-wide occurrence but is not of great importance due to the relative ease with which it can be controlled. It can also attack tall oat grass and barley. The signs of the disease are mainly confined to the panicle on which the spikelets are totally transformed into a black powdery spore mass. Lesions may also develop on the blade of the flag leaf producing spore masses. Normally, these spores, teleutospores, are blown away very soon after the flowering spike emerges but, occasionally, the spores are retained within the remaining flimsy membranes of the spikelet and are not released until threshing. *U. avenae* is very similar in morphology and life-cycle to *U. hordei*, the organism causing covered smut of oats and barley from which it can be distinguished microscopically in that the teleutospores of *U. avenae* are minutely echinulate whereas those of *U. hordei* are smooth. Loose smut is the most common of the two diseases in the United Kingdom although they are not often differentiated.

The primary inoculum consists largely of teleutospores which have lodged between the glumes on the grain either during the course of being dispersed by wind or during the threshing process. It is also known that some ovary infection can occur but the resulting mycelium in the seed coat is not considered to be as important a source of inoculum as the teleutospores carried on the seed. Some spores germinate immediately after being deposited on the grain. The resulting mycelium never penetrates further than the seed coat where it remains dormant until the seed is sown when it can infect the young seedling.

On germination, the teleutospore produces a stout hypha (the promycelium) which functions as the basidium in more conventional Basidiomycetes. The promycelium is four celled by transverse septation. The nucleus of the teleutospore is diploid, the two nuclei from the original characteristic dikaryotic mycelium having fused in the maturing spore. Meiosis takes place as the promycelium is differentiating and one of the four resulting haploid daughter nuclei migrate to each of the four promycelial cells. As an outgrowth at the distal end of each cell a sporidium, or basidiospore, is produced into which passes the haploid nucleus. The sporidia are capable of reproducing by budding. The fungus is heterothallic and the sporidia will be either of + or − mating type. The sporidia do not have the capacity to infect the host but fusion can take place between sporidia of opposite mating type and the mycelium produced on germination is dikaryotic and can infect the developing seedling.

Infection usually occurs through the base of the coleoptile which is very susceptible when young but becomes more resistant with age. After penetrating the cuticle, the mycelium is intracellular at first in the mesocotyl, coleoptile and first leaf. It then becomes intercellular, advancing with the growing point until the panicles are formed where the flower primordia are invaded and teleutospores formed directly from the mycelial cells in which the two nuclei fuse. Because of their mode of differentiation, the teleutospores are often called chlamydospores.

Resistance in the host can be expressed by a failure of the mycelium in the growing plant to keep pace with the culm primordia, in which case the ear remains uninfected. A large number of races of *U. avenae* have been reported showing a great diversity in pathogenicity and some races have been shown to possess genetic heterogeneity sufficient to break down resistance in their hosts. Much breeding work has been carried out in the U.S.A. and many resistant oat varieties produced. However, the disease has been virtually eliminated in most countries by chemical control methods. Seed treatments such as formaldehyde and the various organo-mercurial fungicides have given good control and the systemic oxathiin, carboxin, has been reported to give complete control in France.

Notes

The fungus can be cultured by placing sporidia on PDA or PDA victorgrain extract agar (Narain, Indian Phytopath. **17**; 157, 1964). Infection is favoured by neutral to slightly acid soils and moisture and temperature have large effects with the optimum between 18–22°C. and high soil moisture being more favourable than low soil moisture.

Ustilago hordei (Pers) Lagerh. – Covered smut of oats and barley.

Sori held together by almost intact glumes until harvest. Teleutospores pale yellow or greenish, brown or purplish black en masse, spherical to subspherical, smooth, 7–11 um in diameter. Promycelium transversely septate with lateral sporidia (or basidiospores).

On oats, this fungus was formerly known as *U. kolleri* but, on both oats and barley, this disease is not now very common duo to the ease with which it can be controlled by seed dressings. On emergence, the ears of infected plants have an abnormal blackened appearance due to the masses of dark teleutospores held together by the almost intact but delicate glumes. These spores, unlike those of loose smut of wheat or barley (*U. nuda*) are not released in any great numbers during the flowering period but remain on the ear until threshing. Some spores are liberated in the field and occasional flower infection has been reported and some may lodge on the outer surfaces of the developing grain. *U. hordei* is almost identical in life-cycle and epidemiology to the loose smut pathogen of oats (*U. avenae*). On release, the teleutospores become lodged in crevices on the healthy grain and between the lemma and palea. There is no overwintering in soil as was found in certain soils for bunt (*Tilletia caries*).

The teleutospore contains a single diploid nucleus, it being assumed that the two nuclei of the binucleate cells of the hyphae having fused at spore formation. When the seed is sown the teleutospore germinates to produce a promycelium which becomes septate and, after meiosis, each cell of the promycelium contains one daughter, haploid nucleus. Sporidia, or basidiospores, are produced laterally and they fuse in pairs, presumably according to compatibility in mating type, thus reconstituting the dikaryotic state which is considered normal for most smut fungi. Infection of the germinating seedling is effected by the hyphae produced from the germinating fused sporidia. The fungus then grows, mostly intercellularly, advancing with plant development until the floral primordia are reached where the normal grain tissue becomes completely replaced by the teleutospore masses.

Physiologic races of *U. hordei* have been identified and varietal resistance in oats and barley varies considerably. However, control by organo-mercurial seed dressings has proved very effective in countries where these fungicides are allowed and, along with several other fungicides now used as replacements for mercury compounds, has relegated covered smut to a position of quite minor importance.

Ustilago maydis (DC) Corda – Common smut of maize.

Sori as galls on all above ground parts, mainly embryonic tissue. Galls covered by white, glistening membrane which soon ruptures. Chlamydospores, or teleutospores, black and powdery in mass, globose to ellipsoidal, 8–11 um diameter with heavy spine-like blunt echinulations, germination typically produces a basidium and sporidia (basidiospores) but this is variable. Sporidia increase by budding.

Common smut, caused by *Ustilago maydis*, is found wherever maize is grown although it appears to have been eradicated in Australia and New Zealand. Teosinte (*Euchlaena mexicana*) is also affected. Losses from the disease are generally slight but variable and have been estimated at up to 6% in some localized areas of the U.S.A. Symptoms are often dramatic and unmistakeable as whitish, glistening galls which are variable in shape and size. They occur on all plant parts but are most common on young developing tissues or tissues mechanically injured by hail or detasselling equipment for example. Galls are common in axillary buds, individual male and female flowers and leaves. They are caused by the induction of **hypertrophy** and **hyperplasia** of host cells by the fungus and are usually small on leaves but may be large and grotesque on ears or tassels. The membrane ruptures as the gall develops exposing a sooty spore mass. These spores are able to survive for considerable periods in crop residues and in the soil thus providing the main source of primary inoculum for the following season. The spores are hardy and may remain viable for several years and delayed germination is common. The spores germinate to produce sporidia which are blown to the host plant. These germinate and grow but apparently cannot cause infection until two compatible haploid sporidia have fused giving rise to binucleate infection hyphae. Alternatively, infection hyphae may arise direct from the germinating chlamydospores. Germination of spores takes place in water over a range of temperatures from 10°C. to 35°C. and penetration takes place directly, through wounds or through stomata. Repeated cycles of gall formation, spore production and infection occur through the growing season. Dry weather usually favours smut development but the relationship is not clear. High nitrogen levels, particularly from organic sources such as animal manure, seem to favour the disease and injuries to the plant are also predisposing factors. Because of the hardiness of the spores, control of the disease through crop rotation and sanitation is not practical. Long distance spread is probably by infested seed and so chemical seed treatment is a very necessary precautionary measure. The most effective means of control is through the use of resistant varieties but the fungus exists in physiologic races thus making breeding more difficult.

Notes
The fungus can be cultured on artificial media such as PDA to produce sporidial cultures. Such spore suspensions can be used to spray inoculate plants. It is reported that the spores induce allergic responses in man and are toxic to man and animals although there are other reports to the contrary.

Ustilago nuda (Jensen) Rostrup – Loose smut of wheat and barley.

Sori in spikelets completely replacing ovaries, becoming dispersed soon after ear emergence. Teleutospores pale yellow-brown, dark olive-brown en masse, spherical to subspherical or sometimes irregular, minutely echinulate, 5–9 um diameter.

Unlike bunt of wheat and the covered smuts, loose smut of wheat and barley is still a disease of some significance especially in regions with relatively cool weather during the flowering period. The disease is very easy to diagnose in the field, the smutted ears being obvious as soon as they emerge. Ear emergence in diseased plants is slightly in advance of healthy plants. The naked teleutospores, having completely replaced the flowering parts, are blown away on exposure and provide inoculum to infect healthy florets on other plants as they emerge. On alighting on a healthy stigma or pericarp surface, the teleutospore germinates to produce a promycelium. The promycelial cells are haploid and the normal dikaryotic state is quickly reconstituted by the production of short hyphae, or conjugation tubes, that fuse with compatible cells. It was thought that infection only took place through the stigma but it has been shown to occur more often through the developing pericarp wall (Batts, Trans. Brit. mycol. Soc., **38**; 465, 1955). Following the fusion of cells in the same or nearby promycelium, new binucleate branching hyphae grow out and penetrate the host.

After penetration, the mycelium within the grain remains dormant, chiefly in the scutellum, until the seed is sown the following season. As the seedling germinates the mycelium grows just behind the growing point and eventually invades the first node. Progressively, as each internode expands the mycelium is carried upwards and ultimately reaches the developing ear. Teleutospores are then produced from the mycelium and they completely replace the floral organs so that the rachis, on emergence, is a black mass of powdery spores which are held together very briefly by a flimsy membrane.

The fungus is heterothallic but it tends to inbreed and out-crossing appears to be less common than in most other smut fungi. Physiologic specialization has been reported in many countries but the races have not been standardized on an international basis. The races found in one country seem to differ quite appreciably from those occurring in another although the definition of races has been made more difficult by the non-standardization of host differentials. The forms of the pathogen on wheat and barley are morphologically alike and even have common antigens but there is no cross-infection between the forms on the two hosts.

The disease is of little importance now in many countries due to three reasons. Firstly, seed certification in the United Kingdom and its attendant inspection of the seed crops has resulted in a dramatic reduction in diseased seed although, occasionally, losses of up to 20% have been recorded, mostly due to the introduction of a highly susceptible variety. At present, the disease rarely achieves a 1% level on either wheat or barley. Secondly, the infected seed can be treated in a hot water bath to eradicate the pathogen. One method is to immerse the seed into warm water for times varying from 1·5–2 hours at 49°C. to 5–6 hours at 41°C. in the case of wheat and from 1·5 hours at 49°C. to 5 hours at 41°C. in the case of barley (Doling, Ann. app. Biol. **55**; 295, 1965). The hot water treatment induces the formation of quinones within the seed which, it is believed, account for the fungitoxic activity of this treatment. The third, and probably most effective method of control, is the use of the systemic fungicide carboxin (2,3,dihydro-5-carboxanilido-6-methyl-1,4-oxathiin). This is sold under the proprietary name of Vitavax and has proved successful on both wheat and barley. Resistance to *U. nuda* is known in wheat and in barley. In wheat, resistance has been shown to be controlled by single dominant and independent genes. In certain barley varieties two genes are required to confer resistance. In addition, some barley varieties have closed flowers which provide a mechanical barrier to infection. However, control of this disease in the immediate future would appear to be mainly concerned with the use of systemic chemicals.

Notes
U. nuda can be readily cultured on malt or potato dextrose agar. It can be differentiated from the loose smut of oats pathogen (*U. avenae*) by the absence of sporidia production on potato dextrose agar. The cardinal temperatures for spore germination are 4°C. min., 40°C. max. and 20–25°C. optimum. The optimum relative humidity is 94–97%. Ears of wheat or barley can be inoculated with spore suspensions by using the hypodermic needle method (Poehlman, Phytopath. **35**; 640, 1945) or by a modification of this method utilizing macerated mycelial suspensions as described by Ribiero (Trans. Brit. mycol. Soc. **46**; 49, 1963). Seed can be assayed for infection by staining cleared embryos in trypan blue (Popp, Phytopath. **49**; 75, 1959).

Diseases caused by bacteria and Spiroplasma

Corynebacterium tritici (Hutchinson) Burkholder – Yellow slime or 'tundu' disease of wheat.

An aerobic, non-spore-forming rod, motile with one polar flagellum. Gram-positive, coagulates Litmus milk slowly, gelatin liquefaction slow, starch hydrolysis weak or none, nitrate not reduced to nitrite, optimum temperature ca. 27°C.

This bacterial disease of wheat is mainly found in India, China, Egypt and Iran but has also been reported from Western Australia. The whole or part of the wheat ear appears to be smothered in a yellow slimy bacterial exudate and, in some plants, there is a failure to produce grains. The ears may emerge much distorted or fail to emerge at all. On leaves and sheaths long slimy yellow spots may be seen. The symptoms are very similar to the yellow slime disease of cocksfoot grass (*Dactylis glomerata*) which is caused by another bacterium, *C. rathayi*.

The bacterium is carried with the seed in infected galls of the 'ear-cockle' nematode, *Anguina tritici,* with which it has an obligate association. The presence of the nematode is considered essential for the establishment of the bacteria in the plant and many attempts to inoculate wheat artificially in the absence of the nematode have failed. The bacteria have been shown to be carried on the surface of the galls and they can remain viable for at least five years. The nematode within the galls can remain viable for an even longer period.

The control of this disease involves the elimination of the nematode vector from the seed. Flotation in a 20% brine solution enables the lighter galls to be skimmed off before they become waterlogged and sink. This treatment is effective and is also relatively inexpensive. Hot water treatment, as in the control of loose smut, *Ustilago nuda*, is also possible but great care must be taken to ensure that the germination of the seed is not impaired.

Notes

C. tritici can be readily isolated from the yellow bacterial exudate on infected plants by streaking on to either nutrient or potato dextrose agar. It forms yellow colonies which turn orange or dirty yellow with age. It is very similar to *C. rathayi* in its cultural characteristics differing mainly in its negative reaction to bacteriophages which lyse *C. rathayi* and in its inability to produce acid from mannitol.

Erwinia stewartii (Smith) Dye – Bacterial wilt of maize.

Rod shaped (0·4–0·7 × 0·9–2 um) non-motile, gram negative, occurring singly in short chains. Facultative anaerobe. Colonies on nutrient agar (N.A.) small, round, slow-growing, yellow. N.A. streaks variable, thin, yellow to orange yellow, dry to moist, fluid or not. Growth in broth feeble, whitish ring, yellow precipitate.

Erwinia stewartii causes a bacterial wilt of maize and also of *Euchlaena mexicana* and *Tripsacum dactyloides*. On maize it is also commonly known as Stewart's disease. It occurs mainly in North and Central America but also in Peru, Italy, east Europe, South Africa and China and recently has been recorded in Thailand. It is widespread over the eastern U.S.A. and is common in the warmer areas of North and Central America where it is particularly severe on sweet corn. The disease caused considerable economic losses on sweet corn in the U.S.A. especially in 1930 and 1937. The symptoms on sweet corn are of a typical bacterial wilt that infects the vascular system. The vessels are blocked by a gelatinous mass of bacteria and slime which oozes out from the cut ends of infected tissue. Plants not killed are stunted and tassels may be produced early with the ears small or even missing. Leaf symptoms are more common on the more resistant dent corn types where spread through the entire plant does not generally occur. Long, pale green or yellowish streaks develop from insect wounds and become dry and brown later. Cut ends of leaves placed in water and observed under the microscope show masses of bacterial rods oozing out from the vascular bundles. In severely infected plants, bacteria are carried throughout the vascular system and into cobs, thus infecting kernels which may spread the disease. The main means of spread, however, is by the corn flea beetle (*Chaetocnema pulicaria*) which carries the bacteria in its body and transmits them when feeding; thus the epidemiology of the disease is closely linked with that of the insect vector. The main source of primary inoculum is from the beetle population that emerges from hibernation in the spring and the size of this depends on the severity of the winter. Secondary spread is principally by feeding beetles, the activity of which tends to reach a maximum on dent corn after tasselling and this gives rise to the leaf blight or late infection phase of the disease. In addition, a variety of other insects are able to transmit the organism including the soil-borne larvae of *Diabrotica longicornis* and *Phorbia cilicrura* which can transmit root infections. The use of insecticides early in the season to control the flea beetle populations is partly effective in controlling the disease. High levels of fertilizer nitrogen appear to predispose plants to infection. Seed treatment is not effective as a control measure. The use of resistant hybrids is the most effective means of control. Sweet corn is generally more susceptible than dent or flint types and in both, early and short inbred lines are more susceptible than later, taller types. In sweet corn, Golden Cross Bantam, Country Gentleman and Evergreen are resistant and it has been reported that resistance is governed by two major genes and one minor modifying gene. No bacterial strains with increased virulence on resistant types have been reported.

Notes

The bacterium grows slowly on gelatine but does not liquefy it. Nitrate is not reduced to nitrite. Hydrogen sulphide is not produced. Indole production is slight or absent. Litmus milk is decolourized, not coagulated, not peptonized and is slightly acid. Optimum pH 6·0–8·0, optimum temperature 30°C. (min. 7, max. 39°C.). Thermal death point 53°C. See Dye (N.Z. J.Sci. **6**; 495, 1963). The bacteria can be cultured readily on yeast extract-glucose agar in tubes incubated at 26°C. A simple and effective plant inoculation method is by clipping seedling leaves and dipping the cut ends in a suspension containing 5×10^7 cells per ml. (Lockwood and Williams, Phytopath. **47**; 83, 1957).

Pseudomonas coronafaciens (Elliott) Stapp. – Halo blight of oats.

Motile rods with 1 to several polar flagella; single, in pairs, or in chains, 0·7 × 2·0 um; no spores, capsules formed; white colonies on nutrient agar; gelatine slowly liquefied; H₂S not formed; starch not hydrolyzed; nitrate not reduced; acid produced from many sugars; optimum temp. 22–25°C., Gram-negative.

This disease was first described from the United States of America where oats are widely affected. It has also been reported in Canada, New Zealand and in Europe, especially in Scotland. The causal organism is seed-borne and infected seedlings develop symptoms from the first leaf onwards. Halo blight begins as spots on the seedling leaves but rain-splash and wind spread the bacteria up the developing plant to later infect the older leaves, leaf sheaths and glumes. The lesions produced are very characteristic, beginning as light green oval spots about 4–5 mm in diameter with a small brown, dead centre. Later, the spots may become more irregular and pale green lobes spread out into the leaf. At the same time as the green 'halo' is expanding, the necrotic area in the centre is also spreading. The lesions are commonly found at the leaf margin giving a crescent shape but, in the main, the lesions retain their oval shape.

The bacteria enter the plant via natural openings or injuries and insects are undoubtedly involved in these processes. The bacterial colony is more or less restricted to the stomatal cavity or surrounding the point of injury and there is very little spread between the cells. Chlorophyll production is stopped and the intercellular spaces in and around the infected tissue become water-soaked.

The bacteria abound in the central brown dead tissue and it is thought that the halo effect is due to some diffusable substance, possibly a toxin. There may be one or several lesions on a leaf and the effects vary accordingly, a severe infection often killing the basal leaves. The glumes may also be infected and prevent the spikelets developing. At first, the glumes develop the typical halo lesions but later the whole glume becomes chlorotic and translucent between the veins. The disease is favoured by a cold, wet spring and is checked by the onset of warm, dry weather.

Control of this disease has been concentrated mainly on seed treatment or by the use of resistant varieties. Partial control can be achieved by soaking the seed in formaldehyde but the best control has been achieved by the use of antibiotics, especially streptomycin, after which the seed is air-dried ready for sowing. A comprehensive screening of many oat cultivars for resistance to halo blight indicated that there was much variation which could be utilized by the plant breeders although none of the European varieties had a high degree of resistance. However, a hexaploid form, believed to be a natural cross between A. sativa and A. ludoviciana approached immunity.

Notes

The organism can be isolated from infected material after surface-sterilization using the usual ethyl alcohol and mercuric chloride sterilants. The leaf material is then crushed in sterile water or nutrient broth and streaked out on to nutrient agar where it can be sub-cultured for purification.

The colonies are white, raised, shining, smooth, with slightly undulate thin margins. A diffusable green fluorescent pigment is produced on King's medium B. It is very difficult to distinguish P. coronafaciens from P. striafaciens in pure culture and it would be necessary to carry out Koch's postulates to make a positive identification. Long-term storage is best achieved by freeze-drying, normally on to a small strip of absorbant paper, duly labelled, in an ampoule.

Pseudomonas striafaciens (Elliott) Starr & Burkholder – Bacterial stripe blight of oats.

Motile rods with rounded ends and polar flagella; single, in pairs, or in short chains, 0·66 × 1·76 um; no spores; capsules formed; white colonies on agar; liquefies gelatine, produces H_2S; hydrolyzes starch, acid produced from dextrose, saccharose and laevulose; optimum temp. 22°C.; Gram-negative, not acid fast.

Bacterial stripe of oats is widely distributed on oats in North America, Australia and Russia although its incidence and severity is never very high. The first symptoms are numerous, sunken, water-soaked spots which later coalesce to form a stripe effect with narrow, yellowish margins. Unlike *P. coronafaciens*, a bacterial exudate becomes apparent on the surface of the lesions. The leaf sheaths, pedicels and glumes may also be attacked. Stripe Blight can also be distinguished from Halo Blight by the absence of a halo. Lesions may occur on plants at any stage of development and sometimes the infection is so severe as to kill the entire top of the plant.

Entry is gained through natural openings or through wounds and it is thought that insects may play a part in the transmission of the disease. The bacterial colony develops in a gelatinous matrix and advances between the cells of the infected plant. Dispersal is mainly by wind and rain although the bacteria can remain viable over long periods within the dried up gelatinous matrix in the old lesions on dead leaves. Plant residues from infected crops can thus provide a source of inoculum for a succeeding oat crop but there is also some carry-over on the seed.

Very little research has been devoted to controlling the disease as it is rarely severe. However, seed treatment with antibiotics or formaldehyde can give partial control and crop hygiene will reduce the amount of available inoculum. Very little effort has been placed on the breeding of resistant cultivars although it has been shown that cultivars do vary in their degree of resistance.

Notes

The organism may be treated in exactly the same way as *Pseudomonas coronafaciens.* It has been suggested that the two species are synonomous but *P. striafaciens* has slightly smaller cells, a slightly faster liquefaction of gelatine and does not produce the toxin thought to be responsible for the halo symptom produced by *P. coronafaciens.*

Corn Stunt (*Spiroplasma* Davis & Worley).

Spiroplasma particles are helical, motile, wall-free prokaryotes. The filaments of which they are composed are 0·2–0·5 × 3–15 um, with regular wavelength, often with spherical bodies (0·4–0·6 um diameter) attached and bounded by a unit membrane, most numerous in phloem cells of diseased plants.

Corn stunt is of relatively recent recognition as a disease of maize. It is found in most of the southern states of the U.S.A. and the south-west where it can cause appreciable damage. It is often a limiting factor in maize cultivation in Central and South America where it is known as 'achaparramiento'. The disease was originally thought to be caused by a virus but recently a mycoplasma-like organism has been identified as being associated with the disease. The trivial name *Spiroplasma* has been tentatively assigned to it (Davis and Worley, Phytopath. **63**; 403, 1973) as its helical morphology and contractile movements of the filaments distinguish it from described species of mycoplasmas. In the field, the most striking feature of diseased plants is the bushy appearance caused by proliferation of tillers and elongation of ear stalks at nearly every node. Early infection results in all internodes being shortened, but only upper internodes are thus affected following late infection. Small, circular chlorotic spots develop at the bases of the leaves of young plants and these often coalesce to form discrete or diffuse stripes. As plants become older, reddish-purple stripes are formed and more general chlorosis develops. Proliferation of ear shoots, poor grain filling or barrenness are common on early-infected plants. The organism is transmitted by a number of leafhoppers which vary in their vectoring efficiency and in their geographic range. They include *Dalbulbus maidis* De L & W., *D. elimatus* Ball, *Graminella nigrifrons* Forbes, *Deltocephalus sonorus* Ball and *Baldulus tripsici* Kram & Whit. The incubation period of the organism in its vector, following acquisition feeding, varies with the species of leafhopper and the latent period in the host, prior to symptom appearance following inoculation by the leafhopper, is about 3 weeks. Two strains of the spiroplasma have been reported but this requires confirmation. The best prospect for control would appear to be in the development of resistant varieties. Resistance has been reported as being governed by relatively few genes with strong additive effects. The possibility of chemical control is suggested by the blockage or remission of symptoms following treatment with totracyclines, these compounds being active against other mycoplasma-like organisms.

Notes

Culture of the corn stunt spiroplasma on a simple medium has recently been reported (Liao and Chen., Phytopath. **67**; 802, 1977). This medium (C-3G) contains 20% agamma horse serum, 1·5% PPLO (pleuropneumonia-like organism) broth and 12% sucrose in distilled water. The growth curve is sigmoid on this medium and doubling time of the helices in the exponential phase is 20 hours at 29°C. Motility and helicity are lost below pH 5·4. Colonies within the medium solidified with 0·8% Oxoid Ion agar are granular and occasionally fried-egg shaped.

Diseases caused by viruses

Barley Yellow Dwarf (Virus) (BYDV).

Little is known of the chemical and physical properties. Particles reported as spherical and approximately 30 nm diameter. Circulatory, aphid transmitted. Not mechanically transmitted. Some isolates differ serologically.

Barley yellow dwarf virus (BYDV) is the most important virus of cereals. It is widely distributed and affects over 100 species in the *Gramineae* including barley, oats, wheat and rye. It is economically most important on barley and oats. It was first recognized as a virus in California in 1951 and is widespread in North America, Europe and Australasia. It can be more destructive than the rusts in the U.S.A. where, for example, yield losses in oats have been estimated at 30% in Illinois in 1957. It is considered to be the most important cereal disease in New Zealand and serious outbreaks have occurred in Britain in 1958 and 1971.

Symptoms are many and varied and reflect the systemic nature of the infection. They appear within 10–20 days after inoculation by the aphid vectors. In barley, a bright golden yellowing begins at the leaf tip and rapidly progresses down the entire blade. On some varieties and under some conditions green strips of tissue adjoining the main veins extend into the yellow area in the colour transition zone. A necrotic brown flecking or spotting may accompany the yellowing. The distinct chrome yellow plants stand out amongst surrounding healthy plants in the field. In oats, the main colour change is to shades of red, brown and purple hence it is sometimes called oat red leaf. The first signs are yellowish-green spots or blotches usually near the tip of the leaf which are most easily discerned by holding the leaf up to the light. These blotches enlarge and coalesce, turning various shades of yellow, red and brown. More blotches appear nearer the base of the leaf and eventually the entire leaf is affected with the tip becoming reddish-brown or purple. The symptoms on wheat are similar to those on barley but the chlorosis is more blotchy and diffuse.

Early infection of all three cereals results in severe stunting, excessive or reduced tillering, reduction in the number of flowering tillers, delayed heading or ripening, sterile florets and grain shrivelling. With later infections the effects are progressively less severe to the point where only the upper leaves or the flag leaf may show symptoms. After senescence, infected plants are characteristically invaded by sooty moulds which give a dirty appearance to the plants. This appearance can be used to assess infected plants among healthy ones either in a crop or in segregating breeders' material. Patterns of field infection may either be random within the crop or as circular or angular patches which reflect the patterns of movement of the aphid vectors.

In eastern Britain the distribution of infected plants occurs at random where *Macrosiphum avenae* is the vector but, in western Britain, the common vector is *Rhopalosiphum padi* which gives a patchy distribution pattern. There is vector specificity of isolates, one group being transmitted most readily by *M. avenae* and less efficiently by *R. padi* whilst, with another group, the reverse is true. Another group of isolates, which occurs in the U.S.A., is transmitted most efficiently by *R. maidis* and *Schizaphis agrostis*. All together, about 14 species of aphids transmit the virus. Some strains are more pathogenic than others, in Britain only mild strains being known before 1956 but subsequently more severe strains have become more widespread.

The main source of virus is from infected wild and cultivated grasses and this reservoir makes control difficult. Control is mainly aimed at vector control although, if aphids that arrive on a cereal are already viruliferous, insecticides are of little use except in preventing secondary spread within the crop. Cultural methods are aimed at the control of weed grass species within and around the cereal crop. In barley, sources of genetic resistance to the virus are available from some Ethiopian genotypes in which resistance is conditioned by a single dominant gene which appears to be expressed by retarding multiplication of the virus within the plant. The expressivity of this gene is greatest in rapidly maturing barley genotypes and least in slower maturing, commercially desirable genotypes. Recently, resistance to a strain specifically transmitted by *R. padi* has been reported in maize.

Notes

Acquisition feeding by non-infective aphids normally takes 24–48 hr although a few aphids may acquire the virus within 30 min. After feeding, there is a short latent period within the aphid before transmission can occur. Transmission feeding periods may be as short as 15–30 min but normally 12–24 hr periods are necessary. An aphid will remain infective for several weeks and may infect a number of plants in succession. However, the virus is not passed on to progeny of the aphid. Artificial infections in the field may be initiated by spreading viruliferous aphid-infested plants, produced in the glasshouse, amongst the test plants in the field. Preparations of virus concentrates have been stored successfully for up to 4 years in liquid nitrogen or by lyophilization with no apparent loss in infectivity (Rochow, Blizzard, Muller and Waterworth, Phytopath. **66**; 534, 1976). The BYDV was recovered from virus preparations by letting aphids feed through membranes on samples or by injecting inocula into aphids.

Maize Dwarf Mosaic (Virus) (MDMV).

Maize dwarf mosaic is widespread in the maize growing areas of the United States where it is responsible for significant yield losses especially where maize is grown near the weed johnsongrass (*Sorghum halepense*) which acts as a reservoir for the causal virus, MDMV. Losses have been serious in parts of the south-central corn belt of the U.S.A. and in more eastern regions during the period 1963 to 1967 and in some subsequent years. The typical primary symptom is a variegated light and dark green mottling of young leaves, the pattern and intensity of which varies with host genotype. The mottling may be fine and diffuse or more intense with sharp contrasts between shades of green; the extent of the individual mottles also varies. A more general chlorosis and leaf reddening becomes apparent as the infected plants mature. Plants infected early in their development show the most severe symptoms of mottling, stunting and proliferation of adventitious buds and grain filling is affected which may result in barrenness. Late-infected plants are correspondingly less severely affected. The virus, which is a flexuous rod approximately 750–800 × 15 *nm*, is sap transmissible and is vectored by a large number (at least 12) of aphid species. It is non-persistent and stylet-borne in the vectors. The virus appears to exist as a number of strains which are serologically related, although their relationships are not clear and some workers consider that MDMV is a strain of sugarcane mosaic virus (SCMV). The ambrosia aphid (*Dactynotus ambrosiae*) has been used to experimentally transmit SCMV strain I and MDMV strain A either singly or together from plants of itchgrass (*Rottboillia exaltata*) carrying mixed infections of the two viruses (Koike,

Plant Dis. Reptr., **61**; No. 9, 724, 1977). Control of the disease is by the use of resistant varieties and, although resistance is reported as being partially dominant and governed by few genes, evaluation in the field is difficult. A disease index system has been developed to evaluate resistance under glasshouse conditions (Kuhn & Smith, Phytopath. **67**; 288, 1977) and the index values have been shown to relate to disease incidence and yield losses in the field.

Soil-borne oat mosaic (Virus) (OMV).

The virus particles are fairly rigid rods, 600–700 × 12 nm. In vitro, OMV infected sap remains infective for up to 2 days at room temperatures, is inactivated by heating to 46°C. for 10 min. and loses infectivity when diluted 1 : 1000.

Oat mosaic is most widespread in the United States, the virus responsible being identified there in 1946. More recently it has been identified in Wales, central and south-west England and in New Zealand. It has been reported to cause up to 50% losses in winter oat yields in field situations and virtually 100% losses have occurred experimentally. *Avena* spp. are apparently the only hosts and, although winter and spring types of cultivated oats are susceptible, only winter types show the symptoms when sown normally in the autumn but autumn-sown spring types also develop symptoms. There are apparently two strains which can be separated on symptom type. With both types the first signs of disease appear in the spring when pale green or yellow streaks are seen on the leaves and leaf sheaths. The eyespot mosaic strain illicits streaks that become fusiform and tend to remain discrete. The margins of these streaks are pale green, yellow or grey with dark green centres and are most conspicuous at the base of older leaves. The other strain is called apical mosaic and produces less regular streaks which merge to produce a yellow-green mosaic most evident on the distal parts of young leaves. Plants infected with either strain may be stunted, are dark green and have fewer productive tillers.

Under field conditions, symptoms develop 2–3 months after infection and are most pronounced when temperatures are below 18°C. This long incubation requirement is probably the reason why symptoms do not appear on spring varieties. The fungus vector which invades roots has recently been identified as *Polymyxa graminis*. Infested soils remain so for long periods in the absence of susceptible crops and so rotation is not an effective means of control. Care should be taken to avoid transporting infested soil on machinery. Chemical soil sterilants are effective experimentally but are not practical under field conditions. The best possibility for effective control would seem to be through the use of resistant varieties. The variety Century is highly resistant although the expression of resistance is modified by environment.

Notes
The virus is mechanically transmitted with difficulty, but infection levels are improved if infected sap is sprayed rather than rubbed onto leaves. Symptoms appear on plants thus inoculated within 2 weeks. Plants become readily infected if grown in infested soil and such field nurseries can be used for selecting resistant genotypes or screening segregating populations.

Soil-borne Wheat Mosaic (Virus) (WMV).

syn. Marmor tritici.
The soil-borne mosaic disease of wheat and barley is caused by an RNA-containing virus, the particles of which are stiff, rod-shaped and of two lengths, 110–160 and 300 *nm* and which appear hollow when negatively stained. The virus, which has a host range limited to wheat, barley, rye and a few *Bromus* and *Chenopodium* spp., is transmitted by the soil-inhabiting fungus *Polymyxa graminis* and artificially by sap inoculation. The disease occurs in the winter wheat growing areas of the U.S.A., Japan and Italy. Overall, losses caused by the disease are not significant but severe infections may occur locally in highly susceptible varieties. In Illinois, for example, entire crops have been reported to be almost completely destroyed. Within a field, affected areas show up as yellow or light green patches from a distance and the disease tends to be more severe in, but not limited to, low lying areas of the field.

The virus exists as several strains, one causing a yellow mosaic, another a green mosaic and a third giving rosetting symptoms. Winter wheat occasionally shows symptoms in the autumn but, more normally, the disease is expressed when plants begin rapid growth in the spring. Neither winter wheat nor spring wheat sown in the spring will show symptoms which suggests that symptom expression relates to the rate of plant growth relative to movement of the virus within the plant. The yellow mosaic first becomes noticeable in the spring as new leaves of diseased plants unfold. These appear mottled yellow or light green. The mottling consists of irregular stripes or blotches which vary in size and tend to run parallel with the long axis of the leaf.

Varying degrees of dwarfing may also occur. Plants affected by the green mosaic strain are dwarfed and tiller excessively giving rise to a bushy, rosette form of plant which develops an intense bluish-green colour which may remain until maturity. Severely affected plants remain stunted, shrivel and die leaving bare patches in the crop. Certain varieties, for example those related to Harvest Queen, are particularly liable to rosetting. Symptoms tend to become milder as weather becomes warmer and as wheat plants grow larger, presumably because the plants are growing rapidly away from the virus. Isolates which produce the soil-borne green mosaic of wheat and barley in Japan are serologically related to those from the U.S.A. but the former can infect tobacco and maize. The virus is not seed transmitted but it infects cells of both roots and leaves where three types of cell inclusions have been observed. Control is through the use of resistant varieties.

Wheat Streak Mosaic (Virus) (WSMV).

syn. Marmor virgatum.
Wheat streak mosaic is caused by a virus, the infective particles of which are filamentous rods 670–750 × 14 *nm*. It is sap transmissible and is transmitted in the field by the adult and all nymphal stages of the wheat curl mite, *Aceria tulipae*. It causes a severe mosaic of winter wheat and a mild mosaic in maize. It also infects oats, barley, rye, millets and many wild grasses and is widely distributed in North America and also in Russia, south-east Europe and Jordan. The disease on winter wheat is severe in some of the Great Plains states of the U.S.A. having caused estimated losses of 30 million bushels in Kansas in 1974. Although most infection occurs in the autumn on winter varieties, symptoms usually only develop in the spring with the advent of warm weather. The typical symptom is a characteristic yellowish streaking and mottling of the leaves which becomes more pronounced with continuing warm weather; leaves become yellow and plants are stunted. As affected plants age the mottling disappears and leaves become necrotic, turn brown and die. In maize, the severe necrotic responses do not occur and the characteristic appearance of infected plants is a chlorotic spotting at the tips of older leaves often accompanied by a more general chlorosis. On younger leaves, long, chlorotic streaks with concentric or spindle-shaped patterns are often observed. A reticulate pattern of light and dark green may occur on the ear husks and this may become reddish-purple with maturity. Stunting of plants occurs in inbred lines which are much more susceptible than hybrids. Differences in resistance in inbred lines have been

observed and this seems to offer the best method of control. In wheat, resistance both to the virus and its vector (*A. tulipae*) have been reported. Wheat lines carrying chromosome translocations or substitutions from *Agropyron elongatum* were found to be resistant both to WSMV and *A. tulipae*. Resistance to the vector alone was demonstrated in Salmon, a wheat-rye translocation line and resistance to WSMV alone was detected in a wheat – *A. intermedium* line (Martin, Harvey and Livers, Phytopath. **66**; 346, 1976).

Miscellaneous

Oat Blast (Cause unknown).

Oat blast occurs widely and unpredictably on both winter and spring varieties and commonly results in 5–10% of the potential spikelets being sterile. There is no single cause of blasting and many factors have been implicated especially unfavourable environmental conditions during panicle tissue differentiation. It is likely to result from sudden changes in environment such as large temperature changes or moisture stress during the critical growth period rather than more chronic conditions such as fertilizer imbalance or disease attack, although these may be contributory factors. The characteristic appearance of blasting is a number of white delicate spikelets especially near the base of the panicle when it emerges. Usually, only a few spikelets on the lower part of the panicle are affected although, occasionally, half and rarely the entire head is sterile. Differences between varieties in their tendencies to develop blasted spikelets have been reported but no practical control measures are known.

Deficiency diseases

No matter what the crop, deficiencies of essential nutrients in the soil will result in some form of physiological disorder. Often, these can be readily diagnosed by the morphological, colour or other changes they produce in the host plant. Many deficiency disorders, however, are similar to those produced by biotic factors and their diagnosis is more complicated.

Of the major plant nutrients, *nitrogen* is the most important for the cereal crops. Previous cropping may have seriously diminished the nitrogen level of the soil and wet winters will compound this reduction by the removal of available nitrogen in the drainage water and this results in a condition known as spring yellows. The chief symptoms of nitrogen starvation are stunted and spindly shoots, sparse yellow-green foliage and poor tillering. In oats and barley, the stems may also show red or purplish tints and, ultimately, there is a reduction in grain size. In the United States, nitrogen deficiency can cause the wheat grain to become light yellow, opaque and soft. This condition is known as Yellow Berry and the affected grain is starchy and very low in protein.

Phosphorus is also very easily leached out of soils in high rainfall areas. Plants deficient in this element will have a slow growth rate accompanied by poor tillering and the young leaves become dark bluish green in colour. As the heads appear the colour often changes to purple. Because of the rapid loss of phosphates in certain soils it is always advisable to apply this nutrient at sowing time where it is readily available to the young plants.

Potassium is not a very common limiting factor, deficiencies being mostly found on the lighter sandy and chalk soils. Affected plants usually produce more tillers than normal plants although they are stunted and weak and with fewer tillers. Potash deficiency is also accompanied by a scorching effect on the leaves, especially margins and tips. Barley is particularly sensitive to potash deficiency and affected plants also exhibit purplish-brown spots on the foliage.

Of the micronutrients, *magnesium* can produce certain disorders but most soils have an adequate supply. In rye, deficient plants are characterized by the failure of the leaves to unfold whereas, in wheat and oats there is a striping effect across the leaves which is sometimes referred to as 'tiger-skin'. In general, the affected plants are dwarfed, stiff and somewhat chlorotic. In magnesium-deficient soils a quick remedy has been the application of soluble magnesium sulphate, Epsom salts being a good source.

Copper deficiency is rarely a problem although there are areas in Europe where sowings have been made on newly reclaimed soil which have been affected and it is also known that certain areas in South and West Australia are also deficient in copper. The problem can easily be rectified by a dressing of finely crystalline copper sulphate.

Undoubtedly, the best known deficiency disease of cereals is Grey Speck of oats. This is caused by a deficiency of *manganese* and occurs widely throughout many countries on alkaline soils with a high organic matter content. For this reason, the condition is often found on sewage farms where the sewage has been heavily limed prior to its distribution over the soil as a fertilizer. The symptoms appear on the foliage when the plants are in the very early vegetative stage, often before tillering commences. Affected plants exhibit light green spots or short streaks that later become grey or buff-coloured. As these spots enlarge they coalesce to give a grey striping effect between the veins. The leaf blade often bends sharply across the middle with the upper portions retaining its green colour longer than the lower half. The whole leaf eventually dies and, with root growth also being badly reduced, the affected plant is often reduced to one green shoot surrounded by many dead brown leaves. Plants which survive the early phase develop poorly and produce either blind heads or heads with very few grains. Wheat, barley and rye may also be affected by manganese deficiency although not to anything like the same extent and the symptoms may merely be a reduction in vigour and an associated chlorotic streaking. A surface dressing of manganese sulphate in the spring will normally bring about a rapid correction of this problem.

Compendium list of references
Diseases of Wheat, Oats, Barley and Rye *by Boewe, G. H., Illinois, Natural History Survey, Circular 48, 1960*
Cereal Pests and Diseases *by Gair, R., Jenkins, J. E. E., and Lester, E., Farming Press, 1972*
Diseases of Field Crops *by Dickson, J. G., McGraw-Hill, 1947*
Diseases of Crop Plants *Editor Western, J. H., Macmillan, 1971*
British Rust Fungi *by Wilson, M. and Henderson, D., Cambridge University Press, London, 1966*
Diseases of Corn *by Ullstrup, A. J., in* Corn and Corn Improvement *Editor Sprague, G. F., Agronomy 18, American Society of Agronomy, 1977*
C.M.I./A.A.B. Descriptions of Plant Viruses, *Commonwealth Mycological Institute, Kew, London*
C.M.I. Descriptions of Pathogenic Fungi and Bacteria, *Commonwealth Mycological Institute, Kew, London*

Glossary

Adult plant resistance   Resistance not expressed by seedlings, increases with plant maturity, synonymous with **mature plant resistance.**

Aggressiveness   A term applied to physiologic races of a pathogen that differ in the severity of their effects upon the host plant but which do not interact differentially with host cultivars. Some authorities prefer a neutral qualification of pathogenicity to describe this characteristic.

Allopolyploid   Produced by doubling the chromosome number in a sterile hybrid. The new organism is fertile with polypoloids like itself but infertile with its diploid parental species.

Amphidiploid   A tetraploid produced by allopolyploidy (see **allopolyploid**).

Appressorium   A swelling at the tip of a fungal spore germ-tube. It is normally associated with the mechanism of adherence to the plant surface. Can be formed over the cuticle prior to direct penetration or over a stomate prior to entry via the sub-stomatal vesicle.

Auxotrophic   Describes an isolate or strain of a microorganism which differs from the 'wild type' by having additional nutrient requirements (cf. **prototrophic**).

Biotroph   A parasitic organism which obtains its nutrient supply only from living host tissue regardless of whether or not it can be artificially cultured.

Bridging species   An intermediate species used to facilitate the transfer of genetic material between two species (usually of different ploidy) where direct hybridization is not possible.

Circadian rhythms   A periodic rhythm occurring in all living organisms and normally synchronized to a 24 h cycle. It is normally independent of changes in the environment.

Clone   A group of identical individuals produced either by vegetative propagation or some other method of asexual reproduction or by multiplication from a single cell.

Compensation   The ability of a plant to compensate for the damaging effects of disease. Usually expressed as an increase in one or more components of yield.

Composite cross   A population derived from the hybridization of several parents, either by hand-pollination or by the use of male sterility.

Composite mixture   A mixture of several agronomically similar lines assembled on the basis of their differences in disease resistance factors.

Compound interest disease   A disease which multiplies through more than one cycle within a season in a manner analogous to compound interest.

Differential variety   A host variety, part of a set differing in disease reaction, used to identify physiologically specialized forms of a pathogen.

Dikaryon   An organism with two nuclei per cell (see **heterokaryon**).

Dispersing agent   A chemical added to a fungicide or bactericide formulation to aid the efficient distribution of particles of the active ingredient.

Durable resistance   Resistance that remains effective and stable during the agronomic life of a variety.

Epidemic potential   The biological capacity of a pathogen to cause disease in a particular environment.

Facultative parasite   A mainly saprophytic organism with weakly pathogenic properties.

Facultative saprophyte   A mainly parasitic organism with the ability to survive for a part of its life-cycle as a saprophyte and be cultured on artificial media.

Filiform   Long and thin, threadlike.

Formae speciales   A taxon characterized from a physiological standpoint (especially host adaption).

Fungicidal   The property of being able to kill fungi.

Fungistatic   The property of inhibiting fungal growth.

Genestatic   The property of inhibiting fungal sporulation.

Germ-tube   The initial hypha developing from a germinating fungal spore.

Haustorium   An appendage to fungal hyphae which penetrates the host plant cell. Acts as a rootlet or sucker.

Heteroecious   The requirement of a pathogen for two host species to complete its life-cycle.

Heterokaryon   A fungal strain or hypha in which the cells contain more than one type of nucleus per cell. The dikaryon, with two nuclei per cell is a common example.

Heterothallic   A condition in some fungi where different thalli are required for cross-fertilization. Both male and female sex organs may be present on the same thallus but the thallus will be self-sterile.

Homokaryon   A fungal strain or hypha in which all the nuclei are of one type.

Homothallic   The condition in which a fungal strain is sexually self-fertile.

Hyperplasia   The enlargement of tissues by an increase in the number of cells by cell division.

Hypertrophy   The enlargement of tissues by an increase in the size of the cells.

Hypersensitivity   The response to attack by a pathogen of certain host plants in which the invaded cells die promptly and prevent further spread of infection.

Hyphal anastomosis   The conjugation of two hyphal filaments. This may give rise to a heterokaryon.

Hyaline   Clear, transparent.

Incubation period   The period between infection and the sporulation of the pathogen on the host.

Infection   The entry of an organism or virus into a host and the establishment of a permanent or temporary parasitic relationship.

Infection court   The site on a host plant at which infection by a parasitic organism or virus is effected.

Infection peg   A thickening of the host cell wall in the vicinity of the penetrating hypha. Lignin, callose, cellulose or suberin may be deposited at this site.

Isogenic lines   A series of plant lines genetically similar but which carry different specific genes for resistance to a particular pathogen.

Karyogamy   The fusion of nuclei in sexual reproduction.

Latent period   The period between infection and the appearance of visible disease symptoms.

Lignituber   A thickened structure formed by the deposition of lignin surrounding the tip of the hypha penetrating a host cell and presumably functioning as a resistance mechanism.

Mature plant resistance   See **Adult plant resistance.**

Meiosis   A nuclear division during sexual reproduction in which the diploid nucleus divides to produce four daughter haploid nuclei. This process, also called reduction division, is also accompanied by an exchange of genetic material, or recombination, by the process of crossing over associated with chiasmata formation.

Mitosis   A nuclear division normally associated with cell division. The nucleus divides into two daughter nuclei with identical chromosome complements.

Mitotic recombination   The recombination of genetic material during mitosis and the process of asexual reproduction. The mechanism for the production of variation in heterokaryons.

Monoecy   The condition in plants which have male and female flowers separated on the same plant.

Monocyclic   Describes a test which measures the response of a plant or plants to a single cycle of infection by a pathogen, usually carried out by artificial inoculation (cf. **Polycyclic**).

Multigene variety   A variety which carries a number of specific genes governing resistance to a particular pathogen.

Multiline   A mixture of agronomically similar plant lines each of which differs genetically in terms of the factors governing resistance to disease.

Mutation   A change in the amount or structure of DNA in chromosomes which produces a discrete heritable difference compared with the 'wild-type'.

Mycoplasma   The smallest free-living microorganism. It lacks a rigid cell wall and is therefore pleomorphic. Mycoplasmas cause many diseases in animals and, in plants, many diseases formerly attributed to viruses are now known to be caused by mycoplasmas.

Necrotroph   A fungal pathogen that causes the immediate death of the host cell as it passes through them. A colonizer of dead tissue.

Obligate parasite   A parasitic organism only capable of colonizing living host tissue.

Oligogenic resistance   Resistance controlled by one or a few genes, it should not be used as a synonym for vertical resistance.

Pathogen   An organism or virus with the capacity to cause disease in its host.

Pathogenicity   The ability of an organism or virus to cause disease.

Pathogenesis   The complete sequence of events starting with the arrival of the pathogen at the host surface to the completion of the disease cycle.

Parasexual cycle The recombination of genetic material during asexual reproduction. It occurs in heterokaryons after the fusion of unlike nuclei, often after hyphal anastomosis (see **Mitotic recombination**).

Parasitic Describes an organism or virus which lives on another living organism, obtaining its nutrient supply from the latter but conferring no benefit in return.

Partial resistance Resistance which is expressed by the slower development of fewer pustules or lesions compared with normally susceptible varieties.

Penetration peg A minute protruberance from a hypha, germ-tube or appressorium which effects penetration of the host plant surface.

Phylloplane The microhabitat of the leaf surface.

Physiologic race A sub-division of a parasite species characterized by its specialization to a cultivar or different cultivars of one host species.

Phytoalexin A substance produced in plants as a result of chemical, biological or physical stimuli and which inhibit the growth of certain microorganisms.

Polycyclic Describes a test which measures the response of a plant or plants to repeated cycles of infection, usually carried out by natural infection under field conditions.

Prototrophic Describes an isolate or strain of a microorganism which does not differ from the wild-type in its nutritional requirements (cf. **Auxotrophic**).

Pycnidium A flask-shaped or globose fungal receptacle bearing asexual spores, pycnidiospores.

Pycnium A flask-shaped fungal receptacle, characteristic of the rust fungi, bearing pycniospores which act as spermatia.

Race non-specific resistance Host plant resistance which is operational against all races of a pathogen species. It is variable, sensitive to environmental changes and is usually polygenically controlled.

Race-specific resistance Host plant resistance which is operational against one or a few races of a pathogen species. Generally produces an immune or hypersensitive reaction and is controlled by one or few genes.

Rhizoplane The microhabitat of the root surface.

Simple interest disease A disease which goes through one cycle of multiplication only during the season, analogous to simple interest.

Spreader A substance added to fungicide or bactericide preparations to facilitate better contact between the spray and the sprayed surface. A surfactant.

Sticker Added to fungicide or bactericide preparations to facilitate the adherence of the spray to the sprayed surface.

Stroma An interwoven mass or layer of fungal hyphae.

Tolerance The ability to withstand infection by a pathogen without suffering undue damage or yield loss.

Tylosis The growth of a xylem parenchyma cell through a xylem vessel wall to produce a swelling in the lumen of the vessel. Tyloses are thought to impede the progress of vascular pathogens.

Transgressive segregation The appearance in a segregating population of genotypes exhibiting a character to a more extreme degree than the parents.

Viroid A pathogenic agent, formerly classified as a virus, now known to be a ribonucleic acid of low molecular weight and not a ribonucleoprotein.

Virus A nucleoprotein entity which can replicate within living cells of the host. Passes through bacterium-retaining filters.

Virulence The ability of an individual entity within a group of strains, **formae speciales** or isolates to cause disease under defined conditions.

Index

Note A list of Figs. and Tables will be found at the end of the index.

APDA 54
Acetic:
  acid 73, 74
  alcohol 72
Acid fuchsin: 73, 74
  in chloral hydrate and alcohol 73
  cotton blue in acetic alcohol 72
  in ethanol 74
Aecidiospores of rust 23
Aegilops:
  comosa 47, 114 (Fig. 5.6) (Table 5.3)
  spp 4
  squarrosa (Tables 5.2 and 5.3)
  umbellulata (Table 5.3)
  ventricosa (Table 5.3)
Agar culture, preservation and storage 61, 63
Agropyron:
  elongatum 114 (Table 5.3)
  intermedium (Table 5.3)
  repens 11
Allopolyploids 4
Alopecurus myosuroides 11
Amphidiploidy 4
Anderson and Rowell's spray stain 75
Aphids 69, 70
Apple:
  powdery mildew 149
  scab 141, 149
Appressoria 29, 32, 42, (Fig. 2.2)
Ascomycetes 147, 149
Ascomycotina 23
Ascospores 33
Ascus production 60
Aspergillus nidulans 24
Aureomycin 57
Avena:
  abyssinica 6, 106 (Tables 5.2 and 5.3)
  barbata 5–6, 112 (Fig. 5.5) (Tables 5.2 and 5.3)
  byzantina 6, 106 (Table 5.2)
  canariensis (Table 5.2)
  clauda (Table 5.2)
  damascena (Table 5.2)
  fatua 6, 11, 106 (Table 5.2)
  hirtula 106 (Table 5.2)

longiglumis (Table 5.2)
magna (Table 5.2)
murphyi (Table 5.2)
nuda 6, 106 (Table 5.2)
nudabrevis 105 (Table 5.2)
pilosa (Table 5.2)
prostrata (Table 5.2)
resistance transfer 112
sativa 6, 106, 112 (Fig. 5.5) (Table 5.2)
  var. *Manod* (Fig. 5.5)
spp (Table 5.3)
sterilis 6, 11, 106, 112 (Tables 5.2 and 5.3)
strigosa 5, 6, 105 (Tables 5.2 and 5.3)
vaviloviana (Table 5.2)
ventricosa (Tables 5.2 and 5.3)
wiestii 106 (Table 5.2)

BYDV 70
Bacteria:
  haploid 21
  infection process 25–6
  parasitic 33
  pathogenic 29
  saprophytic 53
  streaking agar plates 55 (Fig. 4.1)
Bacterial:
  diseases 25
  ooze 52, 54
  parasites 16
  pathogens 18
Bactericides 138, 141
Barban 11
Barberry 18, 22, 23, 25, 44, 133–4
Barley: 6–7
  artificial hybridization 103
  brown rust control 149, 156
  control measures 130, 131, 132 (Tables 6.1 and 6.2) *see also* mildew *and* powdery mildew *below*
  covered smut control 150
  cytotaxonomy 106
  disease escape 36
  dwarf 102
  eyespot: 26, 147, 148
    culture inoculation methods 67

genetic male sterility 114
hybrid 114
leaf blotch 67, 148, 156
leaf spot 33
leaf stripe 67, 150
leaves:
  lens-shaped lesions 53
  penetration 32
loose smut 33, 38, 132, 149
powdery mildew:
  assessment 86
  control measures 50, 148, 149, 150,
    151, 154, 160
    integrated 158, 160 (Fig. 6.1)
  epidemic potential 158, 159
  fungicide experiments 92
  population monitoring 88
  resistance: 42, 45, 47, 50, 71, 99, 102
    breeding 101, 116–17
    transfer (Table 5.3)
  resistance breeding strategy 119
  virulence gene frequencies 118–19
nitrogen application 11
resistant varieties 56
scald 67, 158
smut culture 69
standards of susceptibility 158
systemic fungicide 148
varieties:
  Proctor 50, 116
  Vada 50, 125 (Fig. 3.3)
  Vulcan 50
yellow dwarf control measures 133
yellow rust 116, 149
Basidiomycetes 22, 147
Basidiomycotina 23
Basidiospores 23, 44
Benodanil 150
Benomyl 146, 147, 148, 151, 152, 153
Benzimidazole(s) 59, 61, 81, 147–8
Benzimidazole agar 88
Berberis vulgaris 22 see also Barberry
Biotrophs 16–17, 26
Bis-(dimethylamido) phosphoryl group 147
Black stem rust 18, 19, 22, 34, 129, 133, 134
Blackgrass 11
Blasts 17
Blights 17

Bordeaux mixture 136, 140
Botrytis cinerea 152
Blotches 81
Bread wheats 4, 98, 103–5, 111
Brine 135
Brown rust 112, 123, 148, 149, 150, 156, 158
Bunt: 17
  chemotherapeutic action 145
  control measures 136, 138, 141
  host resistance assessment 100
  seed dressing 150, 153
  systemic fungicide 14, 147

Calcium polysulphides 141
Calonectria nivalis 148
Captafol 144
Captan 144, 153, 154
Carbendazim: 148, 152
  dithiocarbamate tank mix 148
  maneb tank mix 148
Carbon disulphide 151
Carboxin: 10, 135, 146, 149, 150, 154
  thiram mixture 138, 150
Carboxylic acid anilides 149–50
Carrot pith 73
Cereal cyst nematode 70, 116–17 (Table
  5.3)
Cereal growth:
  decimal code (Fig. 4.4)
  Feekes scale (Fig. 4.3)
  identification of stages (Fig. 4.5)
Chaetocnema pulicaria 69
Chemical herbicides 11
Chemicals, protectant 14
Chemotherapeutic action mechanism 145
Chemotherapy 137
Chloral hydrate: 73, 74, 75
Chlorenchyma tissue 44
Chlormequat 11
Chloropicrin 151
Chrysanthemums 148
Cladosporium fulvum 143
Claviceps purpurea 19, 26, 33, 36, 114,
  131, 135
Club wheat 105
Cobb scale, disease assessment 85

Cochliobolus:
  carbonum 60
  heterostrophus 46, 60
  sativus 23, 24, 53, 60, 70
  victoriae 45
Cocksfoot streak virus 18
Coffee:
  berry disease 144
  rust 136
Colchicine 112 (Fig. 5.5)
Colletotrichum coffeanum 144
Coloidin 72
Conidia 27, 33 (Figs. 2.1 and 3.2)
Contact fungicides 10
Copper: 144, 153
  compounds 137, 140
  sulphate 17, 136, 138, 153
Corn:
  flea beetle 69
  leaf blight 2, 46
  meal 59
  rust 14
Cotton blue:
  aniline 74
  trypan 74
Couchgrass 11
Covered smut 147, 150
Cross pollination, maize and rye 103
Crown rust 99, 121
Cucurbits 148, 149, 152
Culture:
  and inoculum production 58–60
  mites 61
Cytological barriers to hybridization 98
Cytotaxonomy 103, 105–7
Czapek 55

DNA 18, 22, 24
Dalapon sodium salt 11
Damping off diseases, seed protection 154
Deoxyribonucleic acid *see* DNA
Deuteromycotina 23, 25
Dialkylphosphorothioates 147
Didymella exitialis 134
Differential resistance 116–17, 118–19
Dikaryon phase of rust fungi 21
Dimethirimol 148, 152
Dimethyl metal dithiocarbamates 142

Diplodia:
  macrospora 57
  maydis 57
  zeae 69
Direct penetration 29–30, 32 (Fig. 2.2) *see
  also* Infection process
Disease:
  assessment 75–6, 80, 83, 84, 85, 86
  control:
    biological 134–5
    chemical 135–40, 159, 160
    cultural 132–4
  diagnosis 52–3
  escape 36–7, 44
  forecasting 154–6
  resistance:
    active 39–40
    adult plant 101, 160
    artificial 98
    assessment of value 126
    breeding *see* Resistance breeding
    cell death 43 (Fig. 3.3)
    characterization 96–7, 99–103
    chemical production 42
    composite mixtures 48
    cuticle thickness 43–4
    differential varieties 49
    durable 46
    epidemics 46, 49, 50
    gene for gene 48–9
    gene selection (Fig. 5.1)
    general 39, 50
    genetic control 2, 39, *see also*
      Genetic resistance breeding
    genetics 46–50
    high level 157
    hypersensitivity 43 (Fig. 3.3)
    inheritance 47, 49
    lignitubers 42
    major gene 39, 47–8, 123, 126
      (Table 3.1)
    mature plant 41–2
    mechanisms 36, 39
    monogenic 15, 47, 50
    morphology 102–3
    multigene 48
    multiline 48
    multiple 50

nematodes 50
oligogenic 47
partial 100, 101–2
passive 43–5
physiological 45–6
plant selection (Fig. 5.2)
polygenic 15, 39, 49–50 (Table 3.1)
race:
  non-specific 45, 46, 49, 50, 101, 116,
    122
  specific 45, 48, 50, 101, 116, 126, 152
  specificity 46, 47
retardation 42
seedling tests 99–100
selective breeding 95–7 (Figs. 5.1 and
  5.2)
slow rusting 45
sources 97
sporulation rate 45
structural barriers 36
suberized cells 42
tyloses 42
utilization 103, 105–7
wound barriers 42
tolerance 102–3
diseases:
seed–borne 153
see also Pathogen(s)
Disinfectant chemical control 137
disinfestation 137, 153
Dithane 143
Dithiocarbamates 137, 142, 143–4, 148,
  152, 154
Dithiocarbamic acid 137, 142
Downy mildews 53, 129, 130, 136
Dried host tissue, culture preservation and
  storage 62–3
Durum wheat 4, 105 see also Triticum
  durum
dusting, fungicide application 138

Einkorn wheat 4
Elder pith 73
Emmer wheats 4
Enzymes 17, 30, 32, 45
Epidemic simulators 46
Eradicant chemical control 137
Ergot 19, 26, 33, 36, 100, 114, 135

Ergot sclerotia 131
Erwinia stewartii 69
Erysiphe:
  graminis
    avenae 40, 49, 101 (Figs. 3.2 and 5.5)
    barley variety diversification 120
    conidia 27 (Fig. 2.1)
    conidial chain isolations 58
    cultural control measures 132
    culture:
      inoculation and infection 65, 67
      storage 61
    fungicide insensitivity 152
    hordei:
      epidemic potential 158
      fungicide insensitivity 89
      gene Mlas 118
      host resistance 47, 50
      infection 32 (Fig. 3.3)
      population monitoring 88
      systemic fungicides: 146, 148, 149,
        application timing 151
    host:
      range 19
      resistance 99, 101, 102, 122
        transfer (Fig. 5.5) (Table 5.3)
    infection 27, 28, 34 (Figs. 2.1 and 2.4)
    multigene varieties 117
    systemic fungicide 147, 148
  spp. 56
Ethanol 73, 74
Ethirimol 89, 146, 148, 150, 152
Ethyl:
  alcohol 74, 75
  methane sulphonate 99
Ethylene bis-metal dithiocarbamates 143
Euchlaena mexicana 8, 107
Eyespot 11, 26, 33, 45, 81, 84, 147, 148,
  151

FAA 74
Feekes scale of cereal growth 76 (Fig. 4.3)
Ferbam 142, 143
Fixatives 74
Flag smut 130
Flax rust 48
Flotation, physical control measure 130
Fluotrimazole 149

Foliar:
  diseases, control measures 14 *see also*
      Pathogens, foliar
  spray application 11 (Fig. 1.1)
Formaldehyde 136, 138, 153
Formalin 74
Formol-acetic-alcohol 74
Freeze-drying, culture preservation and
      storage 62
Fuberidazole 148
Fungal:
  fruiting structures 52
  mycelium 52
  spore germination 28
Fungi:
  growth and sporulation 58-9
  haploid 21
  heterokaryosis 23–4
  heterothallic 22
  homothallic 22
  Imperfecti 149
  infection processes 25–6
  pathogenic 16, 29
  root-infecting 19
  saprophytic 53
  stem and root infecting 54
Fungicidal activity, chemical control
      measure 136, 137
Fungicide(s):
  application 11, 138–40
  chemical control measures 137
  contact 10
  eradicant 137, 144 *see also* Systemic
      fungicides
  evaluation 93
  experiments 92
  insensitivity 152
  integrated control 158
  non-systemic 140–4
  organic 141–4
  protectant 137, 140–4
  seed protection 159–60
  systemic *see* Systemic fungicides
Fungistatic chemicals 137
Fungus vectors 69, 70
Fusarium:
  nivale 148
  spp 62, 64, 153

Gaeumannomyces graminis:
  assessment 83, 84 (Fig. 4.7)
  control measures 133, 134
  host:
    range 19
    resistance 42
  infection 26, 30
  inoculation methods 70
  isolation 56
  tritici 74
Gene for gene theory 19
Genestatic chemical control 137, 138
Genetic:
  barriers to hybridization 98
  resistance breeding 2, 13, 95 *see also*
      Disease resistance, genetic control
  vulnerability 14
Germplasm 97–8
Germ-tubes 26, 29, 32, 40 (Figs. 2.1, 2.2
      and 3.2)
Gibberellic acid 145
Glume blotch 34, 46, 83, 148, 152, 158
Glycerol 60, 61, 73, 74
Graminaceous weed spp 11
Gramineae, virus diseases 18
Green manuring, biological control
      measure 134
Growth regulating chemicals, application 11

Haustoria 32, 33, 34, 73 (Figs. 2.3 and 2.4)
Head blight 23
Helminthosporium:
  avenae 99
  gramineum 23
  maydis 62–3
  spp 14, 65, 71, 153
  teres 59
  turcicum 42, 62–3
Hemileia vastatrix 136
Heterocyclic:
  compounds 149
  nitrogen compounds 144, 154
Heterodera avenae 116–17 (Table 5.3)
Heteroecious nature of wheat black stem
      rust 18
Heterokaryons 24
Heterokaryosis 20, 23–4, 48
Homokaryon phase of rust fungi 21

Hordeum:
  agriocrithon 6
  bulbosum 106, 112
  laevigatum 112 (Table 5.3)
  murinum 106
  spp 106
  spontaneum 106, 112 (Table 5.3)
  vulgare 6–7, 106, 112
Host:
  breeding systems 103
  resistance:
    assessment 19, 76, 91, 93–4
    breeding strategy 121–3
    enhancement 145
    see also Disease resistance
  variety 158
Host-parasite:
  interaction symbols 78, 84
  relations 72–5
Hot water treatment, seed-borne pathogen
    control 14
Hybridization of pathogens *see* Pathogen
    hybridization
Hydrated lime suspension 136
Hyperparasites, biological control
    measure 134
Hypersensitivity 43 (Fig. 3.3)
Hyphae 29, 30, 32, 33 (Fig. 2.3)

Imidazole group 149
Infection process:
  colonization process 33–4
  compensation 38–9
  insect vectors 26, 29, 33
  natural openings 32
  penetration: 29–33, 153
    pegs, 29, 30, 32 (Fig. 3.2)
  post penetration 33–4
  pre–penetration 25–34 (Fig. 3.2)
  tolerance 38–9
Inoculation methods:
  direct application 65
  diseased host material 67
  dry inoculum application 67–8 (Fig. 4.2)
  liquid suspensions 68–9
  soil infestation 70
  vectors 69–70
  wounding and physical methods 69

Iron dimethyl dithiocarbamates 142

James keys to disease assessment 85

Kasugamycin 152
Kitazin 147, 151

Lactic acid 54, 74
Lactofuchsin 72
Lactophenol:
  anhydrous 74
  clear 72, 73
  cotton blue: 72, 73, 75
    alcoholic 73
Leaf blotch:
  barley 85, 148, 156
  wheat 38, 50, 158
Leaf:
  diseases 83
  mould, tomato 143
  rust 38, 50
  spot 33
  spotting fungi 17
  and stem treatment, systemic fungicide 151
  stripe, barley, seed dressing 150
Leafhoppers 69
Leptosphaeria avenaria 23
Lime 143
Lime-sulphur 136, 141
Loose smut:
  barley 64, 86, 102, 149
  control measures 131, 132 (Tables 6.1
    and 6.2)
  host resistance 36
  infection 26, 33
  seed treatment 150, 153
  wheat 44, 135
Lycopodium spores 67
Lyophilization, culture preservation and
    storage 62

MBC 144, 146, 147, 148
Macaroni wheat 105
McBride's stain 73, 74
Maize: 8–9
  cross pollination 103
  cytotaxonomy 107
  disease resistance transfer 114

Maize: (*contd.*)
  downy mildew control 129, 130
  F₁ hybrid 5
  inoculation methods 69
  Phytoalexins 42
  regulatory control measures 130
  resistance breeding 101
  seed protectant 154
  seeds, perithecia production 60
Major gene resistance *see* Disease
    resistance, major gene
Malt extract 59
Mancozeb 143, 148
Maneb 143, 152
Manganese:
  deficiency 53
  salt 143
Melampsora lini 48
Mercurial seed dressings 153, 154
Mercury:
  compounds 10, 136, 153
  fungicides 141
Metallic:
  bis-dithiocarbamates 143
  dithiocarbamates 142
Methyl bromide 151
Mexican spring wheat 5
Mildews: 17
  barley *see* Barley mildew
  culturing 59, 60
  assessment 78, 86
  downy 53
  fungicide experiments 93
  host resistance 47, 100
    transfer 112
  infection rate 126
  population monitoring 86
  powdery *see* Powdery mildew
  pustules 58
  spore collection 60
  susceptible hosts 64
Mineral oil, culture preservation and
    storage 61
Mixtures and multilines, resistance breeding
    strategies 120–1
Mobile nurseries 87–9
Mosaics, disease assessment 81
Mounting media 73, 74

Multigene varieties 48, 110, 117, 122
Multiline varieties 15, 48, 110, 120–1
Mutagens 98–9
Mutation of pathogens 19, 20, 21, 48, 98–9,
    152 *see also* Pathogen virulence
Mycoplasmas 18

Nabam 143
Necrotrophs 17
Nematodes 16, 50, 69, 116–17 (Table 5.3)
Nitrogen: 10–11, 12
  heterocyclic compounds 144, 154
  liquid 62
Nutrient growth medium 59

OMV 70
Oat(s): 5–6
  artificial hybridization 103
  black stem rust 19
  covered smut control 150
  crown rust resistance deployment 119
  cytotaxonomy 105–6
  genomic relationships 106 (Table 5.2)
  inoculation methods 70
  manganese deficiency 53
  meal, growth medium 59
  mildew:
    disease assessment 86
    partial resistance 102
  mosaic virus 70
  multigene resistance 118
  powdery mildew *see* Powdery mildew
  regulatory control measures 130
      (Table 6.1)
  resistance: 40, 42, 45, 49, 71, 99, 101, 126
    transfer (Table 5.3)
  seed dressing 153–4
  smut, inoculation methods 69
  standards of susceptibility 158
  varieties:
    Creme 49
    Milford 49
Obligate parasites, isolation 56 *see also*
    Biotrophs *and* Parasites, obligate
Octal system of notation 87
Oomycetes 22
Organic fungicide, seed treatment 153

Organo-mercurial fungicide 89, 138, 141
Organo-mercury compounds 10, 147, 154
Organo-phosphorous compounds 146–7, 151
Ornamentals 149
Oxathiins 149, 150
Oxycarboxin 60, 146, 149, 150

PDA 54
Papilla (Fig. 3.2)
Paraquat 93
Parasexual cycle 20, 24–5, 48
Parasites:
  facultative 16
  non-obligate 16 see also Necrotrophs
  obligate 16, 53, 56, 59 see also Biotrophs
  soil inhabiting 153
Pathogen(s)
  aggressiveness 16
  air-borne 11, 25, 39, 92, 119, 137 (Fig. 4.8)
  bacterial 25, 43
  biotrophic 19, 43, 99
  contamination 153
  culture:
    host-parasite relations 72–5
    incubation and symptom expression 71–2
    inoculation:
      and infection 63–5
      methods see Inoculation methods
    preservation and storage 61–3
    viable inoculum 64
  DNA measurements see DNA
  definition 16
  endemic 117
  enzyme production 30, 32
  epidemic potential 96, 158
  eradication methods 133, 135
  foliar, assessment 100
  fungicide insensitivity 152, 157, 160
  heterokaryosis 20
  host:
    range 18–19
    resistance see Disease resistance
  hybridization 48, 103 (Fig. 5.3)
  hyphae 134 see also Hyphae
  infection see Infection process
  isolation:
    baiting 55–6

dilution 54–5
direct 53
host inoculation 56
induced:
  mycelial growth 54
  sporulation 53–4
purification 56–7
single spore 57–8
soil suspension 55–6
streaking procedure 55 (Fig. 4.1)
karyogamy 22
mutant races 13–14
penetration see Infection process
physiological:
  races 19
  specialization 98, 114
population:
  monitoring 86–9
  stability 124–5
predominance 115–16
recombination 20, 21, 22–3, 47
seed-borne 11, 14, 95
soil-borne 25, 39, 48, 117, 150 see also
  Root diseases
splash-borne 65, 68, 71, 1–2, 117
variability 20–5, 48
virulence: 16, 21, 121, 157, 160 see also
  Mutation of pathogens
  testing 87
Pathogenisis 25–6
Pathogenic:
  infection 33
  variation monitoring 89–94
Pathogenicity 16–18
Pathogenisis 26–7
Pathological experiments, design 90–4
Phenol crystals 74
Phenyl mercury acetate 141
Phosphate application 10
Phycomycetes 55, 147
Physical methods, disease control 135
Physiologic races in isolation 89–90
Phytoalexins 42–3
Phytophthora infestans 144
Phytosanitary certification 130
Picric acid 73
Piricularia oryzae 42 44, 147, 151, 152, 153
Planet Junior 91, 94 (Fig. 4.10)

Plant diseases:
  chemical seed treatment 153–4
  control 128, 156–8 *see also* Resistance
    breeding
Plasmopara viticola 136
Polyethylenethiurum disulphate 152
Polymyxa graminis 70
Post emergence chemical spray 11
Potash application 10
Potato:
  blight 144
  dextrose 54, 59, 61
Powdery mildew(s): 14, 16, 17, 19, 21, 34
  adult wheat and oats resistance 122
  barley:
    forecasting 155
    integrated control 158, 160 (Fig. 6.1)
    prevalence 123–4
    resistance 47, 50
    variety diversification 120
  chemical control measures 140
  conidia, inoculation 60
  cucurbits 152
  cultural control measures 133
  culture, inoculation and infection 65
  grapes 140
  internal observation 73
  isolation 53
  multigene varieties 117
  nitrogen effects 13
  oats 40, 49, 148
  spring barley 150, 155
  systemic fungicides: 146, 147, 148, 149,
    154
    application 150, 151
  wheat 32, 149 (Fig. 2.4)
Prophylaxis, chemical control measure 137
Protectant:
  chemical control 137
  fungicide: 151
    application 139–40
Protection, seed treatment 153
Pseudocercosporella herpotrichoides:
  culture inoculation methods 67
  disease assessment 81, 84
  enzyme production 48
  foliar spray 11
  host resistance transfer (Table 5.3)

infection process 26, 33
parasexuality 24
systemic fungicide: 147, 148
  application timing 156
Puccinia:
  coronata: 24, 62, 71, 118, 121, 126
    (Table 5.3)
    avenae 60
  graminis: 19, 22, 50, 65, 71, 118 (Table 5.3)
    avenae 19
    secale 19
    tritici: 18, 19
      colonization 34
      control measures 129–32, 133, 134
      culture, incubation 71
      parasexuality 24, 25
      passive resistance 44
      penetration 32
      striping effect 44–5
  hordei:
    barley:
      genotypes, inoculation 123
      leaves, surface observation 72
      resistance 101
    contamination 56
    culture techniques 63, 65, 71
    disease assessment (Fig. 4.6)
    epidemic potential 158
    forecasting 156
    germinating uredospore (Fig. 2.2)
    host resistance: 48, 125
      transfer (Table 5.3)
    hyphae development (Fig. 2.3)
    systemic fungicide 148
    virulence variations 117
  polysora 14
  recondita:
    culture techniques 63, 65, 71
    disease assessment 78
    epidemic potential 158
    host resistance: 50, 101, 102, 122
      tolerance 38 (Fig. 3.1)
      transfer 114 (Table 5.3)
    prevalence 123
    spring wheat 102
    tritici: 44
      culturing 59, 60
      uredospores, trapping (Fig. 3.1)

spp 27, 56, 58, 60, 61–2
striiformis:
  contamination 56
  culture techniques 63, 65, 71
  culturing 59
  disease assessment 81
  epidemic: 122
    potential 158
  host resistance: 45, 46, 47, 101, 121, 124
    stability 125
    stabilizing selection 116
    transfer 114 (Tables 5.3 and 5.6)
  isolation nurseries 87, 98
  parasexuality 25
  population monitoring 87
  systemic fungicide 148, 150
  wheat variety diversification 119–20
Pycniospores of rust 23
Pyrenophora:
  avenae 53, 89, 153
  graminea 65, 67, 150
  teres 56
Pyrimidine derivatives 148, 152
Pythium spp isolation method 54, 57

RNA 18
Recombination of genetic material 24, 25, 47
Regulatory control measures 129–32
  (Table 6.1)
Resistance: *see* Disease resistance
  breeding:
    alien gene transfer 110–14
    backcross 110
    bulk hybrid 108
    cross pollinated species 114
    level required 123–4
    mass selection 107
    multigene varieties 122
    pathogen virulence 117–19
    pathological research 102
    pedigree 108 (Fig. 5.4)
    pure line selection 107
    self pollinated species 107–8, 110–14
    stability 124–7
    strategies 114, 116–24
    wheat 101, 117
    transfer 112, 114 (Fig. 5.5) (Table 5.3)

Resistant plants, effect of selection on
  potential yield (Fig. 5.2)
Rhizoctonia spp 54, 153
Rhynchosporium secalis:
  barley, internal observation 73
  cultural control measures 132
  culture techniques 56, 57–8, 65, 67, 71
  disease assessment 85 (Fig. 4.7)
  dwarf wheats and barleys,
    susceptibility 102
  epidemic potential 158
  forecasting 156
  fungicide experiments 93
  host resistance 48, 50
  systemic fungicide 148
Ribonucleic acid 18
Rice: 42
  blast 44, 147, 151
Root:
  diseases 14, 81, 84, 135 *see also*
    Pathogens soil-borne
  rot 23
Root-infecting fungi 19
Rotation, cultural control measure 133
Rust(s):
  see also Puccinia spp
  black stem *see* Black stem rust
  cultural control measures 133
  culture techniques 60, 61, 63, 65, 71, 73
  culturing 59
  disease assessment 78, 81
  flax 48
  foliar 14
  fungi:
    density effect 28
    host resistance 43, 47
    mutations 21
    parasexuality 24–5
    pathogenicity 16, 17, 18
    penetration 32 (Fig. 2.3)
  fungicide experiments 93
  host-parasite relations 72
  leaf 38, 50
  partial resistance 100
  population monitoring 86
  pustules, monospore infections 58
  resistance:
    breeding strategy 118

Rust(s): (*contd.*)
    transfer 98, 112
    Southern corn 14
    spore stages 18, 22, 23
    stripe 119–20
    susceptible hosts 64
    systemic fungicides 149
    yellow 46, 47
    see also Brown rust and Stem rust
Rye: 7–8
    alien gene transfer 110
    black stem rust 19
    cross pollination 103
    crosses with wheat 112
    cytotaxonomy 107
    ergot 26, 36
    regulatory control measures 130
    systemic fungicides 148, 149

Sach's agar 60
Salicylanilide 149
Salt-brine 153
Saprophytes, facultative 16, 53
Scald, barley leaf 67, 158
Schwarzbach sampler for air-borne spores 88 (Fig. 4.8)
Sclerenchyma tissue, lignified 44, 45
Sclerospora sorghi 129, 130
Secale:
    afghanicum 7, 107
    ancestrale 7, 107
    cereale 7–8, 107, 110 (Table 5.3)
    ciliatoglume 7
    dalmaticum 7
    dighoricum 107
    montanum 7–8, 107
    segetale 7, 107
    spp 107
Seed:
    disinfectants 154
    protectants 154
    protection, chemical control measure 136
    rotting organism 154
    treatments 138, 150–1, 153, 154
Seedling disease resistance 160
Selenophoma donacis 33
Septoria:
    nodorum:

    control measures 132, 133, 143, 144
    culture, inoculation method 67
    diagnosis 53
    disease assessment 83 (Fig. 4.7)
    host resistance 46
    infection 28
    seed treatment 153
    systemic fungicide: 148
        application timing 152, 155, 156
    spp:
    cultural control measures 133
    culture techniques 62, 64, 65, 71
    culturing 59
    dwarf wheats and barleys, susceptibility 102
    fungicide experiments 93
    tritici:
    control measures 132
    disease assessment 81
    host:
        resistance 42
        tolerance 38
    infection 28
    quantitative measurement 75
Silicone rubber 72
Smut(s):
    covered 147, 150
    disease assessment 76
    germ-tubes 26
    host resistance 100
    hybrid cereal infection 114
    hybridization 22
    loose, *see* Loose smut
    parasexuality 24, 25
    pathogenicity 17
    population monitoring 86
    seed dressing 154
    systemic fungicide 14, 149
Sodium:
    salt 143
    hypochlorite 54
    oleate 68
Soil:
    sterilants 151
    sterilization, chemical control measure 136
    treatments 151
Southern Corn rust 14

Sphaerotheca fuliginea 152
Spore(s):
air-borne *see* Pathogens air-borne
production:
circadian rhythms 60
quantitative assessment 78, 81
suspensions, streaking agar plates 55,
(Fig. 4.1)
trapping 37 (Fig. 3.1)
Spot blotch 23
Spraying, fungicide application 138
Spreader-bed nurseries, fungicide
experiments 91, 94, 100, 102 (Fig. 4.8)
Spring:
barley:
artificial hybridization (Fig. 5.3)
brown rust control 149
escape mechanism 102
powdery mildew control 148, 149, 150,
152, 155
variety Sultan 118, 125
wheat 102
Stabilizing selection 116
Stains 75
Stem rust 50, 102, 118 *see also* Black stem
rust
Stewart's disease 69
Stomates 32, 33, 44 (Fig. 2.2)
Streaking 55 (Fig. 4.1)
Streptomycin 57, 59
Stripes, disease assessment 81
Stripping 72–3
Sucrose-asparagine-yeast agar 60
Sugar beet 148
Sulphone derivative 150
Sulphur: 135, 136, 140–1
compounds 137
Systemic fungicides: 3, 10, 14, 137, 144–50,
151
application 11, 150–2, 154, 155

Take-all 19, 30, 42, 84, 133, 134
Teleutospores 22, 24, 60
Teosinte 8, 107
Testing centres, pathogen population
monitoring 87
Tetramethylthiuram disulphide 142
Therapeutants 144, 145

Thiabendazole 147, 151
Thiophanate methyl 146, 148
Thiophanates 148
Thiram: 10, 142, 154
carboxin mixture 138, 150
Thiuram disulphides 142
Tilletia:
caries:
chemotherapeutic action 145
control measures 136, 138, 141
pathogenicity 17
seed treatment 150, 153
systemic fungicide 147
spp 14, 28
Tomato leaf mould 143
Toxic action, direct 145
Toxins 17, 34, 45, 145
Tramline drilling 11–12, 138, 140 (Fig. 1.1)
Trap nurseries 86–7
Triadimefon 92, 149, 150
Tridemorph 146, 149, 150, 151–2
Triforine 146, 149
Tripsacum spp 107, 112
Triticale spp 110
Triticum:
aestivum: 4–5
alien gene transfer 110, 111 (Table 5.3)
cytotaxonomy 103, 105 (Table 5.1)
host resistance 98
transfer 112, 114 (Fig. 5.6)
varieties:
aestivum (Table 5.1)
Chinese spring (Fig. 5.6)
compactum (Table 5.1)
Compair (Fig. 5.6)
macha (Table 5.1)
spelta (Table 5.1)
sphaerococcum (Table 5.1)
vavilovii (Table 5.1)
bicorne (Table 5.1)
compactum 105
durum 105 (Table 5.1)
longisimum (Table 5.1)
Monococcum:
boeoticum (Table 5.1)
monococcum (Table 5.1)
spp 4, 110
speltoides (Table 5.1)

Triticum: (*contd.*)
  tauschii (Table 5.1)
  timopheevi: (Table 5.3)
    araraticum (Table 5.1)
    timopheevi (Table 5.1)
  turgidum:
    carthlicum (Table 5.1)
    dicoccoides (Table 5.1)
    dicoccum 112 (Tables 5.1 and 5.3)
    durum 4, 112 (Table 5.3)
    polonicum (Table 5.1)
    turgidum (Table 5.1)
Trypan blue in lactophenol 73
Tween 68

Uncinula necator 140
Uredospores:
  collection 60
  infection 26, 32 (Fig. 2.2)
  pathogenicity 18
  recombination 22
  host resistance 44, 101, 102 (Fig. 3.1)
Urocystis tritici 130
Ustilago:
  avenae 150
  hordei 24, 147, 150
  maydis 24, 25, 69
  nuda:
    control measures 131, 132, 135
      (Table 6.1)
    host:
      resistance 36, 44, 50
      tolerance 38
    infection 26, 33, 64
    seed treatment 150, 153
    systemic fungicides 149
    wheat embryos, internal observation 73
  spp 14, 114
  zeae 28

V8 juice 54, 61
Varietal mixtures, resistance strategy 120–1
Venturia inaequalis 141
Victoria blight 45
Vine downy mildew 136
Viroids 16
Virulence *see* Pathogen virulence
Viruses 16, 18, 25–6, 64, 70

Weedkillers, hormonal 11
Wheat: 4–5
  artificial hybridization 103
  black stem rust 18, 19, 129
  brown rust, epidemic potential 158
  bunt control 138, 141, 145, 150, 153
  compensation 38
  control measure 130, 131, 133 (Table 6.1)
  crosses with rye 112
  cytotaxonomy 103, 105
  disease escape 36
  dwarf 5, 102
  embryos, observation for *Ustilago nuda* 73
  eyespot 26, 67, 147, 148, 156
  F_1 hybrid 5
  genetic:
    male sterility 114
    vulnerability 14
  genomic relationships 105 (Table 5.1)
  glume blotch 46, 67, 148, 152
  host-parasite interaction 78
  hybrid 114
  leaf blotch 38, 158
  leaf rust 38
  leaves, black stem rust colonization 34
  loose smut *see* Loose smut
  Mexican Spring 5
  mosaic viruses, inoculation methods 70
  mutations 99
  nitrogen application 11
  phytoalexins 42
  powdery mildew control 149
  resistance: 42, 45, 50, 71, 75, 101, 102, 124
    breeding 101, 117
    transfer 112, 114
  susceptibility: 102
    standards 158
  systemic fungicides: 148
    application timing 155
  varieties:
    Fulhard 38
    H44 112
    Hope 44, 112
    Kansas 2627 38
    Knox 102, 126
    Red King 47
    Rivet 47
    Thatcher 112

Vermilion 126
yellow rust, population monitoring 87, 149, 150
see *also* Spring wheat *and* Winter wheat
Wild oats 11
Winter:
  barley 150, 151, 152
  wheat:
    brown rust control 149
    powdery mildew control 148
    resistance 71, 125
    systemic fungicides 149
    varieties:
      Cappelle Desprez 46, 125
      Hybride de Bersee 125
      Joss Cambier 122
      Tumult 121

Xanthomonas stewartii 69

Yeast extract agar 55
Yellow dwarf, barley 133
Yellow rust:
  barley 149
  epidemic potential 158
  multiline resistance 121
  wheat:
    isolation nurseries 87, 98
    resistance 46, 47
    systemic fungicides 149, 150

Zea mays: 8–9, 107, 112
  mexicana 107
Zinc:
  dimethyl dithiocarbamate 142
  ethylene bis-metal dithiocarbamates 143
  salt 143
  sulphate 143
Zineb: 143, 152
  tank mix 143
Ziram 142, 143

Fig. 1.1 Tramlines for foliar spraying 12
Fig. 2.1 *Erysiphe graminis* conidia germination 27
Fig. 2.2 *Puccinia hordei* uredospore germinating 30
Fig. 2.3 *Puccinia hordei* hyphae development 31
Fig. 2.4 *Erysiphe graminis* haustorium 31

Fig. 3.1 *Puccinia recondita* uredospores trapped by wheat 37
Fig. 3.2 *Erysiphe graminis avenae* conidial germination 41
Fig. 3.3 Barley response to *Erysiphe graminis hordei* invasion 41
Fig. 4.1 Streaking agar plates 55
Fig. 4.2 Spore settling tower 66
Fig. 4.3 Growth stage key for cereals 77
Fig. 4.4 Decimal code for growth of cereals 79
Fig. 4.5 Cereal growth stages, identification 80
Fig. 4.6 Disease assessment keys for *P. hordei* and *R. secalis* 82
Fig. 4.7 Disease assessment keys for *S. nodorum* and *G. graminis* 82
Fig. 4.8 Schwarzbach sampler for air-borne spores 88
Fig. 4.9 Spreader bed nursery arrangements 92
Fig. 4.10 Modified Planet Junior 93
Fig. 4.11 Planter for clumps of plants 93
Fig. 5.1 Resistance genes, effect of selection on population size 96
Fig. 5.2 Selection for resistant plants, reduction in potential yield improvement 96
Fig. 5.3 Artificial hybridization stages 104
Fig. 5.4 Pedigree breeding method 109
Fig. 5.5 Transfer of resistance to *Erysiphe graminis* 113
Fig. 5.6 Transfer of resistance to *Puccinia striiformis* 115
Fig. 6.1 Scheme for integrated control of Barley powdery mildew 159

Table 3.1 Major gene and polygene resistance 40
Table 5.1 Genomic relationships of wheats 105
Table 5.2 Genomic relationships of oats 106
Table 5.3 Disease resistance factors transferred 111
Table 6.1 UK seed certification for loose smut 130
Table 6.2 Embryo infection by loose smut in seed barley 131

Anthracnose 178

Bacterial stripe blight of oats 248
Bacterial wilt of maize 245
Barley yellow dwarf virus 250
Black stem rust 205
Brown rust of barley 204
Brown rust of wheat and rye 209
Brown stripe downy mildew 227

Claviceps purpurea 169
Cob rot 199
Cochliobolus carbonum 172
Cochliobolus heterostrophus 173
Cochliobolus sativus 175
Cochliobolus victoriae 177
Colletotrichum graminicola 178
Common bunt 233
Common corn rust 211
Common smut of maize 240
Copper deficiency 256
Corn stunt 249
Corynebacterium tritici 244
Covered smut of oats and barley 239
Crazy top of maize 226
Crown rust 202

Deficiency diseases 256
Diplodia macrospora 179
Diplodia maydis 179
Downy mildew of small grain cereals 224
Drechslera avenae 216
Drechslera graminea 217
Drechslera teres 219

Ear rot of maize (*Diplodia* spp.) 179
Ear rot of maize (*Gibberella*) 188
Ergot 169
Erwinia stewartii 245
Erysiphe graminis 181
Eyespot 200

Flag smut 237
Foot and root rot (*Cochliobolus*) 175
Foot and root rot (*Fusarium*) 184
Foot and root rot (*Gibberella* spp.) 186
Fusarium culmorum 184
Fusarium nivale 196

Gaeumannomyces graminis 191
Gibberella avenaceae 186
Gibberella moniliforme 187
Gibberella zeae 188
Glume blotch 194

Halo blight of oats 246
Halo spot of barley 228
Head blight (*Fusarium*) 184
Head blight (*Micronectriella*) 196
Helminthosporium avenae 216
Helminthosporium carbonum 172
Helminthosporium gramineum 217
Helminthosporium maydis 173
Helminthosporium sativum 175
Helminthosporium teres 219
Helminthosporium turcicum 235
Helminthosporium victoriae 177

Kernel rot of maize 187

Leaf blotch 223
Leaf rust of barley 204
Leaf rust of wheat and rye 209
Leaf spot of maize 172
Leaf spot of wheat 198
Leaf stripe of barley 217
Leaf stripe of oats 216
Leptosphaeria avenaria 230
Leptosphaeria nodorum 194
Loose smut of oats 237
Loose smut of wheat and barley 242

Maize dwarf mosaic virus 252
Manganese deficiency 256
Micronectriella nivalis 196
Mycosphaerella graminicola 198

Net blotch 219
Nigrospora oryzae 199
Nitrogen deficiency 256
Northern leaf blight of maize 235

Oat blast 256
Ophiobolus graminis 191

Pellicularia filamentosa 221
Phosphorus deficiency 256
Potassium deficiency 256

Powdery mildew 181
Pre-emergence blight 196
Pseudocercosporella herpotrichoides 200
Pseudomonas coronafaciens 246
Pseudomonas striafaciens 248
Puccinia coronata 202
Puccinia glumarum 212
Puccinia graminis 205
Puccinia hordei 204
Puccinia polysora 208
Puccinia recondita 209
Puccinia sorghi 211
Puccinia striiformis 212
Pyrenophora avenae 216
Pyrenophora graminea 217
Pyrenophora teres 219
Pythium 215

Rhizoctonia solani 221
Rhynchosporium secalis 223
Root rot (*Micronectriella*) 196
Root rot (*Pythium*) 215

Scald 223
Sclerophthora macrospora 224, 226
Sclerophthora rayssiae 227
Sclerospora macrospora 224, 226
Sclerospora sorghi 228
Seedling blight (*Fusarium*) 184
Seedling blight (*Gibberella* spp.) 186, 188
Seedling blight (*Pythium*) 215
Seedling blotch of oats 216
Selenophoma donacis 228
Septoria avenae 230
Septoria nodorum 194
Septoria passerinii 231

Septoria tritici 198
Sharp eyespot 221
Snow mould 196
Soil-borne oat mosaic virus 253
Soil-borne wheat mosaic virus 254
Sorghum downy mildew on maize 228
Southern corn rust 208
Southern leaf blight of maize 173
Speckled blotch of oats 230
Speckled leaf blotch of barley 231
Spiroplasma 249
Spot blotch 175
Spring yellows (*Gibberella*) 186
Stalk rot of maize (*Diplodia* spp.) 179
Stalk rot of maize (*Gibberella* spp.) 187, 188
Stinking smut 233
Stripe rust 212

Take-all 191
Tilletia caries 233
Trichometasphaeria turcica 235
Tundu disease 244

Urocystis tritici 237
Ustilago avenae 237
Ustilago hordei 239
Ustilago maydis 240
Ustilago nuda 242

Victoria blight of oats 177

Wheat streak mosaic virus 255
Whiteheads 191

Yellow rust 212
Yellow slime 244